Interdisciplinary perspectives on modern history

Editors
Robert Fogel and Stephan Thernstrom

Servants in husbandry
in early modern England

Servants in husbandry
in early modern England

ANN KUSSMAUL

Glendon College, York University, Toronto

CAMBRIDGE UNIVERSITY PRESS

Cambridge
London   New York   New Rochelle
Melbourne   Sydney

Published by the Press Syndicate of the University of Cambridge
The Pitt Building, Trumpington Street, Cambridge CB2 1RP
32 East 57th Street, New York, NY 10022, USA
296 Beaconsfield Parade, Middle Park, Melbourne 3206, Australia

British Library Cataloguing in Publication Data
Kussmaul, Ann
Servants in husbandry in early modern England.
(Interdisciplinary perspectives in modern history).
1. Agricultural laborers – Great Britain
I. Title II. Series
301.44'43   HD8039.A29G7   80-41518

ISBN 0 521 23566 9

Contents

v

Figures

Tables

TO MY PARENTS

Preface

It has been seven years since my preliminary thesis notes, ten cassettes, two sleeping bags, a roll of paper towels, a tin of condensed milk, and an English cucumber were stolen from my car in Lyons. The theft brought about the first of several fresh starts to thinking about servants in husbandry. The others were the result of my good fortune in finding a post as lecturer at York University in Toronto, which made it impossible to recall, each May, exactly what I had intended to do the September before. The research, supported for three years by a Canada Council fellowship, took the intermediate form of a thesis between a first set of drafts in 1975–7 and a second set in 1978–80.

In Cambridge from 1973 to 1975 I was able to attend the King's College seminars in social history, organized by Alan Macfarlane and Martin Ingram, and to share thoughts with others, especially Keith Wrightson, John Walter, and David Levine, on what seemed to be an at least theoretically interlocking puzzle, whose parts were the various research projects being done at the time. Back in Toronto, I read preliminary versions of parts of the work at the Economic History Workshop of the University of Toronto and at the Toronto Social History Group, and gained from the critical discussions. I was challenged into the production of a better thesis by John Munro, Andrew Watson, and Scott Eddie, not least by knowing that if I intended to ignore some of their suggestions, I had to present a compelling defence of this position. Karl Helleiner, Abraham Rotstein, John Beattie, Bob Malcolmson, Donna Andrew, Nick Rogers, and Barry Cooper all read the whole or part of various drafts, and offered helpful suggestions, substantive and stylistic. In the two summers since 1978, I was able to return to England, thanks to grants from the Social Sciences and Humanities Research Council of Canada, to continue the research. The revisions took a surprising turn when, in trying to explain the abandonment of farm service in the nineteenth century more amply (Chapter 7), I found myself pulled back into the sixteenth and seventeenth centuries (Chapter 6), where I had begun, by the bank of marriage data drawn from parish registers, kindly made available to me by the Cambridge Group for the History of Population and Social

xi

Structure, just as the 1851 census had earlier pulled me into the nineteenth century.

The Cambridge Group have been the one constant spanning the seven years' work. It was with their collection of parish listings, at the suggestion of Peter Laslett, that I restarted the research in the summer of 1973, and to their aggregative parish register file that I returned in 1979 and 1980. Peter Laslett, Roger Schofield, Richard Smith, Richard Wall, and Tony Wrigley encouraged and helped me at each stage of the work. Keith Snell and David Souden, research students at the Group in 1979, freely offered extensive and valuable suggestions based on their own research.

I visited too many county record offices to risk slighting some by praising others. None was unhelpful; I shall single out for specific thanks only one, the Lincolnshire Archives, and Miss Judith Cripps, then archivist there, and do so because it is hard to separate the joy of finding a rare record, in this case the astonishing Holland Statute Sessions lists, from gratefulness to those who made the discovery possible.

I must not be the first author to have been handling editor's queries about the consistency of form of the bibliography and endnotes whilst writing the preface: I believe I will be very grateful to the staff of the Cambridge University Press in a few months' time. Bernice Eisenstein typed the draft that became the thesis in great spirits, and the typing pool at York must be glad that it is all about to end. Oh yes, the thesis notes were eventually recovered and mailed to me by the Lyons police. No trace was found of the cucumber.

Cambridge, August 1980

PART I

Servants and labourers

1   *Servants: the problems*

This is a book about servants, as 'servant' was understood in the past. To the modern mind, 'servant' evokes images only of grooms, house-maids, cooks. Three centuries ago, it would have called forth the image of a host of ploughmen, carters, dairymaids, and apprentices. Servants were youths hired into the families of their employers. Hundreds of thousands of them were accounted for by Gregory King, and then concealed in his famous table of 'Income and Expense of the Several Families of England, Calculated for the Year 1688', subsumed under the caption 'Heads per family', just as the servants themselves were contained within the households of farmers, tradesmen, artisans, handicraftsmen, Temporall and Spirituall Lords.[1] Servants consti-tuted 13.4 per cent of the population in sixty-three scattered listings of parish inhabitants, dating from 1574 to 1821;[2] from the figures avail-able we can infer that servants, most of whom were youths, constituted around 60 per cent of the population aged fifteen to twenty-four.[3] In other words, most youths in early modern England were servants; that so few are now is one of the simplest differences between our world and theirs.

That so many youths *were* servants has many consequences. As Macfarlane put it, 'the institution of servants and apprentices helped solve the problem of what to do with children between puberty and marriage'.[4] While servants and apprentices waited for marriage, they had opportunities to learn skills and save their wages, free from the responsibility of maintaining themselves.[5] They formed a large and distinctive part of the labour force, differing from adult wage-labourers in the nature of their contracts, their residence, and their marital status. Because service was widely practised, farmers, craftsmen, and tradesmen could compose their household labour force independently of the numbers and skills of their children; their productive households could survive the death of any of its members; parents could send the children they could not support into the households of others.[6] For all these reasons, this is not a book simply about servants: it is also concerned with population, family structure, inheritance, economic organization and agricultural practices.

Early modern England contained many varieties of service. Some

3

servants were what the nineteenth century would come to call 'domestics', hired to establish and maintain the status of the family and to attend to its personal needs. These became, by the later nineteenth century, the overwhelming majority of all servants, and thus bequeathed to modern language the present meaning of 'servant'.[7] They are not the subject of this study. Our servants were called by Adam Smith 'productive', hired not to maintain a style of life, but a style of work, the household economy. Whereas most domestic servants were women and girls, more productive servants were male, and here the balance between numbers of males and females was more even. In 1851, for example, the ratio of male to female domestic servants was 13:100, while the ratio in farm service was 213:100.[8] In the set of sixty-three parish listings referred to above, the overall ratio of male to female servants is 107:100, and the ratios in farmers' and craftsmen's households are 121:100 and 171:100.[9]

Within the category of productive service, marked distinctions existed. Rural service differed from formal urban apprenticeship. The masters of apprentices were paid by the parents of the apprentices to lodge, board and train their children; rural servants were paid by their masters.[10] Formal apprenticeship tied master and apprentice, by written contract, to a term of several years; rural servants and masters were bound by verbal or tacit contracts for shorter terms, typically a year. Of rural productive servants, servants to farmers were the most numerous. Agriculture was early modern England's dominant occupation; farmers were more apt to hire servants than were craftsmen and tradesmen.[11]

Service in husbandry was marked by several characteristics that distinguished servants from all other workers in agrarian society. Their annual contracts and continuously available labour set them apart from day-labourers. Their residence in the farmhouse protected them from changes in the cost of living. Unlike day-labouring, service in husbandry was the permanent occupation of only a small minority. For most servants, it was a transitional occupation, specific to their transitional status between childhood and adulthood. No one was born a servant in husbandry, and few expected to die as servants.

Between one-third and one-half of hired labour in early modern agriculture was supplied by servants in husbandry, and most early modern youths in rural England were servants in husbandry. Yet service in husbandry has been, heretofore, the subject of no intensive study. This is, at first sight, puzzling. Laslett and Macfarlane have provided introductions to the understanding of service, but Hasbach's study of the agricultural labourer, written three-quarters of a century ago, remains the most systematic treatment of farm servants.[12] Most general works on English agriculture draw distinctions between the various forms of agricultural labour, and then ignore the economic, demographic, and social implications of the existence of a large group of youthful wage-workers, fed and lodged by their employers.[13]

The reasons for the disregard of service in husbandry are legion. Records of farm servants are scarce and fragmentary. Had servants in husbandry been more literate, we might have had scores of diaries, journals and memoirs to ransack for glimpses of the *mentalité* they reveal.[14] Had servants been householders, we might have found them named in assessments for the hearth tax, window tax, and land tax.[15] Had servants not been clustered in two of the three healthiest age-groups, and had they possessed property, we might have found their possessions listed in post-mortem inventories. What dead servants left behind, when recorded, is of interest, but few records exist. More often, we glimpse their lives through the diaries, account books, and inventories of their employers. Henry Best's inventory, for example, included 'the servant's bed in the stable' among the nine beds at Elmswell.[16] Had service been compatible with marriage, we might have found marriage registers in which 'servant' was a common occupational designation. Because servants were highly mobile, their appearance in one record, whether poll-tax assessment, account book, census, or militia list, usually precludes their appearance in the next.

More serious than the problem of evidence is the problem of interpretation. Modern language and modern categories fail us. In their terms, service in husbandry is so ambiguous that it can hardly have existed. Consider, first, the language of the institution. When a seventeenth-century yeoman wrote of his 'family', he meant his wife, children and servants; when he wrote of his 'servants', he meant his carters and dairy-maids. 'Servant', 'labourer', 'domestic', 'menial', 'family': each word conveys a meaning to us that it did not bear in the past.

'Servant', as we have seen, now connotes a 'domestic' servant, a personal servant. In early modern England, the word had a doubly broadened set of meanings. The first, specific use was to denote all those who worked for one master, and were maintained by that master. William Harrison wrote in 1587 of the yeomen who keep 'servants (not idle servants as the gentlemen do, but such as get both their own and part of their master's living)'.[17] No simple distinction was possible between productive servants and the servants Harrison called idle and Smith called unproductive. Ploughman and groom, dairymaid and housemaid: all were simply 'servants'. Fitzherbert's advice on the management of servants goes further, making no clear distinctions between the farm servants and personal servants of 'the yonge gentlyman that entendeth to thryve'.[18] All were, moreover, 'menial' or 'domestic' servants. The adjectives meant only that they lived in their master's house. Thus Blackstone distinguished between '*menial servants*, so called from being *intra moenia* [within the walls], or domestics', and labourers 'who do not live *intra moenia*, as part of the family'.[19] The poll tax of 1688 required masters to pay the taxes of defaulting 'menial' servants.[20] The Select Committee on Agriculture heard evidence, one and a half centuries later, of the farmers who were ridding their houses of 'domestic servants' and having 'recourse to labourers'; the Report on Women and Children in Agriculture of 1843 noted the 'house servants' who provided all the labour on graziers' farms in the Yorkshire Dales.[21] 'Menial', 'domestic' and 'servant' were narrowed to their modern meanings only when productive workers ceased, while butlers and housemaids continued, to live in the houses of their masters.

The second early modern meaning of 'servant' extended still further to include all those who worked for others. Used in this general sense, 'servant' comprised both servants, in the specific sense of the word, and day-labourers. The two synchronous meanings can be confusing. Putnam found 'serviens' to have been most ambiguously used in the fourteenth century; it meant, she decided, both household servants and agricultural labourers.[22] The 1495 Act against vagabonds and beggars referred to the 'apprentice, servant of husbandry, laborer, [and] servant artificer', and to the 'maister of any the seid servaunts'.[23] The chapter in Burn's *Justice of the Peace* (1755) dealing with all labour is entitled 'Servants', and under this heading are discussed labourers, journeymen, artificers, and servants. In an earlier chapter, however, Burn explicitly gave 'servant' its specific meaning: 'in general, the law never looks upon any person as a *servant*, who is hired for less than one whole year; otherwise they come under the denomination of labourers'.[24]

'Labourer', not 'servant', became the general term denoting wage-workers only in the nineteenth century. Earlier, 'labourer' had a restricted, specific meaning. The *Farmer's Magazine* in 1779 defined 'labourer' as 'a man hired to work by the day or week, or employed by the acre, rod, pole, etc.'.[25] It was in this sense that 'labourer' was used in most wage assessments taken under the Statute of Artificers from the sixteenth to the eighteenth centuries. By the middle of the nineteenth century, 'labourer' had nearly displaced 'servant' in common usage. The framers of the 1851 census, working in the midst of the change in usage, confused enumerators and enumerated alike by asking first that 'farm servants' be distinguished from 'agricultural labourers' on the basis of residence or non-residence in the farmer's house, and then that farmers report the 'number of labourers' employed on the farm, meaning in this context 'all kinds of workmen employed on the farm, whether they sleep in the house or not'.[26]

Variant usages of 'servant' occasionally appear. On large estates in the northeast, married men, living in cottages provided by their employers, were called 'servants'.[27] It is likely that these were the early modern successors to the *famuli* of medieval England, full-time workers on a manor's demesne whose duties were centred on live-stock.[28] The process of ridding a farmhouse of its servants in husbandry gave rise to another variant. As a first step, servants often continued to be hired for the year, but were paid 'board wages', a money payment in lieu of room and board, in addition to their normal money wages, and were expected to fend for themselves. Sometimes the board wages were paid directly to a housekeeper who boarded and lodged several of a farm's servants.[29] These workers were still called servants; later, presumably when the memory of their having lived with the farmer had faded, they came to be called constant labourers.

It is fortunate for us that despite the several uses of 'servant' and 'labourer' the words were most often used only in their specific mean-ings in early modern works touching on agriculture. 'Servant' generally denoted a worker hired for the year, resident with the farmer; 'la-bourer' a worker hired for a shorter term and resident elsewhere.

'Family' presents the modern reader with a more difficult problem. We have little trouble extending our notion of the family to include the co-resident kin of the extended family. But to read that servants were part of the early modern family is to be tempted to think that they did not belong there, that they were not 'proper' members. To do so is to ignore both the early modern *mentalité* and the development of the meaning of 'family' before 1600. Slaves, *famuli*, were the original *familia*, a group of *famuli* living under one roof.[30] 'Family' later came to include all those, not just the slaves or servants, who lived under the authority of the *pater familias*;[31] later still, the husband joined the 'family' of wife, children, and servants.

Early modern English had no word whose meaning was 'only kin', or 'all in the household except the servants'. 'Family' included them all. Mayo wrote in 1693 of the 'middling kind' of servants 'making up a part of every family'.[32] To illustrate his scheme for a public granary, Yarranton imagined a 'family' of seven: 'the Self, Wife, a Man, a Maid, and Three Children'.[33] When Arbuthnot described the house-hold of a large farm, he was at first ambiguous in his usage: 'His family will consist of himself, a wife, three children, 12 servants, and 10 labourers, each with a wife and three children'.[34] Whatever confusion this may have caused his readers, his tally of the number in the farmer's family makes its composition clear: 'Thus the farmer's family – 17.' Manuals of household government spoke of servants as they did of wives and children: all were subservient members of the family.[35]

The problem of language can be solved. Servants include ploughmen and dairymaids, families include servants, and labourers live separately.[36] The problem of categories remains. Service in husbandry is, in terms of modern categories, painfully ambiguous. Servants in husbandry, wage-earners, were hired by contract into a status relationship, and became members of the family. But how, we may ask, can they really have been both family members and wage-workers?

Nature abhors a chimera. Macpherson dealt with the paradox by dismissing one of its elements. He argued that the 'annual patriarchal relation' of master and servant was incidental to the market relation between property-holders and those who 'had to sell their labour-power to others to make a living'.[37] Everitt dismissed the other half. On the first page of his major essay on farm labour,[38] he carefully distinguished between the farm workers who lived in the farmhouse and those who did not, but by the second page, the concept of farm servants appears to have evaporated, as if their living with the farmers' families made them unimportant as agricultural labour. Except for mentioning that servants might have been better fed than labourers, none of his subsequent discussion concerns servants. But because his estimates of the size of the labour force were based, in part, on the combined numbers of servants and labourers, he was left with another paradox, the 'intense patriarchalism' of a countryside in which one-third of the people were farm workers. Patriarchy begins at home, however, and it was in farmers' families that many of these farm workers lived.

The place of servants in the early modern social order is equally difficult for us to understand. Servants had no independent place within it. In this sense, their taking of wages was seen as incidental to their dependency within their employers' families. Chamberlayne's Body Politique has as its Feet 'the lowest member ... the Day Labourers'.[39] Servants, wives, and children were discussed by him in a separate section; their place was derived from their dependence upon their masters, husbands, and fathers, and from the status of their masters, husbands, and fathers, in the social hierarchy proper.[40] King's economic ordering of the English population ranked adult male householders according to the net contribution of their families, and simply attached the total of wives, children and servants to the ranks attained by the householders. The 1801 census was similarly compiled by listing households by the occupation of the householder and counting the number of males and females within each household.[41]

Servants did not understand themselves, and were not understood by early modern society, to be part of a labouring class, youthful proletarians.[42] Servants were not unfree simply because they had been reduced to the status of wage-takers. As members of the family, they were politically invisible. Of course they controlled no property: they were unmarried youths, not adults. Of course they were subject to the political authority of their masters: they lived as dependent members of their families. Families at every level of early modern society sent their children into the households of others, and families at all but the lowest levels brought others' children into their own.[43] The opinion that all youths, whether children of nobles, gentry, yeomen, craftsmen, labourers, or paupers, became members of the labouring class by entering service was inconceivable.

This chapter began by stating that the existence of service in all its forms in early modern England is one of the simplest distinctions that can be drawn between the modern and early modern worlds. It is also one of the greatest obstacles to the simple application of modern categories to early modern experience. How large was the early modern proletariat? If we mean by proletariat a class of poor labouring families, having the power to produce, by themselves, only children, our account must exclude servants. The Hammonds, in *The Village Labourer*, and E. P. Thompson, in *The Making of the English Working Class*, are scrupulous in their usage.[44] When they write of the increasing differentiation between classes, they mean the growth of a class of ever more propertyless labourers. What was the condition of the working class? If we mean by this the condition of all wage-workers, we must differentiate between the condition of constantly employed servants, boarded by their employers, and seasonally unemployed labourers, feeding themselves and their families.[45] How large was the early modern labour force? If we mean by labour force the numbers willing to work for wages, we must include servants, which means in practice prising them out of the categories into which many early modern records placed them.

The problems of language and categories begin to evaporate in the nineteenth century, as 'servant', 'labourer', and 'family' take on their modern meanings, and as servants in husbandry come to be seen, in the south and east of England, as labourers in an unimportantly variant guise. By the mid century, most servants were female domestics. By the 1830s, most servants in husbandry in the southeastern half of England were sons and daughters of labourers, destined to become labourers themselves. The social and economic gap between servant-supplying and servant-hiring families widened, stretching to the breaking point the notion that servants became members of their employers' families. By 1851, few servants in husbandry were hired in the south and east. Most poor youths worked as day-labourers; only a few were plucked from this mass and placed at the farmer's table.

In the final chapter of this book, the decline in the practice of service in husbandry, its virtual extinction in the south and east, is explored. The five chapters that precede it are a search for an understanding of the place of service in husbandry in early modern England.

2   Incidence and understanding

Service in husbandry was a major form of hired labour in early modern agriculture and the typical experience of rural youths. By the mid nineteenth century, however, this was not true of the south and east of England. This second statement is far simpler to demonstrate, thanks to the wealth of detail provided by the 1851 census. Our best early modern estimates, by contrast, are drawn from samples resulting from historical accident.

Local censuses of parish populations were compiled for reasons as varied as tax assessment, the mustering of militias, and inquisitiveness. Relatively few survive. Fewer still are detailed enough to identify servants in husbandary, day-labourers, and farmers. Of the several hundred listings collected by the Cambridge Group for the History of Population and Social Structure,[1] only fifty-five, dating from 1599 to 1831, contain both occupational designations of the heads of households and the identification of the status of those within each household (Table 2.1). The simplest conclusion to be drawn from the listings is the large number of farm servants, especially in relation to the age group (15 to 24) in which most servants were concentrated. At most, approximately 19 per cent of the population was of this age.[2] The listings, moreover, reflect only the momentary status of individuals and households, and thus underestimate the proportion of youths who were at some stage servants in husbandry. The servants were diffused throughout each parish's households. Almost half (46.4 per cent) of the households of farmers contained servants, and most of these held no more than two servants (59.0 per cent). Once again, the momentary estimate represents the minimum figure for the proportion of farmers who ever employed servants.

The relative importance of servants in the agricultural labour force is more complicated to gauge. We are concerned with the functional categories of farm servant, day-labourer, and farmer, while the list-makers were concerned with the status of those listed. When we map the status designations of the lists into our own categories, errors of estimation arise. The number of farmers will be greatly under-estimated. Any of the gentlemen, clergymen, widows, craftsmen, and tradesmen of the lists may have been farmers, either as their principal

Table 2.1. *Servants, labourers and farmers, from parish listings, 1599–1831*

Date	Place	P Population	S Servants of farmers	L Labourers	F All farmers	Fw Farmers with servants	$\frac{S}{S+L}$	$\frac{S+L}{F}$	$\frac{Fw}{F}$	$\frac{S}{P}$
1599	Ealing, Middlesex	427	39	1	48	12	0.98	0.83	0.25	0.09
1688	Clayworth, Notts.	412	46	24	28	18	0.66	2.5	0.64	0.11
1695	Hutton Roof, Westmorland	141	17	5	12	9	0.77	1.8	0.75	0.12
1697	Hothorpe, Northants	100	5	7	9	3	0.42	1.3	0.33	0.05
1697	Killington, Westmorland	250	12	7	30	7	0.63	0.63	0.23	0.05
1697	Kirkby Lonsdale, Westmorland	552	70	12	35	22	0.85	2.3	0.63	0.13
1697	Donhead, Wilts.	280	4	37	14	2	0.10	2.9	0.14	0.01
1705	Adisham, Kent	125	28	7	9	6	0.80	3.9	0.67	0.22
1705	Ash (Chilton), Kent	701	47	46	25	14	0.51	3.7	0.56	0.07
1705	Ash (Overland), Kent	438	38	37	29	12	0.51	2.6	0.41	0.09
1705	Stadmarsh, Kent	54	8	6	3	2	0.57	4.7	0.67	0.15
1752	fforthampton & Swinley, Gloucs.	288	43	22	11	10	0.66	5.9	0.91	0.15

Year	Place									
1777	Carlton Rode, Norfolk	726	43	37	34	20	0.54	2.4	0.59	0.06
1787	31 Westmorland parishes	—	387	169	609	249	0.70	0.91	0.41	—
1790	Corfe Castle, Dorset	549	28	62	26	17	0.31	3.5	0.65	0.05
1792	Barlborough, Derbyshire	682	43	47	33	18	0.48	2.7	0.55	0.06
1796	Ardleigh, Essex	1,145	72	97	35	28	0.43	4.8	0.80	0.06
1800	Melbury Osmond, Dorset	334	5	32	6	3	0.14	6.2	0.50	0.01
1801	Sturminster Newton, Dorset	1,406	16	100	29	12	0.14	4.0	0.41	0.01
1801	Barkway & Reed, Herts.	995	38	108	28	18	0.26	5.2	0.64	0.04
1811	Smalley, Derbyshire	618	21	29	17	11	0.42	2.9	0.65	0.03
1811	Littleover, Derbyshire	353	25	25	14	11	0.50	3.6	0.79	0.07
1811	Mickleover, Derbyshire	580	39	39	16	15	0.50	4.9	0.94	0.07
1821	Digswell, Herts.	202	12	30	2	2	0.29	21.0	1.00	0.06
1831	Melbourn, Cambs.	1,474	22	137	23	15	0.14	6.9	0.65	0.01

Source: CG, Parish Listings Collection.

or secondary occupation, but we cannot know.[3] Servants in husbandry cannot be identified with precision. We can know only the numbers of servants employed by those designated as farmers, yeomen, graziers, and husbandmen. That estimate will overstate the true number of servants in husbandry, because some servants to farmers were personal servants, and were neither farmworkers nor engaged in ancillary tasks such as the management of the servant-holding family. More importantly, it understates the true number by excluding the servants in husbandry who were employed by gentlemen, clergymen, widows, craftsmen, and tradesmen. Parson Woodforde's household, for example, regularly contained at least two servants principally engaged in agriculture, but it is unlikely that a parish listing of Weston Longeville would have styled Woodforde as a farmer. An unusually detailed listing of the population of Murton, Westmorland, in 1787, illustrates the difficulty.[4] The list-maker noted the occupation of every member of the household, and we find that, for example, the family of Joseph Idle, weaver, contained his wife, described as house-keeper, and four others: Robert Dent, servant, husbandman; Elizabeth Bowen, servant, manager of dairy; Betty Robinson, servant, spoolswinder; and James Harrison, servant, shepherd. Without the unusual detail, we would have missed Idle's by-employment in farming, and failed to know that three of his four servants were servants in husbandry.

Our estimate of the size of the day-labouring population can only be derived from the number of householding labourers. Resident children of labourers, craftsmen, and tradesmen who worked in farming must go unrecognized. No part-time labourers can be identified, because the lists designated them by their primary status of wife, child, carpenter, husbandman. Partially counterbalancing these omissions were the alternative opportunities for work available to those termed 'labourer': not all labourers were constantly available to work for farmers.

Farm servants and labourers, moreover, were not all of identical strength and skill. In some instances the inequality will be unimportant: we shall be concerned only with the numbers in each category. But to say something about the relative contribution of labour made by servants and labourers, it would be useful to be able to adopt a standard unit of measurement, and adjust the raw data to this standard. Unfortunately, this is nearly impossible. Most records do not include the ages of individuals, so we cannot know which servants were very young and therefore unskilled and weak, and which labourers were old and weak. The possibility of providing weighted totals is discussed in detail in Appendix 2; the unweighted totals will be used in all the calculations that follow.

Table 2.2. *Farm servants, agricultural labourers and women (1851 census, five counties)*

Counties	Ratio of all servants to all labourers	Percentage deviations from column 1	
		All women excluded	Female labourers excluded
Devon	0.66	− 30	3
Cornwall	0.65	− 29	11
Cumberland	0.95	− 25	18
Westmorland	1.24	− 35	2
E. Riding	0.72	− 10	3

Source: 1851 census, PP 1852–3, LXXXVIII.

That so many women were, at some time in their lives, productive farm servants is of importance, because women were to lose much of this productive role in agriculture as a result of the decline of farm service. Female farm servants can be identified in these early modern listings, and in the 1851 census, and their numbers, where available, will be included in the total of all farm servants. Female agricultural labourers, however, cannot be identified, except in the 1851 census. Early modern recordkeepers invariably considered the status of a woman in relation to a man, as daughter, servant, wife, or widow, to be more significant than the woman's occupation.

Including female servants while necessarily excluding female la- bourers from the totals introduces an apparent asymmetry. The asym- metry, however, is less important than the error that would result from excluding female servants. The proportion of women among farm servants was much higher than among full-time agricultural labourers, a proposition which can be demonstrated using the 1851 census, the first systematic record that includes totals of female labourers. Table 2.2 shows the ratio of all farm servants, male and female, to all agricultural labourers, male and female, in five of the counties in which farm service survived through the nineteenth century. The 'true' ratio is then compared with the errors that would arise, first, if all females were excluded from the totals, and second, if only female labourers were excluded. The errors introduced by excluding all women from the estimate range from a 10 to a 35 per cent underestimation of the true ratio of servants to labourers, while the exclusion of women labourers causes an overestimation of the true ratio of only 2 to 18 per cent.

Taking, therefore, the total of servants to yeomen, husbandmen, graziers, and farmers as the best estimate of servants in husbandry, and the total of householding labourers as the best estimate of day-labourers, we can measure the composition of the early modern hired labour force in agriculture before 1800. Figure 2.1 shows the highly dispersed distribution of the ratio of servants in husbandry (S) to the total of servants in husbandry and day-labourers (S + L) in the parish listings of Table 2.1.[5] The median of the distribution is 0.56; that is, in half of the parishes, servants were at least 56 per cent of the hired force.[6] The size of the labour force relative to the number of farmers was high in none of the parishes (Figure 2.2). In the median parish, there were 2.65 hired workers per farmer.

These estimates can now be compared with those drawn from three more problematical early modern sources. The first, muster rolls and militia lists, are deficient because they excluded all women, and all men above and below the ages at which they were liable to be called into service. The Muster Roll of 1608, 'Men and Arms for Gloucestershire', was used by the Tawneys in their study of occupational structure, and listed males aged twenty and older.[7] In every parish, yeomen and husbandmen were listed together with their sons and male servants; labourers were listed separately. We selected a 10 per cent sample of the more than 400 parishes, and then arbitrarily narrowed this sample to include only those parishes in which the number of craftsmen and tradesmen was not larger than the number of yeomen and husbandmen, in order to limit errors in the estimation of the number of 'labourers' employed in agriculture. In these twelve parishes, there were 245 farmers, 78 male servants, and 96 male labourers. The ratio of servants to all hired workers was thus 0.45, and the ratio of all workers to farmers 0.71. Both figures underestimate the true relations, because nearly half of all male servants would have been too young to be mustered.

The militia lists date from the second half of the eighteenth century. Those of Hertfordshire and Northamptonshire are similar: they consist of yearly listings, made under the frequently amended Act of 1757, of men available to be drawn into the militia.[8] The minimum and maximum ages were fifteen and forty-five (lowered from fifty in 1762). Unlike the 1608 Muster Roll, therefore, these lists more systematically underestimate the true number of labourers than of servants. Once again, only those parishes in which farmers formed the majority of non-labouring occupations were selected, and only the first listings in each county were used, in order to avoid undercounting older labourers who

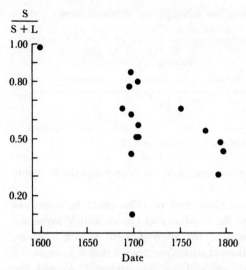

2.1. Servants relative to all hired workers in agriculture, 1599–1796.
Source: Table 2.1.

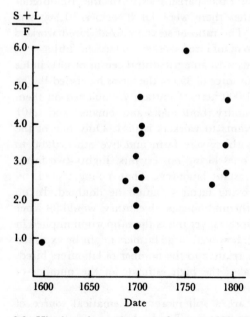

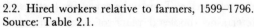

2.2. Hired workers relative to farmers, 1599–1796.
Source: Table 2.1.

Table 2.3. *Composition of labour force from militia lists for Hertfordshire and Northamptonshire*

		Parishes	Servants to all hired workers	All hired workers to farmers
Hertfordshire	1758–9	11	0.39	4.5
Northamptonshire	1762	24	0.48	3.2

Source: Northants RO; HRO, Militia List Collection.

might have become exempt from the militia in a previous draft. Table 2.3 presents the findings.

The Buckinghamshire Posse Comitatus of 1798 might be called, in imitation of the 1608 Muster Roll, 'Men and Horses and Wagons for Buckinghamshire'.[9] It claimed to list all men aged fifteen to sixty, together with their occupations and infirmities ('Francis Simons ... glazier ... nervous' was a resident of Great Missenden).[10] As with the militia lists of Hertfordshire and Northamptonshire, servants to farmers cannot be distinguished from other servants (although apprentices were grouped separately in each parish's list). In the 102 predominantly agricultural parishes there were 1,190 farmers, 1,360 servants, and 1,750 labourers. The ratio of servants to all hired workers was thus 0.438, and the ratio of all hired workers to farmers 2.61.

Arthur Young presented us with an agricultural census of sorts in his tours. He recorded the labour force of 355 of the farms he visited.[11] The farms ranged from 30 to 11,000 acres. Constantly employed on them were 1,482 servants in husbandry (both males and females) and 1,401 labourers. The ratio of servants to workers is 0.51. Only one of the farms hired no labour; this thirty-acre farm and five others (200 to 1,000 acres) were the only ones hiring no servants. Eighty-two farms (23.1 per cent) hired no constant labourers. That Young visited, by preference, large and improving farmers cannot be doubted. In no county in England, even in the mid nineteenth century, would 99.7 per cent of farmers have hired workers, yet this is the proportion implied in his lists. As we shall see later, however, large farmers might be expected to have hired fewer servants relative to the number of labourers hired. Young's bias, therefore, makes the high estimate of the number of servants even more impressive.

Settlement examinations are a still more problematical source of information on the incidence of service. They were taken by Justices of the Peace in order to determine the legal place of settlement of a pauper – that is, the parish in which the pauper was entitled to poor relief. One year's service or apprenticeship in a parish made it the place of legal settlement, and each year of service nullified the prior settlement. Examinations therefore often inquired into the history of service of the pauper, and provide us with fractional biographies of the former servants. Women are systematically underrepresented in the examinations, for a woman took on both her husband's name and his place of settlement when she married. Paupers are not representative of all those who had been servants, since the poverty of adults was often tied to the poverty they experienced as children, before they entered service, but it is likely that more paupers had been servants than had the general population.

Nonetheless, the examinations reveal a very high incidence of service from the late seventh nth to the early nineteenth century.[12] A sample of 2,201 examinations from eleven southern and eastern counties reveals that 81 per cent of the examinants had been servants.[13] Often, the examination does not specify the occupation of the former employer of the servant; thus, in Oxfordshire, Berkshire, and Hampshire, the percentage of those earning their settlement through farm service, as contrasted with apprenticeship, productive service to craftsmen and tradesmen, and domestic service, must lie between 44.4 per cent (where farm service was specified) and 68.2 per cent (farm service plus unspecified service).

Taken as a whole, the seventeenth- and eighteenth-century sources show the strong presence of farm servants in English agriculture. The 1851 census does not. The first census to have asked the right questions from the point of view of this study, it reveals two Englands, the south and east with relatively few servants, and the north and west, with relatively few labourers (Figure 2.3).[14] The enumerators were instructed to complete schedules for every household, and to include in them the name, age, marital status, sex, occupation, and position within the household of each inhabitant. The example given to enumerators was a hypothetical household containing 'Tho. Young, servant, unmarried. *M. 19*. Farm labourer.'[15] The 'Farm Servants (in door)' in the summary tables were drawn from these household schedules, and were defined as 'all labourers in agriculture ... living in the house of the farmer'. The 'Agricultural Labourers (out door)' were defined as 'all labourers in agriculture (except shepherds) not living in the farmhouse'. The mean number of agricultural workers per farmer is shown in Figure 2.4.[16] The regional pattern of Figure 2.3 has been almost exactly reversed. Counties with small numbers of servants relative to labourers had large numbers of all workers relative to farmers.

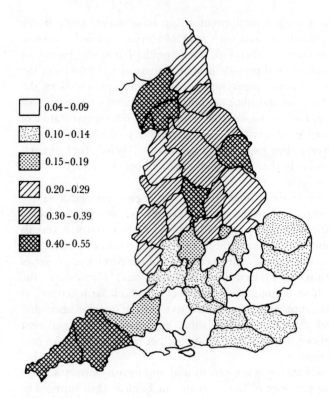

2.3. Farm servants as a proportion of farm servants and labourers (male and female), by county, 1851.
Source: 1851 census.

There is a great difference between the 1851 census and the various pre-census listings in terms of their reliability and national coverage. None of the biases in the earlier records, however, could have been responsible for the marked change in the incidence of service between the two sets of records. In nearly all the early listings for the counties in which service was insignificant in 1851, servants were a far higher proportion of the labour force. The mean parish ratio of farm servants to all hired agricultural workers in the Cambridge Group's parish listings was 0.49; in Arthur Young's sample, it was 0.51. In the 1851 census, the mean county ratio was 0.21. Hertfordshire and Northamptonshire, in 1851, had ratios of 0.04 and 0.07: these were the lowest and second lowest county ratios in all of England. In the eighteenth-century militia lists, the ratios for these counties were 0.39 and 0.48.

If one breaks down the distribution of pre-1800 parish ratios in

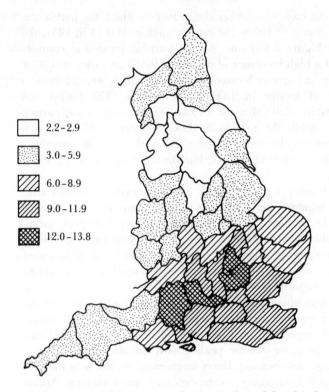

2.4. Servants and labourers per farmer (male and female), by county, 1851.

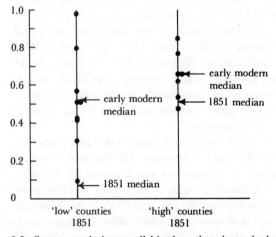

2.5. Servants relative to all hired workers in agriculture, early modern and 1851.

Figure 2.1 on the basis of whether the county in which the parish was located scored above or below the county median of 0.15 in 1851, the distribution of Figure 2.5 results. All the parishes located in counties which retained a high incidence of service in 1851 had ratios of 0.48 or more; the ratio in parishes located in counties which were to show a low incidence of service in 1851 range greatly. The lowest was Donhead, Wiltshire (0.10), but the median of this southern and eastern group was 0.51, while the median for those counties in 1851 was 0.08, lower than even the Donhead figure. The median for the northern counties also fell, from 0.68 to 0.51, but the fall was not as marked.

Service in husbandry was the life of many an early modern youth; servants in husbandary were the work force of many an early modern farmer. Why? In ecological terms, the economic, technological, social, and demographic environment of early modern England was one in which the institution of service in husbandry flourished: it favoured the demand for, and supply of, servants, and restricted the supply of their chief competitors, day-labourers.

No English agriculture was so seasonal that it required no constant attention, and it was to continuous tasks that servants, hired on annual contracts, were especially well suited. Pastoral farming was least seasonal. The need for labour peaked only in the spring, during lambing, calving, and shearing. Dairy farms required not only the care of the herds but daily milking and butter- and cheese-making. Arable farming was more seasonal: weeding, hoeing, mowing, and reaping were tasks of the summer and early autumn. But continuous labour was required there as well. Most farms were large enough to permit the use of draught animals, and unlike modern farm machinery, oxen and horses needed daily attention, whether or not they were used daily in ploughing, harrowing, and carting. Where the farmer's family could not provide the necessary constant labour, servants were hired. Arthur Young described the masters of two-plough farms who '*universally* (unless they are remarkable hard working men themselves, or have sons men grown) keep a man servant'.[17]

Commons and wastes, small farms, and rural crafts and trades all restricted the assured supply of day-labourers. All provided potential labourers with alternatives to continuous employment by farmers. 'Commons', complained a Board of Agriculture report of 1794, gave labourers 'the means of subsisting in idleness'.[18] William Marshall called cottagers 'fickle' for their power to refuse offers of employment. Arbuthnot wrote in exasperation that 'if you give them work, they will tell you that they must go to look up their sheep, cut furzes, get their

cow out of the pound, and perhaps say that they must take their horse
to be shod, that he may carry them to a horse-race or cricket-match'.[19]
A century earlier, Adam Moore had described wastes as the excuse for
the poor to develop 'strategems to avoid work'.[20] The ideal cottager,
praised for his industry in 1785, would have had neither the necessity
nor the time to labour constantly for others, with his two or three milk
cows, two or three calves, forty or fifty sheep, two or three hogs, and
three acres of rental land.[21] Putting the children of farmers and
cottagers on annual contracts and bringing them into the farmhouse
ensured their reliability. 'One in the house is worth two at a distance',
as Marshall put it.[22]

The mixture of small- and medium-sized farms typical of much of
early modern England enhanced both the supply of and the demand
for servants. Small farmers could reduce the burden of supporting their
adolescent children by sending them into service. Larger farmers did
not hire so many workers that it was difficult to lodge them within the
farmhouse.

Rural crafts and trades similarly made servants necessary and
labourers scarce. They were alternatives to wage-work in agriculture,
and had low set-up costs. Alehouses, as Thirsk reported, were often no
more than 'the parlours of the cottage'.[23] Farmers in regions with many
rural crafts and trades therefore had to compete with these opportunities for the attention of householding adults. By-employment in
agriculture and rural industry could also make hired labour necessary.
A by-employed craftsman–farmer could not have given his constant
attention to farming: he relied on his family to provide the agricultural
labour.[24] Farm servants were hired into the family to replace the
labour of the householder. It was the household, not the householder,
that was by-employed. The household of Joseph Idle, mentioned
above, was by-employed in this sense. A Norfolk man testified at his
1827 settlement examination that he had once been hired by a
carpenter and farmer 'to look after his farm'; other settlement examinations show farm servants having been hired by brickmakers, linen-
weavers, and inn-keepers.[25]

It is likely that the combination of rural crafts, pastoral farming,
small farms, and dispersed settlement that characterized the 'horn and
thorn' north and west made servants in husbandry especially necessary.
Where farms were isolated, tied labour was essential, because independent labourers were not within the easy call of farmers. Thomas
Hitt found day-labourers preferable to farm servants only where
labourers lived in close proximity to farmers.[26] In East Yorkshire, two
centuries after Hitt published his treatise, day-labourers predominated

in nucleated settlements, and farm servants in areas of isolated farms.[27]

Demography and family structure also influenced the keeping of servants in husbandry. Service was uniquely suited to a farming environment of nuclear families, high rates of mortality, and a high age at marriage. The labour a nuclear family could supply, and the labour it required to meet its needs, constantly changed, and the change in its labour supply was often out of phase with the change in needs.[28] A family of two able adults soon became a family of two adults and small children, who needed both attention and food; this then became a family of adults and able adolescents. Nalson has called the inevitable cyclical imbalance between labour and needs 'the basic problem of family farming'.[29]

Several structural solutions to the problem have been known. The laterally extended family did not experience the cyclical change as sharply, because the family cycles of the constituent couples tended to overlap, and thus cancel one another. While one couple's children were being born, another's might have been becoming productive. These joint families were less confronted by cyclical imbalance than by a long-term disparity between overall family size and the size of each family's holding.

The redistribution of land, either in a system of *métayage* or in the Russian *mir*, described by Chayanov and later by Shanin, solved the cyclical problem in another manner.[30] As the family's needs changed, a changed amount of land was made available to it. More effort had to be applied by the family's workers, but the return to their labour was greater than it would have been if they were applying it to a fixed amount of land. Markets in land could have served the same balancing function, where credit was made available to young families as their needs grew.

Service in husbandry solved the cyclical problem by eliminating it. The family was simply redefined.[31] Youths were hired into the family to bring its labour into balance with the land available to it; youths were sent out to be servants for other families, for even when a farmer needed extra labour, he would not always have found his sons and daughters suited, by their strength and skills, to the farm's particular tasks.

Farm service could have existed in the absence of money, markets in commodities, and differences in the sizes of holdings. The only formal requirements would have been the desire of families to maintain constant average levels of consumption and effort, and holdings just large enough that the marginal contribution of a servant's labour was equal to the marginal cost of maintaining the servant. Cost and product could both have consisted of real goods rather than money. Family cycles alone would have given rise to the advantageous transfer of youths. Wages could have been paid to the servant in food, lodging, and livestock.

The picture of a moneyless world of equally sized holdings is abstract; it is not entirely fanciful. Occasionally, English servants in husbandry received, in lieu of money wages, the right to keep their sheep with their employers' flocks for the year of the contract. In chronically money-short and labour-scarce New France, *censitaires* brought the children of their neighbours into their service, boarded and lodged them for several years, and gave them a cow when they left service to marry.[32] In this respect it is interesting that the keeping of a servant's livestock as a condition of employment was far more common in the sixteenth-century court rolls of Ingoldmells, Lincolnshire, than it was in any eighteenth-century record.[33] Wherever service in husbandry was practised, it solved the problem of a farm's cash-flow by delaying money payments for work done until after the harvest, and by paying much of the real wage in food, drink and lodging. The 'forced saving' of servants represented an advance of credit to their employers for the year of the contract.

Habakkuk and Anderson have further linked youthful departures from home to customs of impartible inheritance.[34] Habakkuk reasoned that impartible inheritance promoted the permanent migration from home of all but the heir, while partible inheritance promoted seasonal mobility from the fixed base of home. Anderson found servants in rural Lancashire in the nineteenth century to have been a reflection of single inheritance and the scattering of the rest of the children.

The titles of both studies suggest, however, the primacy of preferences for family structure over formal systems of inheritance. Inheritance practices can accommodate themselves to a variety of desired ends. Formal partible inheritance can be used to maintain nuclear or stem families, and need not lead to the division of land. Sabean found that while all legitimate children of peasants in southern Germany in the sixteenth century had a claim to the property, in practice only those heirs who remained in the village could press their claim. Informal institutions were therefore required to determine who would stay and who leave.[35] Charles Varley's autobiography echoes this practice, two centuries later. He came to fear that if he remained too long away from home, his ill-natured stepmother would persuade his father to change his will in favour of her daughters.[36] Impartible inheritance would similarly have led to the division of property when the will ordered the principal heir to provide for his siblings, and when the disposal of part of the property was the only means of accomplishing this.[37]

Service in husbandry also provided a solution to several problems posed by the unpredictable hand of death. A farm servant could have been quickly hired to replace the farmer or his wife in the farming household. Without this ready remedy, death often occasioned the collapse of the family economy and the dispersion of the surviving members.[38] Larger joint families were better able to redefine tasks in response to the death of one member. Wrigley has recently related the function of service to a wider demographic problem. 'Family planning' can be a modern euphemism for contraception and abortion only because the planning of births can be taken to be equivalent to the willing into existence of an ultimate family size. In an age of high rates of mortality, however, the careful planning of births would have had only a weak relation to the resultant size of the family, because the timing of deaths could not be predicted. The institution of service was a form of *ex post facto* family planning. Once the family knew that it had too many surviving children to be employed or maintained within the family, the surplus could be sent to the family that now knew that it had too few surviving children to help with the farm.[39]

A high age at marriage favoured the existence of service in husbandry. The higher the proportion of the adult population that remained unmarried, the larger was the potential supply of servants, and the smaller the potential supply of married adult labourers. A high age at marriage, coupled with farm service, also allowed youths to save before facing the costs of establishing an independent household.[40] The delaying of marriage was also the other side of Wrigley's early modern 'family planning': aggregate population growth was slowed more by a high age at marriage than by contraception within marriage.

Service in husbandry was an elegant solution to the many problems posed to the nuclear family. It preserved the form of the nuclear (or stem) family while allowing the family to balance its labour and its needs.[41] It was not common where joint families were the desired family structure, as in southern and eastern Europe, nor where formal systems of redistribution of land existed.[42] It was instead common over much of northern and western Europe in early modern times, wherever nuclear or stem families predominated. Laslett has identified service as one of the three characteristics of the western family, along with a high age at marriage and a nuclear family structure.[43] Service has, moreover, survived in parts of Europe while becoming rare in England.[44]

Service in husbandry was an institution imbedded in a particular environment. Nurtured by that environment, it also affected it. That farm servants married late, and could save, supported the demand for small farms and checked the growth of supply of their competitors in the labour force, propertyless adults. The economies of nuclear families were protected from the random hand of mortality. The growth of the population as a whole was slowed. Finally, the redefinition of the family that service made possible insured a higher level of labour productivity than would have resulted if each farm was limited to the use of its own children.

Servants in husbandry were available to, and hired by,* Richard Baxter's Poor Husbandman,[45] Arthur Young's sorry farmer of twenty acres,[46] and by large farmers, accumulating ever-larger holdings from their neighbours while employing their neighbours' children as farm servants. Servants came from the families of· cottagers, craftsmen, tradesmen, and farmers. The institution was, in early modern times, wonderfully adaptable, filling both the roles of family-balancer to small farmers, and labour force to larger farmers. It declined when its environment deteriorated.

We have drawn two statistical sketches of the incidence of service in husbandry, the first, early modern, in which the practice was wide-spread, the second, modern, in which the practice had ceased in half of England. In the final two chapters, they will be redrawn, revealing changes in the incidence of service within early modern England, before the final slide towards extinction in the south and east. As broad outlines, however, the sketches of this chapter are accurate enough. The next chapters are concerned not with changing incidence, but with the nearly static form and practice of the institution.

PART II

Form and practice

3   *Life and work*

The notion of an institution implies a certain rigidity of form. Its rules, once learned, become the tacit regulators of the behaviour of the people whose actions are the institution itself. Service in husbandry was a simple institution with three rigid rules, three defining characteristics:

1. It was not an adult occupation, but a status and occupation of youths, a stage in the progression from child living with parents to married adult living with spouse and children.
2. It was a contractual institution; the contract was annual and renewable.
3. Servants in husbandry were maintained in the farmer's family.

These characteristics were found wherever the institution was common and unquestioned, both in sixteenth-century Middlesex and twentieth-century Yorkshire.

Within these constraints, modest variations in behaviour were possible, and can be observed at all times. The argument of the next three chapters is that until the late eighteenth century, and after that in the north and west, the form of the institution retained its useful tacit rigidity. Part II is thus devoted to a description of service in husbandry as it was normally practised; the two chapters of Part III, which are devoted to change in the incidence of the institution, will demonstrate, first, how important was the rigidity of form in early modern England, and second, how complete was the decay in form in the south and east after 1790.

Contract and law

For the most part, service in husbandry was a private institution, practised within the farmer's family, defined not by law but by custom. Law touched only upon the formation and maintenance of the relationship of master and servant. Contracts were normally verbal;[1] the fact that a verbal contract had been made, however, was at some times and in some places recorded at Courts Leet, Hundred Courts, Petty Sessions, and Quarter Sessions.[2] Master and servant customarily

31

sealed their agreement with the offering and taking of a token
payment, the 'earnest', 'hiring penny', 'fastening penny', or 'God's
penny'.[3] The term of the contract, unless otherwise stated, was one
year. It began at the habitual regional hiring date, and contracts made
after that date usually ran only through the end of the customary year,
and not for a full twelve months.[4] The contract implicitly bound the
servant to serve the master for the year, and to obey his reasonable
commands, and it bound the master to maintain the servant for the
year and to pay the wages agreed upon, whether or not there was daily
work for the servant, and whether or not the servant remained fit to
work.[5] As Burn advised Justices of the Peace, 'if a servant retained for
the year falls sick, or is hurt or disabled, by act of God or the master's
business, he is not to be put away nor his wages to be abated'.[6] The
large number of Quarter Sessions' orders to take back sick and injured
servants and to maintain them to the end of the term attests both to
the enforceable nature of the contract and to the frequency with which
it was broken.[7] Some orders were more explicit than others. Anthony
Gray, for example, was ordered to keep and maintain one Jeffrey
Salmon, his servant who had become sick and subject to 'strange fits of
lunacy', until the 'full end and expiration of the term of his said service'.[8]
In Hereford in 1666 a servant made complaint that she had been
disabled by a beating received from a fellow servant, and 'by the
severity of her said mistress was enforced to quit her said service and
now her said mistress doth not only deny to pay her the wages arrears
for the time she served but also detains her cloaths from her'. The case
was referred to the next sessions.[9] Pregnant servants were not to be
turned away, but in many cases they were.[10] Quarter Sessions
sometimes compromised, ordering masters to maintain their pregnant
servants for one month after the birth of the child.[11] The rigidity of the
contract could work against the interests of servants as well as masters:
pregnancy and sickness were not sufficient legal causes for a servant's
departure.[12] As might be expected, the part of the contractual
arrangement least palatable to masters was the requirement that they
continue to pay wages to a disabled servant. A master may have felt
Perkins' 'Christian Duty' to maintain a sick servant ('If the servant in
time of his service be sicke, the master's care must be by all means
possible to procure for his recovery'), but he often felt no such duty to
pay wages to a servant who could not work. Thomas Parkyns, a Justice
of the Peace for Nottinghamshire, recognized this reluctance. He
suggested that the responsibility for maintenance was unchanged by
the servant's illness, but that wages could rightly be abated.[13]

In law, the contract had a rigid annual form. In practice, it often did not. Contracts could be broken with cause. Michael Dalton counselled that the decision of one Justice of the Peace was sufficient to terminate a servant's contract with cause; in the parish records of Gissing, Norfolk, is a set of orders dating from 1726 and 1743, each signed by one justice, terminating the contracts between masters and servants for 'sufficient cause'.[14] A single termination order appears in the parish records of Norton, Suffolk, for 1733: 'Upon hearing of the matter between Joseph Clark of Norton [,] Farmer [,] and Hether Parker his servant I do discharge them from one another and give the same Hether Parker liberty to serve elsewhere according to the statute in that case made and presided.'[15] Furthermore, judging by the evidence of settlement examinations, contracts were often annulled with only the mutual consent of master and servant. Arguments often precipitated the mutually agreeable partings; it is impossible to do more than speculate over the coercion involved in gaining the servant's consent.[16]

Farm servants were, in many respects, invisible to the state. While under contract, they were submerged beneath the broadly circumscribed authority of their masters.[17] As Lawrence Stone has recently suggested, service was itself partly political in its function, maintaining good order among potentially unruly adolescents and young adults by assigning them to the governance of their employers.[18] The normal relation of servants to the state was indirect, mediated through their masters. They were subject to personal taxes, such as the subsidy, poll tax, and marriage tax, but their masters were either responsible for paying the tax, deducting it from wages, or liable to pay the tax in case of default.[19] Masters were required in 1540 to supply their sons and male servants aged seven to seventeen with bows and arrows and to deduct the cost from the servants' wages (33 Hen. VIII, c. 9). During the Interregnum, householders were ordered to keep their sons and men servants in quiet and peaceable order, and to report to the militia any absence of more than twelve hours.[20] Servants were personally subject to all general statutes, but the infrequency with which they appear in records of presentments to, and orders of, Quarter Sessions, except in cases of bastardy, refusal to serve, and grave public disorder (like that described recently by E. P. Thompson), suggests that the maintenance of the good order of servants was effected by their masters, and not by the larger state.[21]

Some aspects of the activities of servants, however, were not captured within the bounds of immediate patriarchal authority. Vagrancy, unwillingness to work for 'reasonable' wages, and absolute refusal to serve affected the entire community. All these concerned 'masterless men', and could be controlled only by the greater community. Their eradication was the object of much statute law from the fourteenth to the nineteenth century. Statutes regulating wages and prohibiting vagrancy were common in the years following the disruption of the Plague. Much of this law was repeated in piecemeal fashion in the fifteenth century; the scattered legislation was gathered together and standardized in the great Statute of Artificers of 1562–3 (5 Eliz. I, c. 4).[22] Two major institutions existed to enforce the statutes concerning servants. The first, which has been mentioned obliquely, was the ordinary government of the county. Parish constables, appointed by Justices of the Peace in the sixteenth century, were the local agents of the law dealing with the complaints of breach of contract and other offences. Differences that could not be settled by them were brought before the Justices of the Peace of the county, meeting in formal Quarter Sessions (hence the amount of information on enforcement available in Quarter Sessions Rolls). The second institution was, however, more specific to the practice of service. Masters and servants in many places in England were obliged to appear before the High Constable or Justice of the Peace at an annual sessions in order to ensure, first, that all contracts made were within the bounds of the statutes, and second, that all servants had masters. These Statute Sessions, also called Petty Sessions, were later to become the better-known hiring fairs.[23] They were the one public institution in England wholly concerned with servants, and they will be considered below, in their relation to hiring and mobility, in Chapter 4.

Tasks

Most of the rules governing the practice of service in husbandry were customary, and resulted in several regular patterns of behaviour. The tasks performed by a servant, and the annual wages received for them, were fairly strict functions of the sex and age of the servant. Women generally ran the dairy, milked the cows, cared for small animals, especially poultry, weeded, and performed the principal tasks ancillary to agriculture, ale-making and cooking. Men traditionally cared for and worked with the draught animals, cattle, and sheep. They ploughed and carted, harrowed, and so forth; Henry Best's carters made regular trips to market.[24] In southwest Wales around 1900 ploughmen did the 'highest work' of any hired worker. The status of these young, unmarried servants was reported by Jenkins to have been higher than that of older, married labourers because the latter were not entrusted with the farmer's horses. Marshall betrayed his ignorance of the mental world of his servants when he expressed surprise at the contempt in

which his servants held oxen.[25] The association of status with horses led
to friction between master and servant. Servants stole grain from their
masters' stores to supplement the horse's feed. Banister thought farm
servants experts in deception: they stole corn 'to pamper a favourite
team'. Marshall called carters 'the greatest thieves in the world ...
they are thieves to a man, and glory in their thievery'.[26] Fred Kitchen
worked on a farm where the horses were so 'sorry-looking' that he felt
ashamed to be out in public with them, and stole pig and bullock feed
from his master to get their coats to shine.[27]

Young boys were not entrusted with draught horses or oxen; they
lacked the strength to manage them. Instead, they performed a
multitude of odd jobs. Fred Kitchen's first 'missus' hired him because
she wanted 'a lad to live in an' help wi' the bits o' jobs'. A typical day's
work at thirteen consisted of cleaning the stable, milking the cows,
feeding the calves and other stock, helping to cart turnips, leading the
plough, and milking the cows and cleaning the stable once again.[28]

Kitchen's workday began at five in the morning and was over at
nine at night. Three and a half centuries before Kitchen wrote his
memoirs, Tusser admonished housewives to

> Call servants to breakefast by day starre appeare
> A snatch and to worke fellowes, tarry not here.[29]

Markham described a typical winter day's labour: servants and farmers rose at four, foddered the cattle, cleaned the stable, rubbed down
the cattle, curried the horses, watered and fed the beasts and breakfas-
ted at six. They ploughed from seven until two or three, came home for
dinner, and returned to the stables at four to repeat their pre-breakfast
tasks. Supper was taken at six-thirty, and then servants mended shoes,
beat hemp, stamped apples for cider, ground malt, threshed corn,
sharpened the plough irons, or repaired ploughs until eight, when they
returned to the stables to clean the stalls and replace the straw in
them.[30] Servants were expected to do a variety of odd jobs in the
evening after the day's ploughing and dairywork were completed. The
author of the *Boke of Thrift* observed that the more carters and
ploughmen could do minor craftsmen's jobs, 'the more are these two
sorts of servants to bee enterteyned'. Bailiffs were instructed to make
servants 'to labour about the yarde, to thresh corne, or to make walls,
ditches, hedges, or other necessarie workes about the house, for the
sparing of money'.[31]

Wages

Wages were, at least in legal theory, regulated by statute. The first
explicit regulation of servant's wages was the ordinance 'de

Servientibus' of 1349 and the 'Statute of Labourers' of 1350–1 (25 Ed. III, Stat. 2), enacted in the first years of the Black Death. Wages were ordered frozen at the levels that had prevailed before the Plague. By 1388, it had become clear that this rule was not enforceable, and specific rates of wages were proclaimed (12 Ric. II, c. 4). These rates remained in force until 1444–5 (23 Hen. VI, c. 12); the new rates were double the 1388 rates. They were revised slightly upwards again in 1495 (11 Hen. VII, c. 22); and repeated in 1514–15 (6 Hen. VIII, c. 1). No more legislation regulating wages appeared before 1562–3: the Statute of Artificers placed the responsibility for establishing maximum wages on the Justices of the Peace, in Quarter Sessions, and removed it from Parliament. Noting that the assessed wages were too low, the Statute ordered Justices of the Peace to meet annually and set wages for the coming year for their county. Extant proclamations of wages in Quarter Sessions from 1563 to 1566 show great variation from county to county. Some assessments were double the old levels; others showed increases of only a tenth to a third.[32] The legislation remained in force for 250 years, repealed only in 1813 (53 Geo. III, c. 40).

Records of proclamations of wages abound;[33] it is less easy to know whether wages were held to the assessed limits. There are a few presentments in Quarter Sessions for giving wages in excess of the assessed rates: Essex Quarter Sessions, for example, ordered an inquiry into excessive wages in 1566; several masters and mistresses were presented in North Riding Quarter Sessions for giving high wages; Elizabeth Gooch of Caxton, Cambridgeshire, was presented in 1670 for taking higher than prescribed wages.[34] Few records of wages paid in the later sixteenth and seventeenth centuries exist; of those that do, fewer still can be paired with coincident wage assessments for the counties involved. By comparing the wages paid to the farm servants of Henry Best in 1641, of Robert Loder in 1614, and to the farm servants of a Kentish estate from 1616 to 1704 with the closest available county assessments, it can be seen that in general the wages received did not exceed the assessed wages, with the exception of the wages of some men on the Kentish estate, where their wages of £6 were higher than the £5 maximum for bailiffs in 1724.[35] The servants enrolled in Petty Sessions in Essex and in manorial rolls in Lincolnshire in the late sixteenth century were all given wages within the bounds established by the closest assessment,[36] but that should not be surprising, for Petty Sessions were an agency of enforcement of assessments. More Quarter Sessions presentments concern hiring outside Petty Sessions or Statute Sessions than they do the payment of excessive wages; prevention of illegal contracts was simpler than punishment after the fact.

Just as tasks varied with sex and age, so did wages. Women systematically received only a fraction of men's wages. In a sample of sixteenth- to eighteenth-century Quarter Sessions assessments, the median ratio of maximum male to maximum female wages was 1 to 0.60.[37] In the Spalding, Lincolnshire, hiring fairs, the mean annual male wage from 1768 to 1785 was £6.5.0; the female wage was £2.15.0 (Figure 3.1); an account book from Tetney, Lincolnshire, shows the same pattern.[38]

Very young servants might receive no wages at all; rather, they would only have been maintained by the farmer for the year. The minimum age for which wages were specified in Quarter Sessions assessments varied from ten to twenty for men, and from twelve to sixteen for women.[39] Servants would not receive adult wages until they were in their late teens or early twenties.[40] In the eighteenth century, the normal age of transition from juvenile service was often taken to be sixteen. *Annals of Agriculture* reported in 1798 that the Wrexham Agricultural Society had established a prize for the long service of men servants, beginning at sixteen; ten years later the Kent Society was offering a prize for best boy in husbandry under seventeen.[41] In the

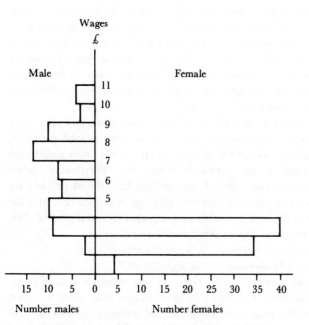

3.1. Annual wages at Spalding, Lincolnshire, 1786–7.
Source: LAO, Holland QS D2.

sample of Quarter Sessions assessments, the minimum age at which adult wages could be paid to men ranges from fifteen to twenty-four; the median is twenty. The range for women was the same, but the median was eighteen.[42] The wages reported in eighteenth-century settlement examinations show similar differences, within broad limits. The mean wage for male servants under fifteen was £2.10.0 ($n = 18$, S = £1.10.0); the mean wage for those twenty and older was £5.15.0 ($n = 34$, S = £2.3.0).[43] Bloom Stimpson came to the Spalding hiring fairs for four consecutive years (1770–3) and received wages of £6.8.0, £6.12.0, £6.18.0, and £8.2.0; William Eason jumped from wages of £3.10.0 in 1776 to wages of £7.12.0 in 1779.[44] The often dramatic increases also appear in an account book of a farm probably located in Tetney, Lincolnshire. The annual wages of the second men (that is, not the main male servant) who remained at Tetney for more than one year increased at a median rate of 17 per cent for each year they remained at Tetney; the wages of the first man often did not increase at all.[45] If it can be presumed that a change in the 'earnest' from 2s 5d to 5s represented an attainment of adult status (because low male wages are associated with the 2s 5d earnest and high wages with 5s), then the median of the once and for all increase upon attainment of maturity was 23 per cent. Similar patterns can be found in settlement examinations, and in the Spalding hiring fairs. The wages of individual males at Spalding increased at a median rate of 18 per cent per year, in a period (1768–85) when overall wage levels at Spalding were nearly constant. All women's wages were low, showing very little increase with age. The median annual increase at Tetney was zero; at Spalding the median was 3 per cent.

Wages were annual, but payment was often more frequent. The usual arrangement was that servants could request partial payment, and that the balance would be paid at the end of the contractual year (in Kitchen's case, at the breakfast before the 'Martlemas' hiring fair).[46] An Essex servant reported that he had been hired in 1801 for £3, and that he had received fourteen shillings in November, and the rest as he wanted them.[47] Many Tetney servants received part of their wages during the year. Tusser instructed farmers to

> Paie weeklie thy workman, his household to feed
>
> Paie quarterlie servants, to buie as they need.[48]

The annual payment of wages bears an interesting and ambiguous relation to the ability of servants to save. Wages that were not paid until the end of the year represented 'forced' savings, an extension of credit by the servant to the farmer. It probably mattered little to servants, who had no expenses in maintaining themselves other than clothing and ale, whether they or their masters hoarded their savings. One of the advantages Andrew Yarranton claimed in 1698 for his scheme for a public granary was that money 'now in the servant's hands, both men and maids (which at present lies dead in their chests)' would 'tumble' into the bank.[49] Some servants apparently collected no annual wages until they left the master's service. Sussex Quarter Sessions in 1649 ordered a master to pay a female servant £5.5.0 for five and a quarter years' service.[50]

Servants had the opportunity of saving their lump sum wages in preparation for leaving service, but also had the opportunity of spending them immediately. The year's wages were paid immediately before the largest festive occasion in the servant's year, and could easily be spent on immediate pleasures and clothing rather than saved. Fred Kitchen referred to 'Martlemas' as the first holiday in twelve months, when servants were let loose with purses full of golden sovereigns.[51] Nash Stevenson counselled farmers to pay their servants quarterly to prevent annual binges.[52]

Money savings were simply hoarded. Another form of payment to servants, however, allowed servants to earn a kind of interest on their savings. Male servants often, as Best put it, 'condition to have soe many sheepe wintered and sommered with theire meisters'.[53] Best docked eighteen pence per sheep from the wages of the servants whose sheep he kept. Several sixteenth-century records show the same form of saving. An eighteen-year-old youth was hired in 1574–5 in Essex for twenty shillings and pasture for two sheep;[54] many hiring agreements registered in petty sessions at Ingoldmells in Lincolnshire in the late sixteenth century mention the keeping of sheep and lambs by servants.[55] Eighteenth-century settlement examinations and hiring fairs furnish later examples. A Bury man had been hired at seventeen for undisclosed wages and the 'going' of half a score of sheep; another had been hired at twenty for two guineas and the keeping of thirty-four sheep.[56] A Lincolnshire servant was hired at the Spalding Martinmas session of 1782 for £4.4.0 and the keeping of two sheep.[57]

Both forms of saving appear in the rare instances of post-mortem inventories of servants' goods. Most of these inventories list only purses, chests, and clothing, a few list livestock. A Lincolnshire servant left behind him in 1696 a purse, some clothing, eighteen sheep and eight lambs; a later servant died leaving a purse, clothing, four heifers, thirteen ewes, and nine lambs.[58] Small flocks accumulated in this way could provide either the basis of a separate flock when the servant left service, or an easily realizable stock of money.

Food and lodging

The meals and beds farmers provided for servants were in some ways extensions of the wages they paid them. In this sense, farmers paid servants half, or two-thirds, or whatever proportion of their wages in money, and the rest in kind.[59] An OECD study of farm servants in husbandry and labourers in Europe estimated that board and lodging were 20 to 42 per cent of total wages.[60]

The servants of small farmers shared the same standard of living as the rest of the family. They often ate at the same table, and slept in the same rooms (and beds, upon occasion). Literary evidence for this shared life is stronger in the modern period than in the early modern, but it is likely that only in the later period did the practice become worthy of remark. Gervase Markham published a recipe for a coarse bread suitable for the farmer or his hinds (farm servants);[61] Robert Loder, in trying to prove to himself that keeping servants was too expensive, adopted the assumption that all eight members of his household, including his five servants, ate equal shares of the food purchased and consumed equal shares of candles and firewood. He calculated that each person cost the household almost ten pounds a year.[62]

Even when the servants did not eat with the master, they seem to have been fed well. This would have been in the interest of the masters, in two ways. Better fed servants worked better; a poorly nourished servant was the liability of the farmer for the year.[63] There was, moreover, no way better calculated to encourage servants to renew their contracts than to feed them well. The farm whose food Kitchen remembered with the most pleasure was the farm on which lads always stayed 'until they grew too big to be lads any longer'.[64] But not all farmers cared in this way. Mayo wrote of the discontent servants were apt to feel 'to be laid in some cold out-house, or meanest Loft, of a Poor Cottage, to have the leavings of coarse fare there'.[65]

There were those who, like Loder, were worried about the expense of maintaining servants, and who argued that farm servants were fed too well on larger farms. Tusser had a rhyme to cover this, as he did for every occasion:

> Let such have ynough
> That follow the plough
>
> Poor seggons halfe sterved, worke faintly and dull,
> And lubbers doo loiter, their bellies too full.[66]

Banister used a similar argument in condemning the overfeeding of horses by servants, and was sure that servants themselves were overfed in the south of England, where masters were unwilling 'to rusticate' themselves and eat the same coarse diet.[67] Marshall was appalled at 'that luxurious style which farming servants in this county [Surrey] expect to be kept in':

> discharge a grumbler, – one who pretends to be dissatisfied, tho' in fact *satiated*, and he will return to his bread-and-cheese with, perhaps, equal *health* and equal *happiness*. He sits down to his master's table with a resolution to eat voraciously of the best, – to do himself justice; but, at his own, he eats sparingly of the meanest, to save his money. His motive, in both cases, is the same: – self-interest![68]

Contemporary reports of diets show some regional variation, with meat being more common in the south in the later eighteenth and early nineteenth centuries. The information has been gathered together in Table 3.1. The meals are not extravagant, but they go well beyond the diet of bread and cheese that Marshall smugly pictured his day-labourers eating.

Sleeping arrangements are as difficult to document as diets and for the same reason. Because servants often slept, as they ate, with the rest of the family, there were often no rooms in the farmhouse reserved for them. Henry Best kept at least eight farm servants; inventories of the house made at the death of Best's son in 1668 list nine 'standing beds', trundle beds, or bedsteads at Elmswell. Four were almost certainly servant beds: the one in the west garret, next to the thirty cheeses, the 'servant's bed in the stable', and the two beds in the kitchen. The other beds were in the east and middle garrets and the parlour and middle chambers.[69] Two hundred and fifty years later, in southwest Wales, little differentiation between family space and servant space existed. Sons and male servants slept together in an outbuilding, although daughters and maid servants did not sleep together.[70] Barley pointed to the numerous seventeenth-century references to chambers over oxhouses, similar to the ones described by both Jenkins and the inventory takers at Elmswell.[71]

Little else definite can be said about living conditions. Did male and female servants sleep in the same room? Morgan says that they did in Colonial New England.[72] How many people slept in a bed? Kitchen called the drunken servant George his 'bedmate'.[73] The most illuminating evidence of privacy, or rather its lack, is provided by the unfortunate results of the fight between the Parson of Alphamstone, Essex, and his wife, as reported in Essex Quarter Sessions in 1572. Joan Reyner was their servant. The Parson's house had only three beds; after the argument, the Parson took one bed and his wife the second, displacing the wife's son, Symond Callye. Joan was forced to sleep with

Table 3.1. *Diet of servants*

Place, date and source	Morning	Noon	Night
South			
Bedfordshire, 1808 (Marshall, *Review and Abstract*, p. 589)	Milk, bread, cheese or meat	n.a.	n.a.
Hampshire, 1810 (Vancouver, *GV Hants*, p. 384)	n.a.	Fresh meat (Sundays), wheat bread, pickled pork, vegetables	n.a.
Middlesex, 1807 (Middleton, *GV Middlesex*, p. 509)	Bread, cheese, fat pork	Coarse joints of beef, boiled with vegetables	Cold pork, bread and cheese, small beer
Northamptonshire, 1813 (Pitt, *GV Northants*, p. 224)	Cold meat, cheese, bread, and beer	Roast or cold or boiled meat	Same as breakfast
West and north			
Cumberland and Westmorland, 1833 (PP 1833, V, 306)	n.a.	Barley bread, potatoes, milk, and bacon	n.a.
Gloucestershire, 1789 (Marshall, *Rural Economy of Gloucs.*, vol. II, p. 29)	n.a.	Bacon, vegetables	n.a.
Yorkshire, E. Riding, 1812 (Strickland, *GV East Riding*, p. 261)	Milk, cold meat, fruit pie, or cheesecake	Hot meat pie or boiled meat and dumpling, small beer	Same as breakfast
Yorkshire, E. Riding, c. 1900 (Kitchen, *Brother to the Ox*, p. 126)	Boiled bacon, boiled milk, bread and butter, apple pasties, currant cake	Roast or boiled meat, vegetable, Yorkshire pudding, ale	Tea, bacon, bread and butter

For full sources, see abbreviations to Notes and Bibliography.
n.a. = no information available.

Symond from two weeks before Christmas to Candlemas, and 'not having the feare of God before her eyes, being overcome with the entyceing and alurement of the same young man, consenting to his wicked demand, is now become with child by the same Symond'.[74] The Parson was ordered to keep Joan for the rest of the year.

Recreation

Workdays varied in their intensity. Bad weather might halt all outdoor work, servants might be called on to accompany the master or mistress to market. More certain opportunities for recreation existed, however. Sunday was generally a day of reduced work. Fred Kitchen joined other ploughmen in inspecting the straightness of each other's ploughing; he also went hunting rats and sparrows, visited his mother, and went to chapel.[75] The only outright vacations from the household authority of the master occurred at hiring times. Kitchen got a week's holiday at Martinmas; Best's servants got two to three days 'with their friends'; Skinner, writing in 1861, called Martinmas the only time of the year when children returned home.[76] Jenkins found that servants who were changing masters got one week off, while those staying on got less time off.[77]

Everyday escapes from masters and work took place in the stable and the alehouse. In dispersed settlements, such as those in which Kitchen laboured, servants from the few nearby farms would gather in the stable after supper. Kitchen described the singing and games with which they entertained themselves until nine or ten at night.[78] The alehouse provided a site for recreation removed from the workplace. The ubiquitous alehouse, as Wrightson argued, held a 'prominent place in the social lives of servants and young of both sexes'.[79] He gave examples in two presentments from Lancashire and Essex records: in Essex in 1639 an alehousekeeper was charged with 'detaining men's servants from their masters' houses'; in Lancashire, a master testified that he found 'his children and his servants drinckinge and playinge with other men's servants' at an alehouse at midnight.[80] The absence of the master and mistress provided opportunities for more unusual revels. In Cheshire in 1666, a female servant was charged with breaking into a closet to steal keys while her master and his wife were gone at Christmas. She was reported to have taken strong beer from the cellar, nuts, apples and cheeses from the store room, to have made bread from oatmeal and wheat flour, and to have invited servants from other households to drink the master's beer.[81]

The sexual activities of servants were not regularly recorded. The Board of Agriculture may occasionally have reported the diets of servants, but never their sex lives. A glimpse of practices comes only from worried moralists and from bastardy examinations. Banister wrote of the female servant, 'the ploughman's sweetheart', who took the keys to help the ploughman steal the corn to overfeed the horses.[82] Richard Mayo explained in 1693, with increasing shrillness, the danger inherent in the close proximity of young men and women servants:

undue Familiarity between servants of different sexes in a Family has had fatal and tragical Effects. How often has Opportunity and Privacy exposed Men and Maids that live together to the Devil's Temptations. And in houses, where the Masters have set *battlements on the roof*, they have leap'd over into the ditch, (*for a Whore is a deep ditch, and he that is abhored of the Lord shall fall therein*, Prov. 22:14).[83]

Privacy was not necessary. Margaret Bull, a servant, was delivered of a bastard child in Staffordshire. She testified at the bastardy examination that the father was Ralph Lees, the husbandman who lived next to her master. Ralph, she said, 'had to do with her both in the [master's] house and chamber' on several occasions. Later, when he was in his own stable, he called to her and 'would have had to doe with her … she answered I feare you have done to much alreadye'.[84] In seventeenth-century Lancashire, according to Wrightson's sample of bastardy examinations, 24 per cent of the mothers of bastards were servants; in Essex, the figure is 61 per cent. Many fathers of bastards resided in the same family as did the mothers: the Lancashire figure is 24 per cent, the Essex figure 52 per cent. Of fathers identified by their status within the family, however, half were masters, not fellow servants, and others might have been the masters' sons.[85] This raises the question, impossible to answer, of the extent to which coercion was central to the sexual relationships.

In other cases, however, the pregnancy resulted from the normal courtship of servants, or at least from promises of marriage. Wrightson reported that around one-quarter of the mothers of bastards had been promised marriage by the fathers.[86] Most servants expected to marry soon after they left service, and pregnancy often determined when exit from service and marriage would occur. Service, some may argue, was a way of avoiding incest, but if it was, it was also a wonderful opportunity for non-incestuous sex.

Resentment

The annual patriarchal relation of master and servant was not always easy. Little information exists on the attitudes of servants and masters to each other, but what information there is shows the strain. Almost all we know about discipline and resentment was written by masters. Settlement examinations seldom reflect the problems of the year, because it was the serving of the year alone that was the object of investigation. We have the testimony of Fred Kitchen, pointing to the thrill of the Martinmas hiring fair, when once a year masters and servants met on the same footing.[87] But agricultural manuals and the diaries of farmers are the main source of information.

Farmers wrote little about servants, compared to the pages they devoted to new crops, new techniques, and new machines; but when they happened to mention servants, they were not reticent in expressing their opinions. 'There is not', wrote Nourse, 'a more insolent and proud, a more untractable, perfidious and a more churlish sort of people breathing, than the generality of our servants.'[88] Farmers were not insensible to the value of their farm servants. Nourse continued, calling servants 'the Hands by which the Good Husbandman does subsist and live';[89] Marshall, with atypical generosity, allowed that 'the most valuable animal of harvest is a good carter'.[90] But the difficulties in dealing with servants on a daily basis apparently overcame whatever abstract thankfulness farmers felt for the servants' presence.

The constant battle over the feeding of horses has already been mentioned. Best recorded the doggerel he heard a servant repeat when he was asked what he could do by a prospective master:

> I can sowe
> I can mowe
> And I can stacke
> And I can doe
> My master too
> When my master turnes his back.[91]

The prizes for long-standing servants referred to their good character, not their skill.[92] Young looked to physiognomy to determine the character of prospective servants.[93] Tull and Banister have already been observed complaining about their servants: Tull's were impudent, Banister's thieves. No writer, however, of any century, can match William Marshall in self-righteous peevishness. Marshall was proud that he, unlike his arch-rival, the 'aerialist' Arthur Young, was a successful farmer. He passed on to his contemporaries not a theoretical treatise on methods, nor a collection of designs for new implements, but a diary of the daily challenge of managing a 300-acre farm. To read Marshall is to think that no challenge was greater than that of working with his servants without being tempted to throttle them.

When he started farming, soon before beginning his *Minutes* in 1774, Marshall was not an experienced farmer. Born into a farming family in the North Riding, from the age of fifteen he was 'trained to traffic, and wandered in the way of commerce in a distant climate [the West Indies] for fourteen years'. By July of 1775, he would be calling the preceding twelve months 'an Apprenticeship of farming'.[94] He saw himself not as an 'Aboriginal Farmer' (an 'illiberal sloven, illiterate economist, ape-gentleman' etc.) nor as an 'Aerialist' ('he had read the TOURS, and seen the PATENTPLOW!'), but as a 'scientific' farmer, who learns from 'EXPERIMENT and OBSERVATION'.[95] Marshall had more to learn than most farmers, and he expected his servants, who were, after all, more experienced than he was, to help him: 'The Author commenced farming with high expectations of the happiness he·was about to receive from a virtuous MANAGEMENT of virtuous SERVANTS ... How far reality confirmed his expectations, may be gathered from a review of the Minutes incident to Servants.'[96] Marshall was shocked to find that they would not help him become a good farmer.

The servants understood his predicament. Marshall was placed 'by the law of *right*'[97] in a position of authority, but was at the mercy of his servants. He rewarded servants who taught him new methods,[98] but reflected that 'A THINKING SERVANT is very valuable; but rarely to be met with.'[99] His servants were not cooperative, and almost certainly took advantage of him. About his foreman, he said 'all along he has been *siding* with the men; instead of assisting me to manage them, he has been assisting them to manage me'.[100] But it was not the servants' responsibility to see that the farm was well run; it was Marshall's.

Marshall blamed each of the many small disasters that befell him on either the carelessness of servants or his own failure in managing them: 'you may talk of your *Farmer This* and your *Farmer That* but I say, FARMER SELFATTENDANCE is the best farmer in all this country'.[101] He blamed accidents on carelessness whenever he was ignorant of the cause. A harrow overturned, and the horse died as a result of the injury, 'through CARELESSNESS, no doubt'.[102] A servant set a coulter wrong and made a mess of ploughing.[103] Marshall was unsure, in the former instance, whether the ploughman was obstinate or ignorant, but he was punished for failing Marshall. A new bull was christened (with ale) 'David', after the ploughman. Marshall reminded himself to '*Remember to notice the effect.*' Four days later Marshall was jubilant: 'Just so – he was the laugh of the whole yard ... He has, since, been perfectly pliable ...'[104] Marshall wrote too soon. In the first week of April he caught David stealing oats for the horses. Marshall took David's team away, and ordered him to thresh. David refused, held out all day, and by evening had reduced Marshall to allowing him to thresh for only half an hour in return for his team. Marshall thought that he had won: 'A manoeuvre of this kind saves a great deal of that *damning*, which indoor farming servants habitually expect'.[105]

At times the punishment he meted out was more traditional. He horse-whipped a 'puny' lad who had begun the progression from 'idle excuses' through 'falsehood' on his way to '*thieving, – murder, –* and the *gallows*', but with little effect.[106] More often, he behaved as W. S. Gilbert's Lord High Executioner would have counselled. In the instance of the dead harrow horse, Marshall gave his ploughmen 'A mute

lecture on carelessness':[107] he put the dying horse on a sledge opposite
the stable door, and labelled it 'See the shocking consequence of
CARELESSNESS! Let this be a warning to you all.' He 'saved the ears and
dock to nail over the stable-door, as a perpetual caution to the
carters'.[108] He did not record the effect.

Marshall was forced to substitute aphorisms for knowledge and
authority:

–Good usage makes bad servants
–The best team spoils the carters
–One man among women, one woman among men.[109]

This last command was a reference to the advantage of placing one
woman in a field of working men, or one man in a field of working
women: the man would silence gossip, the woman invigorate slug-
gards.[110] On the whole, however, his experience with servants was his
greatest disappointment in farming. He wrote that in preparing his
journal for publication, he was 'more embarrassed in the selection of the
Minutes on Servants, than in the choice of those on any other
subject'.[111] He hoped and believed, as he put it, that he had been
'unfortunate in the neighbourhood he happened to fix in';[112] at another
point he wrote that 'the writer is either very difficult to please, or very
much out of luck, or else a good Bustler is a Being rarely to be met
with'.[113] How truly unfortunate and out of luck, however, were his
servants.

Nourse, like most writers, believed that servants worked better on a
small farm.[114] Not only did their masters work and live as they did, but
often the masters would have been servants themselves before becoming farmers, and would have understood something of the relationship.
The relationship was not inevitably antagonistic. Jenkins wrote of the
image of 'friendly uncle' that servants had to the farmer's children.[115]
Josselin recorded in his diary that a former maid servant came to nurse
his daughter when he and his wife were away.[116] But the opportunities
for niggling and serious abuses were great. A Suffolk farmer docked two
shillings from a servant's wages for her having been gone for three days
with her family at Christmas and Easter. The two shillings represented
more than three hundred per cent of her prorated daily wage at three
and a half guineas a year.[117] Farmers docked shillings, even sixpences,
to deny servants their settlements.[118] Far more seriously, as previously
noted, masters could rape their servants and then coerce them into
silence. Essex Quarter Sessions recorded the unusual circumstance in
which voice was given to the abuse: the husbandman 'did not only in
most vile and detestable and uncomely manner abuse her, causing her
by oath to conceal and keep secret his abominable lewdness (which now

God of his goodness has opened and made manifest to the world)'.[119]
Even in this case, however, the master had also detained her wages,
and one wonders whether God of his goodness would have made the
case manifest had the wages been paid.

4   *Hiring and mobility*

The mobility of farm servants set them apart from all others, both literally (because mobility broke those social bonds that depended on contiguity) and conceptually (because no other group shared this characteristic movement).[1] The militia lists of Hertfordshire should have been an excellent source for the calculation of the distance travelled between hirings, because the lists are continuous from 1758 to 1765 and include almost all Hertfordshire parishes. So one parish, Westmill, was chosen as a base for 1758 and 1759, and the names of the eighteen male servants of Westmill in those years were sought in the subsequent lists for Westmill and fifteen surrounding parishes.[2] By 1765, all but four names had disappeared from all sixteen parishes (see Table 4.1). None of the four was still a servant; all were labourers in 1765. Some servants may have been drawn into the militia (which was, after all, the purpose for which the list was made), but the others had disappeared. Three kinds of mobility defeated the attempt to measure any one of them. Servants were mobile over time, in moving frequently; they were mobile over space, in moving some significant distance; and they were mobile socially, in changing their status when entering and eventually leaving service. The temporal and spatial aspects of the movement of servants from master to master are the concern of this chapter.

Farm servants changed masters, and farmers changed servants, often. The timing of the change was influenced, in most regions, by the customary dates on which the annual service contracts began and ended. During the conventional term of the contract, little movement occurred. When the terminal date arrived, the country roads swarmed with servants moving to new hirings, and when the new term began, movement ceased as abruptly as it had begun. The annual regularity of mobility served two ends. It differentiated job-seeking servants, legitimately abroad in the country at year's end, from vagrants, 'masterless men', who could be compelled into service. It was also a convenience to master and servant alike to know, without newspaper advertisements or widespread literacy, that at one time in the year masters would be seeking servants and servants new places.

Masters and servants were drawn into the annual pattern, and were

49

Table 4.1. *The eighteen male servants of Westmill, Herts, in 1758 and 1759 and their persistence in Westmill and fifteen nearby parishes, 1760–5*

	Occupation in 1760–5				
Year	Servant	Labourer	Craftsman	Farmer	Total
1758–9	18	—	—	—	18
1760	9	0	1	1	11
1761	9	2	1	0	12
1762	6	2	1	1	10
1763	1	4	1	1	7
1764	0	4	0	1	5
1765	0	4	0	0	4

Source: HRO, Militia Lists: Ardley, Aspenden, Bengeo, Braughing, Cottered, Great Hormead, Layston, Great and Little Munden, Sacombe, Standon, Stapleton, Throcking, Walkern, Watton, and Westmill.

penalized for failing to conform to it. An agent of the Duke of Buccleuch wrote to his employer in June of 1797 to explain why no dairymaid had yet been hired on one of the Duke's farms: 'I have not yet heard of a young woman properly qualified for the management of a Dairy that I can properly recommend – it unfortunately happens this is not the Time of year when good and useful servants in this part of the county are likely to be out of place.'[3] William Marshall felt keenly the pains of unconventionality:

> Paid off *David, Will, Jack, Joe*: Tyburn never sent Hell a more finished group! ... Last year, I was obliged to take such as I could get; – their lodgingroom was not finished at Michaelmas; – and I was obliged to pick up the starving refuse in Winter. – This year, I have culled in time – I expect them more ignorant, but less vicious.[4]

A witness before the Parliamentary inquiry into the depressed state of agriculture in 1821 said that he made no eleven-month hirings to prevent settlement becoming possible because it was difficult to find good servants after Michaelmas.[5]

Michaelmas was the conventional hiring date for much of the south and east of England; in the north, Martinmas, a month later, prevailed. The time of changing thus corresponded to the slack after the major grain harvest, and sometimes also followed the autumn ploughing.[6] In areas specializing in grazing, such as the fens of Lincolnshire and the west, the annual time of hiring and mobility was generally May Day. Some areas may have had no traditional times of hiring: Marshall reported this to be true of the southwest.[7] Settlement exam-

Table 4.2. *Hiring dates, seventeenth to nineteenth centuries, from settlement examinations*

| | Percentage of hirings | | | | | |
Place	Michaelmas	Martinmas	May Day	Lady Day	Other	Total hirings
Yorks., N. and E. Ridings	0	92	8	0	0	24
Northants and Leics.	91	7	0	2	0	44
Cambs. and Norfolk	98	1	0	0	1	120
Lincs.	0	7	90	0	3	72
Wilts. and Gloucs.	96	1	0	1	1	85

Source: SE Coll., CRO, ERRO, LAO, LRO, Northants RO, NRO, NRRO; CSE; Arthur J. Willis, *Winchester Settlement Papers, 1667–1842* (Hambledon, Kent: 1967).

inations, largely dating from the eighteenth century, reveal the common regional dates of contract (Table 4.2). The contractual year began and ended at Michaelmas, Martinmas, or May Day in more than 90 per cent of all instances.

When the time came for contracts to end, most servants did not renew their agreements. They left and moved to a new master. Evidence ranging from statute law to farm account books all point to that conclusion. The Act establishing a tax on marriage, baptism, and burial in 1696–7 made masters liable to pay the duty for their servants, because 'bachelors and widows that are servants in husbandry by their frequent removals are returned as fugitives and escape the duties to which they may be liable by the same Act' (8 and 9 Wm. and Mary, c. 20). Dydsey, in Herefordshire, returned the names of nine defaulters to the poll tax of 1678; six were servants.[8] On a farm near Tetney, Lincolnshire, 68 per cent of the 128 servants hired over the fifty-year period between 1780 and 1830 remained at the farm for only one year; only 16 per cent renewed their contracts for three or more years.[9] A similar account book from Berkshire shows 80 per cent of 99 servants leaving after one year and only 5 per cent staying for three or more years (Table 4.3).[10]

The same high frequency of movement appears in settlement examinations. Sufficient information exists in 809 settlement examinations from Hertfordshire, Essex, Norfolk, Bedfordshire, Northamptonshire, Leicestershire, Suffolk, and Lincolnshire to measure the number of years spent with one master. The results are shown in Table 4.4: 76 per cent of the hirings lasted only one year.

Table 4.3. *Continuous years of service*

Maximum number of years served	Percentage of servants		
	All	Male	Female
(a) Tetney, Lincs. farm accounts, 1780–1830			
1	68	54	77
2	16	22	13
3	7	14	3
4	2	2	3
5	3	2	3
6 or more	4	6	3
Number of servants	128	50	78
(b) Three farms in Radley, Berks., 1797–1819			
1	80	84	72
2	15	15	16
3	4	1	9
4	0	0	0
5 or more	1	0	3
Number of servants	99	67	32

Source: (a) LAO, Misc. Dep. 161; (b) HFR, Reading, BER/13.5.1.

Table 4.4. *Continuous years of service, settlement examinations, seventeenth to nineteenth centuries*

Maximum number of years with same master	Total servants	Percentage of servants
1	613	75.8
2	124	15.3
3	40	4.9
4	15	1.9
5	6	0.7
6	6	0.7
7	3	0.4
8 or more	2	0.2

Source: SE Coll., BRO, ERO, HRO, NRO, Northants RO, SRO(B).

A more complex measure of movement, the annual rate of mobility, can be calculated from consecutive parish listings by noting the persistence, in subsequent lists, of names appearing in a first list. The

Table 4.5. *Rates of mobility in Cogenhoe, Northants, 1618–28*

Year 0	Year t	N_o	N_t	r_m
1618	1620	28	1	0.81
1620	1621	15	0	1.00
1621	1623	16	1	0.75
1623	1624	20	10	0.50
1624	1628	23	2	0.46

Source: Figures provided by Peter Laslett.

annual rate of persistence (r_p) is the proportion of names surviving from one year to the next; the annual rate of mobility (r_m) is the proportion disappearing, or $1 - r_p$. The rates are cumulative. If half the names were to disappear after one year, three-quarters would have disappeared after two years, and so forth. The number of names (N) expected to persist after t years is given by

$$N_t = N_o(1 - r_m)^t$$

where N_o = number of names in original list, and N_t = number of those names still in the list t years later. This formula can be transformed to yield the annual rate of mobility, r_m:

$$r_m = 1 - \left(\frac{N_t}{N_o}\right)^{1/t}$$

As an example, assume that a list made in 1700 contained one hundred names, and that fifty of these names reappeared in a list of 1703. Then $N_o = 100$, $N_t = 50$, $t = 3$, and the annual rate of mobility, r_m, is

$$1 - \left(\frac{50}{100}\right)^{1/3} = 1 - 0.7937 = 0.2063$$

In other words, 21 per cent of the listed individuals would be estimated to have departed each year.

The calculated rates of servant mobility were far higher. In Cogenhoe, Northamptonshire, the rates ranged from 1.00 to 0.45 (see Table 4.5).[11] An unusual surviving pair of poll-tax assessments for the little parish of Orby, Lincolnshire, yield an estimated rate of mobility of 0.61: of thirteen servants listed in 1692, only two remained in Orby to be listed in 1694.[12] Three Hertfordshire parishes were examined, using militia lists as evidence.[13] In Great Amwell, the best estimate of annual mobility is 0.60; in Sacombe, 0.58; in Westmill, 0.65 (see Table 4.6). More than half of these male servants left the parish after one

Table 4.6. *Annual rates of mobility in three Hertfordshire parishes, 1758–65*

Number of successive years	Observed persistence	Predicted persistence
(a) Great Amwell: $r_m = 0.60$		
1	38	(38)
2	15	15.2
3	3	6.1
4	2	2.4
5	0	1.0
(b) Sacombe: $r_m = 0.58$		
1	68	(68)
2	28	28.6
3	14	12.0
4	5	5.0
5	2	2.1
(c) Westmill: $r_m = 0.65$		
1	71	(71)
2	28	24.9
3	8	8.7
4	3	3.0
5	1	1.1

Source: HRO, Militia Lists.

year's service. Similar rates can be calculated for the Tetney and Radley account books; the annual rate of mobility in Tetney was 0.52, that in Radley 0.77. These figures are all consistent with the estimation that of any group of farm servants, between one-half and two-thirds of them would have changed masters at the end of the hiring year.

Not all of the calculated mobility represents true movement from master to master. The names of some servants failed to recur because they died, and of others because they left service. The non-persistence of names arising from these factors, however, could not have accounted for the high calculated rates. Farm servants, whose median age ranges from eighteen to twenty-two in records dating from 1599 to 1851, were members of an age group with low rates of mortality;[14] most servants remained in service for a number of years, so that the proportion leaving service altogether in any one year was low.[15] Most of the calculated r_m was caused by the movement of servants to new masters.

Median age, aggregate mobility: so much variation is hidden within these single-figure estimates of behaviour. 'Aged retainers' existed among farm servants. Arthur Young's *Annals of Agriculture* often listed prizes given by county agricultural societies for long service of farm servants (the Bath Agricultural Society awarded three guineas in 1785 to five servants who had served between eighteen and fifty-two years with a single master).[16] Two-thirds of the servants in Tetney may have remained with the farmer for only one year, but it was in only eight of the forty-nine years covered by the account book that all servants were newcomers to the household.[17] In most years, some continuity within the group of servants was maintained despite the high average rates of mobility.

Why did servants move so often? The simple answer to this is 'why not?'. Nothing inhibited mobility.[18] Contracts terminated at the end of the year, servants had few possessions to carry from place to place and no dependants, and agricultural techniques were sufficiently common to allow servants to be interchangeable with one another in farming.

Parson Woodforde, the 'Clerical Glutton', hired five servants each year, a farming man, a footman, a housemaid, a cook and dairymaid, and a boy. In his twenty-six years in Norfolk, thirty people filled these five posts. Five were with him when he died, in 1802, so twenty-five servants left his employ in this period. He records the reason for the parting of master and servant in his diary for fifteen of the twenty-five departures. Eight might be called the unequivocal decisions of Woodforde, on grounds of the servant's drunkenness, incompetence, foul mouth, illness, and pregnancy; seven were the decisions of the servants, to leave because they were too old to fill the post of a boy, or to go to a better service, to enlist, and to return home.[19]

The range of possible motives for departures was wider than those shown by Woodforde. Nash Stevenson, a critic of the abuses of hiring fairs, wrote in 1858 that servants ran off to them at the end of the year as if freed from bondage.[20] So much could be wrong with a servant's situation: the food could be stingy, the alehouse distant, the master or mistress vicious. The hope that any change would be a change for the better might have motivated many moves. More generally, just as servants might have left home to prevent conflicts of authority with their parents and to avoid incest (see Chapter 5), a master grown too familiar might give rise to quasi-parental conflicts and quasi-incestuous temptations; frequent mobility ensured that the master was a stranger. Servants might have hoped that their bargaining position would be stronger with a master ignorant of the last wage they had received. Servants were, moreover, members of a hierarchical order; in it, to move up was to move to a more responsible position, or to a larger and better-run farm. Kitchen left a good farm at seventeen to go to a run-down one, because on the latter he could be a waggoner instead of a mere horse-lad.[21] Jenkins wrote of a similar hierarchy of farming services in southwest Wales.[22] The *Commercial and Agricultural Magazine* counselled young people to move from place to place to learn a variety of farming techniques in a variety of geographical settings.[23] Older servants may have been seeking marriage partners as they moved.[24]

Masters were sometimes annoyed at the frequency of change. Tusser voiced his displeasure in rhyme:

> The stone that is rolling can gather no mosse
>
> For master and servant, oft-changing is losse.[25]

Marshall complained, in the peevish tone that permeates all his comments on farm servants, of the 'fickleness' that hiring fairs encouraged.[26] Farmers, however, had two reasons to be pleased with the custom of frequent change. Most tasks on the farm were skill- and age-specific. Small boys were not hired to drive plough teams, and young adults were not hired to scare crows. Each farm had a fixed set of tasks, but servants did not remain similarly fixed in their capacities. They grew and expected their wages and the status of their tasks to grow with them. Kitchen, it should be recalled, worked on a farm so pleasant that 'most lads stayed with them until they grew too big to be lads any longer'.[27] The little farms that Arthur Young described sometimes hired a lad; they would not need the same growing lad, year after year, but rather a succession of different lads.[28] The great change in Woodforde's household came at the post of 'boy'; in the Tetney account books, no lad remained at the farm for more than three years.[29]

Servants gained a legal settlement in a parish by serving there for a year, but lost that settlement if they served a subsequent year somewhere else.[30] Encouraging servants to move on to new masters may have seemed to farming ratepayers to be a way of reducing new settlements in their parish. Indeed, farmers occasionally went further than simply condoning mobility. Robert Gibbons testified at his settlement examination in 1773 in Groton, Suffolk, that after he had served Mr Thomas Underwood of Milding for a year, Mr Underwood said to him, 'Robin, you have lived a year with me, I own, now get yourself another service out of this parish, and live one year, I will give you a shilling.' The examination does not reveal whether Robin took the shilling, but he never served another year in any parish, and Milding was determined to be his place of settlement.[31] Many such hopes must have been dashed: nearly all servants eventually quit service altogether, bestowing upon the unlucky ratepayers of the parish in which they last served lifetime responsibility of their poor relief.

When servants changed masters, they most often travelled far enough to leave the parish in which they had last served, but not much further. This spatial component of mobility is very difficult to measure, but the two sources that can be made to yield statements about the distance and direction of movement, settlement examinations and a highly unusual set of records of a hiring fair, agree that movement over long distances was rare, and that mobility did not tend to be random and cumulative, but directed and bounded.

Of the many hundreds of settlement examinations preserved from Suffolk and Hertfordshire, only 192 are detailed enough to reveal both place of birth and the place of last farm service, and only 32 also give details of movement within farm service. The straight line distances between the residences of successive masters is shown in Table 4.7. The medians of these highly dispersed distributions are 4 km in Hertfordshire and 5 km in Suffolk. There was no 'typical' distance of movement; we can say only that most moves were shorter than 15 km.

The records of the Spalding Statute Sessions provide an interesting contrast. These lists of servants hired, dating from 1767 onward, can be used to calculate the distance travelled because they record the names and residences of both the old and the new masters.[32] The sample size is far larger: between 1767 and 1785, 844 male and 722 female servants were hired at Spalding. The distances travelled are significantly larger than those recorded in the settlement examinations (Table 4.8).[33] The mean distance between successive masters of male servants, 12.32 km, is larger than the mean distance travelled by females, 10.78 km. The difference is caused not by a slight tendency of all males to travel a few kilometres farther to their new hirings, but rather by a marked tendency of some males to travel considerable distances: 18 per cent of males travelled 20 km or more, while only 8 per cent of females did.[34] Wages are listed for each hiring at the Sessions, making possible an indirect test of the influence of age on mobility, because higher wages are associated with older servants. The mean distance for the 95 males earning £9 or more, 12.77 km, is only slightly larger than the mean distance of the 749 lower paid males. Once again, however, it can be shown that the greatest difference between the two groups appears in the propensity to travel more than 20 km between masters. While 24.2 per cent of males earning £9 or more travelled this distance, only 16.7 per cent of other males travelled as far.[35]

The difference between the distances travelled in the Spalding record and those recorded in settlement examinations is large enough to demand an explanation. Perhaps all that is being shown by this test is the distance between fen- and marsh-separated farms in the Spalding region, but it is possible that the difference arose from methods of

Table 4.7. *Distances between successive masters, from settlement examinations*

	Distance (kilometres)							
	0–3	4–7	8–11	12–15	16–19	20–23	24 or more	Total
Hertfordshire	9	7	4	3	0	0	0	23
(proportions)	(0.39)	(0.30)	(0.17)	(0.13)	(0.00)	(0.00)	(0.00)	(0.99)
Suffolk	7	8	6	2	2	1	1	27
(proportions)	(0.26)	(0.30)	(0.22)	(0.07)	(0.07)	(0.04)	(0.04)	(1.00)

Source: SE Coll., HRO, SRO.

Table 4.8. *Distance between successive masters, Spalding, Lincs., 1767–85*

	Distance (kilometres)							
	0–3	4–7	8–11	12–15	16–19	20–23	24 or more	Total
Male	129	133	151	163	120	83	65	844
(proportions)	(0.15)	(0.16)	(0.18)	(0.19)	(0.14)	(0.10)	(0.08)	(1.00)
Female	107	140	158	160	95	39	23	722
(proportions)	(0.15)	(0.19)	(0.22)	(0.22)	(0.13)	(0.05)	(0.03)	(0.99)

Source: LAO, Holland QS D2

hiring. All the Spalding records pertain to hirings at a Statute Sessions; in three of the settlement examinations we are told that the hiring occurred at a Statute Session, and in all three the distance travelled (7, 8 and 27 km) is larger than the county medians for Suffolk and Hertfordshire. This conjunction provides only faint support, however, for the argument about to be presented, that the mode of hiring influenced the direction and distance of movement. The other forty-seven Hertfordshire and Suffolk servants may also have been hired at Statute Sessions, and have lacked only Justices inquisitive enough to record it.

The distance travelled from master to master and the directedness of the movement should have been influenced by the manner in which farmer and servant found each other. Door-to-door searches for employment, reported by William Marshall in 1796 to have been common for farm servants in the southwest, and by John Neve in 1833 to have been common in Kent, could be expected to have had no purposeful direction, but to have been limited by the time-consuming

nature of the search.[36] Word of mouth spread information in predictable ways, through the patrons of alehouses, for example, or through
those who attended local markets. Fred Kitchen moved to one farm
because other servants had told him of a vacancy there; he moved to
another because the farmer had learned that Fred wanted work.[37]
Mobility, in these instances, should have been bounded by the information networks. Kin sometimes effected hirings. Servants found places
with their own kin; masters found servants through theirs. John Ward
covenanted in 1572 to serve his brother as a farm servant at the behest
of their dying mother.[38] A Hertfordshire labourer testified in 1784 that
he had worked one year for a farmer, and the next for the farmer's
brother.[39] Gough described a combination of both networks: a servant
found a place for his cousin with the son-in-law of the servant's
master.[40] These hirings can be considered to have been both directed
and bounded, in the sense that if we knew the shape of the kin-
network, we would know the boundaries and direction of mobility.

Statute Sessions, or Petty Sessions, or hiring fairs, as they came to be
called in the nineteenth century, seem, unlike the other three methods, to
have been designed to promote mobility over long distances.[41] Strangers
until the day of the Sessions, a servant from one edge of the catchment area
of the Sessions could meet a master from the edge opposite, and when, at
day's end, the agreement had been sealed by the earnest, or God's penny, or
fastening penny, the distance between the old and new master could be as
great as the diameter of the circle of attraction of the Sessions.[42] When the
catchment areas of nearby Sessions overlapped, servants could have found
themselves moved, year after year, over sizeable distances.[43] The spread of
county newspapers led to the spread of advertisements for hiring fairs. The
Suffolk Mercury, or St Edmundsbury Post for Monday, 30 August 1725, carried
a notice for Stow Hundred:

> A sessions will be holden by the High Constables of this Hundred at the
> Maypole and Three Crowns at Wetherden upon Monday the 13th of
> September, 1725, being the only sessions that will be holden for the said
> Hundred. It is expected to be the largest Petty Sessions that have been
> seen for many years.[44]

The earliest notice in the *Norwich Mercury* was that for 1743; after that
date, the issues of late August and September contained many notices
for Petty Sessions to be held in a large part of Norfolk. The issue for
Saturday, 12 September 1761, advertised the sessions for Depwade,
Forehoe, and Wayland; a week later, the notices for South Greenhoe
and Shropham hundreds appeared. The notices were treated as all
advertisements were; the Forehoe notice was sandwiched between a
notice to the 'Principal Inhabitants' of Holt to come to the Coronation

Party and an advertisement for the sale of a good secondhand wagon. The effect of the advertisements was that any servant willing to travel could know where and when distant fairs would be held. Before the spread of newspapers, notices had been sent only to the towns within each hundred.[45]

Sessions were annual or semi-annual, corresponding to the conventional hiring date (and its bi-annual twin) of the region. In some areas, hiring sessions were held in only one place; in others, there were several sessions in nearby villages in the space of a few weeks. They varied greatly in the numbers in attendance, and in their area of attraction of masters and servants. Marshall guessed that two to three thousand servants came to the Polesworth, Warwickshire, Statute of 1784.[46] At Spalding, the main springtime sessions averaged eighty-two hiring agreements each year (1768 to 1785); the autumnal fair was smaller, averaging forty-seven agreements, and the nearby Holbeach Statute averaged fifty-three springtime agreements.[47] The maximum distances travelled to the Spalding springtime Statutes of 1773 and 1784 were 22.5 km for masters, and 37.5 km for servants; the median distances were 9 km for both masters and servants. The maximum distance travelled by masters alone to a variety of Gloucestershire, Oxfordshire, Worcestershire, and Wiltshire sessions, as indicated in Cheltenham settlement examinations of 1815 to 1826, was 25 km; the median distance was 6 km.[48] Henry Best travelled to sessions 9, 8, 5, and 3.5 km distant from his East Riding farm to register his servants.[49] Fred Kitchen recalled that people came to the Doncaster Statute around the turn of the twentieth century from southern Yorkshire, northern Lincolnshire and Nottinghamshire, and Derbyshire.[50]

Statute Sessions were widespread. No exhaustive list of sessions and fairs exists, and none can be compiled. The reader will find in Appendix 4 a list, by county, of the sessions and fairs encountered in the course of this research. None was found in Somerset and Cornwall, but this does not prove that none was held there. A preliminary search through Quarter Sessions records, *Annals of Agriculture*, *British Calendar Customs*, and guide books to fairs showed twelve counties without fairs. Among them was Lincolnshire; it was in the Lincolnshire Archives, however, that the excellent Spalding Statute Sessions records were later encountered. *Caveat lector.*

Fairs and sessions served a variety of social, administrative, and economic functions. The obvious one of matching servants without places with masters needing servants was not always principal among them. The purpose and functions of sessions changed greatly from the sixteenth to the nineteenth centuries. In the earlier period, the administrative function was foremost. As John Cowell reported in 1607,

> Statute sessions, otherwise called petit sessions, are a meeting in every hundred of all the shires of England, where of custome they have been used, unto which the constables doe repaire, and other both householders and servants, for the debating of differences between masters and their servants, the rating of servants' wages, and the bestowing of such people in service, as being fit to serve, either refuse to seek, or cannot get Masters.[51]

Servants and masters were required to gather annually under the supervision of a Constable or Justice to make public the contracts made between them and to show that the new contracts fell within the bounds established by statutes.[52] In this early period, master and servant generally met and came to an agreement before the sessions. The session served only to ratify a prior agreement, and to record the contract before witnesses. This is the procedure described by Best: only a few hiring agreements were initiated at the sessions, the rest having been made weeks earlier.[53]

Thus the Statute Sessions, which might have been thought to have been markets for labour, were instead principally administrative. They 'bestowed into service' only the minority of servants who had not already agreed to serve. They were not wage-setting markets. The market was 'cleared' not through bargaining, but through compulsion. Masters and servants came to hear the year's wages pronounced, not to participate in setting them.[54]

The administrative nature of the sessions could not survive the decline in the practice of wage assessment in the eighteenth century, which saw the flowering of free and open markets in agricultural labour, centred around the hiring fair, the successor to the statute session. Fairs probably grew larger as they came to serve as distributors of servants to farmers. Both the Leicestershire and Derbyshire reporters to the Board of Agriculture complained of the strangers that farmers were forced to hire at fairs.[55] Wages were now set by the bargaining of servants and masters. If satisfactory wages could not be obtained at an early fair, servants knew that there was always a later fair nearby. An order made by Nottinghamshire Quarter Sessions in 1723 was prefaced by a complaint of the 'several great abuses that have been committed from time to time by Servants running from one Statute to another, and thereby put great inconveniency upon their Masters that have hired them by letting themselves to other masters after they have been hired at a former statute.'[56] The Board of Agriculture reporter for the East Riding noted a related problem in 1812: '[Servants] are hired at

statutes, here called "sittings", held at the market-towns and principal
villages on different days, three or four weeks before the expiration of
their year, and claim a right to go from one to another until they are
hired, thus wasting their master's time.'[57] He also complained that
servants 'cabal' to raise wages.

Servants preferred hiring in the open market. It was there, removed
from the obscurity of the household, that they could be powerful
collectively.[58] Servants could discover what working conditions and life
with a particular master would be like by asking other servants.[59] Fred
Kitchen asserted, on the basis of his experience at the Doncaster hiring
fair, that the fair 'was the only time when master and man met as
equal and separate units'.[60]

Masters as well as servants could learn the characteristics of their
prospective work partners before entering into an annual contract with
them. Servants, however, knew they had more to lose from a bad
master than farmers did from a single bad servant, for they were
preparing to submit themselves to the household regimen and absolute
authority of a master. Kebble reported the following exchange at a
hiring fair:

> *Farmer:* I shall inquire into your character and you shall know my decision
> in the afternoon.
>
> *Servant* (some hours later): Since I saw you this morning I have inquired
> into *your* character, and my decision is to have nothing more to do with
> you.[61]

The fair also impartially reflected the underlying conditions of supply
of, and demand for, farm servants.

Another function of fairs explains their popularity: 'Statute fairs
functioned most obviously as labour exchanges, but the evidence
suggests that they were of at least equal importance as social occasions.'[62] Malcolmson's book contains an excellent discussion of fairs
in the social life of servants. They were, in most regions, the first festive
occasion after the harvest, and for servants, the only vacation from the
household of a master in the year. Kebble called the fair 'a combination of the *utile* and the *dulce*'.[63] Games, diversions, and sex were
not the only social events that followed upon the large congregations of
servants. A letter to Sir Joseph Banks of Lincolnshire, dated 11
November 1796, informed him that difficulties were being experienced
in collecting militia lists: 'the country seemed very quiet until the
evening of the seventh at Leak Statutes when a conversation on the
Riot at Horncastle and the supposed success attending it induced
several men to incite in a determined resistance of the Law for
Augmenting the Militia'.[64]

Just as the decline in the practice of wage assessment in the eighteenth century transformed the purpose of the sessions, so the decline in the use of servants in the south transformed hiring fairs into pure fun fairs. In this form, they survived in many places through the nineteenth and into the twentieth century. The few servants who continued to be hired were often hired at the fairs, but the principal purpose of the fair was to serve as one of the round of annual fairs and wakes for agricultural labourers. Howitt noted in 1838 that, unlike other fairs, which were a pleasure to all classes, Statutes (or statties, or statis, or statice) were the labourers' own.[65] The Rev. James Skinner, quoting the Archbishop of York, found Statute fairs to be 'nurseries of crime and powerful incentives to vice'. After the hiring, servants gave themselves up to tobacco, beer, spirits, 'and the maddening results of dancing and music'.[66] Skinner recognized in 1861 that servants needed a vacation, 'a time for brothers and sisters to gather under their father's roof, after having been dispersed since childhood in distant villages as farm servants'; a vacation 'allows them to remember that this is a land, not of American Republicanism, but of glorious liberty'.[67] Skinner wished only to end the evil of public hiring, and replace it with register offices. He was, however, commenting on fairs in Yorkshire, where the institutions of farm service and Statute fairs remained strong throughout the nineteenth century.

Statute Sessions and hiring fairs may thus have served to increase both the frequency of movement from master to master and the distance travelled. More often than not, unfortunately, we cannot know the way in which servants and masters were matched, and we cannot know how common each method was. There are no lists of farm servants in the region around Spalding against which the importance of the Spalding Sessions can be measured; settlement examinations only sporadically note the method of hiring. Eighteen per cent of the old hirings registered at Spalding had previously been registered there as current hirings, but nothing certain can be inferred from this. If servants had been so perverse as to use the Sessions to find employers every second time, the proportion of old masters previously registered would have been nil.

The silence of most settlement examinations on the method of hiring prevents us from asserting that the shorter distance of movement recorded in them, compared to the distances recorded at Spalding, demonstrates unequivocally that Sessions moved servants over greater distances than did other methods.[68] The settlement examinations do indicate, however, that the mobility of the servants was not random in its direction, as we might expect mobility mediated by hiring sessions to have been. Thirty-two examinations include place of birth, place of first farm service, and place of last service; there is no significant tendency within them for the place of last service to be farther than the place of first service from the place of birth. The mean distance to the place of first service is 5.92 km $(s = 4.94)$; and the mean distance to the place of last service is 6.31 km $(s = 4.65)$; the small difference between the means is not significant.[69] Eight of the thirty-two servants were back in the parish of their birth for the last full year they served; 50 per cent were within 7 km of their place of birth.

The Spalding records do not note the place of birth, but by linking consecutive records, we can follow the path of some servants as they moved from master to master.[70] Letting M_1 stand for the residence of the first master in any linked series, M_2 for the second, and so on, we can measure the tendency towards cumulative mobility (Table 4.9). There is none: the small difference between the mean distances is not significant.[71] It is possible that no tendency existed because the hiring sessions created its own boundaries to mobility: servants could be moved only as far as the residences of the masters who came to the Sessions. Some servants came from farther afield to the Spalding Sessions than did masters, but the number is small: in 1777 and 1778, only six male servants (5.88 per cent of the total) came farther than any master.[72] Mobility was constrained by more than this, however. In the course of calculating the distances travelled, it was noted that a number of servants were not using the whole Sessions area as a market for its labour. The three servants whose patterns of mobility are illustrated in Figure 4.1 were not flung randomly about Spalding by the hiring sessions, but rather were returned, year after year, to their own smaller areas.[73] A chi-square test was devised to determine whether the impression of constrained mobility was borne out generally. The region around Spalding was divided into four wedges, and a contingency table constructed to test whether the region to which a servant went was independent of the region in which he or she had just served. It was not: the chi-square value for the 1,013 cases (1779–85) was 23.16 (9 d.f.), which indicates significant non-randomness at a level of error of 0.0058 (Table 4.10).[74]

Should we be surprised at this finding? In some ways, we should. Eighteenth- and nineteenth-century complaints about public hirings stressed their anonymity; anonymity, in turn, should have ensured the random pairing of masters and servants.[75] It was perhaps the fear of anonymity that caused mobility to be directed in some cases. Servants and masters both might have asked their fellows about their prospective work partners, preferring slight knowledge to complete ignor-

Table 4.9. *Cumulative mobility, male and female ser-*
vants, from Spalding Statute Sessions

	Mean distance (km)	s	N
M_i to M_{i+1}	10.75	7.34	546
M_i to M_{i+2}	11.23	8.10	148

Source: LAO, Holland QS D2.

ance; it is likely that their circle of acquaintances was far smaller than the number who attended the annual fairs. It would rather have been determined by the numbers regularly present at social centres, such as alehouses, and by the numbers who regularly attended local markets. G. William Skinner has described such a market-defined community in China. His 'standard marketing communities' had radii of 3.4–6.1 km; they comprised, on average, eighteen villages and 1,500 households. Each adult, Skinner reported, had at least a nodding acquaintance with every other adult in this large community.[76] If any pattern similar to this existed in the Spalding area, the hiring fairs would have drawn together masters and servants from many 'standard marketing com-

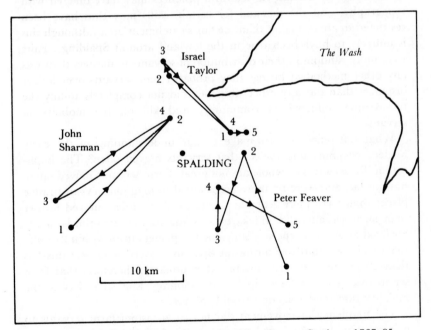

4.1. Mobility of three servants hired at Spalding Statute Sessions, 1767–85.
Source: LAO, Holland QS D2.

Table 4.10. *Origin and destination of 1,013 servants, Spalding Statute Sessions, 1779–85*

From	To			
	Spalding	North and northwest	South and southwest	East
Spalding	30	8	45	73
(expected values)	(23.6)	(14.6)	(41.3)	(76.5)
North and northwest	33	39	66	112
(expected values)	(37.8)	(23.5)	(66.1)	(122.7)
South and southwest	28	10	56	92
(expected values)	(28.1)	(17.4)	(49.2)	(91.3)
East	62	38	101	220
(expected values)	(63.6)	(39.4)	(111.4)	(206.6)

Source: LAO, Holland QS D2.

munities';[77] mobility would tend to be restricted to these communities, even though the place of hiring, the fair, might be distant from the community. Servants, more simply, may have attempted to stay near their parents or friends. Agricultural practices may have differed with topography, and the demand for certain skills may thus have been restricted to areas smaller than the fair's catchment area (although this is unlikely to have been true in the lowland around Spalding). Fairs were more random in their distribution of servants to masters than was any other method of hiring; they probably sent servants over longer distances than did any other. But they did not completely nullify the pre-existing influence of community and kin on the mobility of servants.

What difference does it make to our understanding of the early modern economy and society that servants moved often? The implications for society as a whole are not great. Farm servants moved often, but not far, and were no more accustomed to long journeys to strange places than were more sedentary workers. Apprentices moved farther than farm servants did. Buckatzsch estimated that two-thirds of the Sheffield apprentices she studied came to Sheffield from within 21 miles (34 km);[78] two-thirds of hirings at Spalding moved male servants less than 20 km to their next master. It is unlikely, therefore, that farm service was a major factor in 'preconditioning' English society to the mobility that modernization would call for.[79]

The frequency of movement did not so accustom farm servants to moving that they continued the pattern for life. On the contrary, the frequency of mobility ceased when farm servants left service. The

Table 4.11. *Annual rates of mobility of non-servants and servants*

			Rate of mobility (r_m)	
Years	N_o	N_t	Non-servants	Servants
(a) Cogenhoe, Northants, 1618–28				
1618–20	157	121	0.12	0.81
1620–1	135	126	0.07	1.00
1621–3	138	130	0.03	0.75
1623–4	154	138	0.10	0.50
1624–8	153	113	0.07	0.45
(b) Orby, Lincs., 1692–4				
1692–4	59	50	0.08	0.61

(c) Sacombe, Herts., 1758–65, males of militia age

	Farmers		Labourers	
Successive years in list	Observed persistence	Predicted persistence, $r_m=0.20$	Observed persistence	Predicted persistence, $r_m=0.26$
1	63	(63)	70	(70)
2	51	50.4	53	51.8
3	39	40.3	38	38.3
4	25	32.3	26	28.4
5	18	25.8	15	21.0

Source: (a) See Table 4.5; (b) LAO, LD 35/2; (c) HRO, Militia Lists.

contrast between the mobility of servants and the mobility of the rest of society was great. The annual rates of mobility of farm servants (the proportion of servants who would depart from the parish at year's end) were calculated above to range from 0.45 to 1.00; Table 4.11 compares the rates for servants with rates calculated for the rest of the population. Men and women were, *after* they left service, 'of all sorts of baggage the most difficult to be transported'.[80] In some senses the greatest implication of the differences in rates of mobility is the warning it should give to researchers such as Rich against using aggregate figures to calculate a true estimate of 'the mobility of English society', for though one part was mobile, another part was not.[81]

The mobility that was the special characteristic of farm servants was not destabilizing to society, despite the fact that servants alone had no direct bonds to the community other than their temporary contracts. Their mobility occurred as if in a closed container of customs and agricultural practices. Within that container, servants moved from place to place and permitted the most efficient allocation of labour in agriculture. Mobility helped communities maintain their customary practices; they found it convenient to use the labour of young adults before they 'settled down' and added new mouths to the community.

A more restricted question about the implications of the mobility of farm servants opens up still more areas of ambiguity. What was the effect of mobility upon agricultural technology? There were two contradictory effects. First, constant mobility implied rigid agricultural practices. Without them, farm servants would not have been as interchangeable. Methods and implements of sowing, manuring, ploughing, etc., all had to be familiar and largely unchanging in order for servants to fall easily into any farm's routine. Servants, further, resisted change. Tull railed against the servants who opposed his improvements, complaining that ploughmen did not follow their master's new ideas, but instead taught their masters.[82] Kitchen told the story of the Yorkshire farmer who tried to persuade his servants to use a new plough. They refused: the new plough, while faster, did not make neat furrows, and a well-ploughed field was a ploughman's badge of status.[83]

At the same time, however, mobility promoted technological change. The spread of new techniques, it has been argued, was not accomplished through the publication of descriptions, nor through the distribution of new tools or seeds. Cipolla has called the printed descriptions of inventions the stepchildren, not the parents, of innovative activity; he saw the migration of skilled workers as the main channel of innovation.[84] Farm servants and skilled agricultural labourers were occasionally such a channel. The Board of Agriculture reporter for the Isle of Man described the men servants who had been brought to the island from England and Scotland to improve ploughing, potato-drilling, and turnip-growing.[85] The famous Norfolk plough was of little use without a Norfolk ploughman who knew how to use it. Matthew Peters commended the good sense of Mr Mumford, of Hampshire, 'who has not only brought this utensil of husbandry from thence very prudently, but a Norfolk servant also, who will do his duty'.[86] Arthur Young's *Annals of Agriculture* published an essay in 1784 on Coke of Norfolk's farm at Holkham, which recalled that Coke had sent a Norfolk plough, a pair of horses, and a ploughman to a tenant of his brother, telling him to replace his six horses, ploughman, and leader with this rig. He did, very successfully, but 'the practice . . . scarcely travelled beyond his own hedges'.[87] William Marshall was convinced of the futility of publishing diagrams of the construction of the wonderful plough:

Nay, the very implement . . ., constructed in Norfolk in the most complete manner, and furnished with every necessary appendage, has lain useless upon a soil it suited, until a Norfolk plowman was sent to hold it! How useless, then, to expect utility from a drawing of it . . . Whoever wishes to introduce an implement which is in some use in some distant District . . . cannot [ensure] success . . . unless a person accustomed to the working of it accompanies it, and sets it to work . . . [88]

Within a single village, one servant might have been promoting technological change through her or his mobility while fifty others were inhibiting it, again because of their mobility. Stevenson captured the ambiguous relation of servants to technological change when he observed that they knew the best prevailing cropping systems, but were prejudiced against new practices.[89]

Service in husbandry is an institution fraught with ambiguity. Servants were hired workers and family members. Hiring fairs both promoted mobility and contained it. Now we can add to the list the contradictory effects of mobility on technological change. The examination of entry into farm service and exit from it will be no simpler.

5   *Entry into and exit from service*

Service in husbandry was the usual occupation of early modern rural youths. They left their parents as children, and departed from service as adults. The progress in status from child to servant to householding adult is conspicuous in the few parish censuses that include information on age and occupation (Table 5.1).[1] Ealing's pattern is the most striking. All males and females aged 10 to 14 were children resident at home, but only 21 per cent of males 15 to 19 were. The rest were servants. Householding then began to take the place of service among the 25–9 age group. Fewer women appear to have left home before their marriage, and they married younger. In Corfe Castle and Ardleigh, the progression is repeated. The proportion of males aged 15 to 19 who were farm servants was higher than the proportion of females, and the rapid movement away from service into householding came between the age groups of 20–4 and 25–9.[2] The median age of servants to farmers ranges narrowly in the three listings from 19 to 21 for males, and from 19 to 20 for females. The median ages of householding farmers and labourers in the three listings ranged from 36.5 in Corfe Castle (labourers) to 55 in Ealing (yeomen).

Entry into service in husbandry

There was no fixed age at which children left home to become servants in husbandry. The normal age in the north of England in 1843 was, as one observer put it, 'ten to twelve to fourteen'.[3] Christopher Tancred assumed in his scheme for registering the hirings of all servants that thirteen was the ordinary age of entry.[4] Charles Varley wrote of the poor farmer whose 'children be of no use, but rather a burden to him, till they be thirteen or fourteen years old that they go to service'.[5] A Cambridgeshire labourer testified at his settlement examination of 1789 that 'when at proper age he lived in several places'.[6] The modal age of entry into farm service, taken from ninety-one settlement examinations, was thirteen to fourteen: 23 per cent of all servants entered service at that age (Figure 5.1). An additional 22 per cent entered when aged fifteen to sixteen. The age distributions of servants in the Ealing, Ardleigh, and Corfe Castle listings (and in the 1851 census) are consistent with a typical age of entry around fourteen or

Table 5.1. *Distribution of agricultural population by age and status*

	Proportions							
	male				female			
ages	C	S	H	N	C	S	H	N
(a) Ealing, Middlesex, 1599								
0–9	0.96	0.04	0.00	25	1.00	0.00	0.00	23
10–14	1.00	0.00	0.00	12	1.00	0.00	0.00	8
15–19	0.21	0.79	0.00	14	0.71	0.29	0.00	7
20–4	0.17	0.83	0.00	6	0.14	0.57	0.29	14
25–9	0.13	0.38	0.50	8	0.11	0.22	0.67	9
30–4	0.00	0.17	0.83	12	0.13	0.25	0.63	8
35–9	0.00	0.60	0.40	5	0.00	0.00	1.00	6
40+	0.00	0.09	0.91	33	0.00	0.00	1.00	20
(b) Corfe' Castle, Dorset, N. and S. Divisions, 1790								
0–9	1.00	0.00	0.00	37	1.00	0.00	0.00	37
10–14	0.85	0.15	0.00	13	0.95	0.05	0.00	20
15–19	0.50	0.50	0.00	14	0.64	0.36	0.00	11
20–4	0.50	0.30	0.20	20	0.08	0.67	0.25	12
25–9	0.17	0.00	0.83	12	0.18	0.06	0.76	17
30–4	0.00	0.00	1.00	9	0.00	0.14	0.86	7
35–9	0.00	0.06	0.94	16	0.00	0.13	0.88	8
40+	0.00	0.03	0.97	31	0:00	0.05	0.95	22
(c) Ardleigh, Essex, 1796								
0–9	1.00	0.00	0.00	71	1.00	0.00	0.00	111
10–14	0.96	0.04	0.00	26	0.91	0.09	0.00	35
15–19	0.43	0.57	0.00	37	0.71	0.29	0.00	38
20–4	0.41	0.38	0.21	34	0.38	0.19	0.43	42
25–9	0.22	0.04	0.74	23	0.15	0.10	0.75	20
30–4	0.19	0.04	0.77	26	0.04	0.00	0.96	23
35–9	0.15	0.00	0.85	13	0.00	0.00	1.00	9
40+	0.00	0.03	0.97	77	0.00	0.05	0.95	57

Source: CG, Parish Listings Collection, Dorset, Essex, Middlesex.
C = resident children of yeomen, husbandmen, farmers, and labourers
S = servants of yeomen, husbandmen, farmers, and labourers
H = householding of yeomen, husbandmen, farmers, labourers and their wives
N = number in age-group

fifteen, although the early Ealing listing suggests a somewhat older age.

The nature of farm service influenced the minimum age of entry. Farmers may have been impelled, in part, by motives of patronage in bringing the children of their neighbours into their families, but most

Number

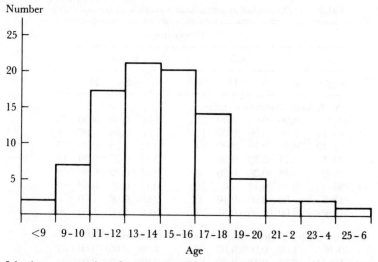

5.1. Age at entry into farm service (from settlement examinations); n = 91.
Source: SE Coll., CRO, ERO, HRO, LRO, LAO, NRO, Northants RO,
SRO.

farmers hired servants to help them work their farms. They resisted
hiring anyone who could not contribute enough to the production and
life of the farm to recoup the wages that would be paid and the cost of
maintaining the servant for the year. As the *Farmer's Magazine* put it,
'Farmers have no use for hired infants.'[7] The wages of younger
adolescents were low; in the sample of settlement examinations used,
the mean wage of ten- to fifteen-year-old male farm servants was less
than half the mean wage of servants over twenty. But the farmer had,
in addition, to lodge, freed, and sometimes clothe the servant. Until
children were old enough to 'earn their own living', they could not
expect a farmer to hire them. Instead they worked for farmers during
the day and returned to their own homes at night, as Fred Kitchen
did. A Norfolk settlement examination of 1826 neatly encapsulates the
transition. The labourer who was being examined had been 'sent out
to be employed amongst the farmers' when he was seven, and went
into yearly farm service when he was twelve.[8]

When rural children left home to enter farm service, they did not,
typically, travel far. A comparison of the distances involved, taken from
several sources, is shown in Table 5.2. The Hertfordshire and Suffolk figures
are derived from settlement examinations, and represent the distance
between the place of birth and place of first service of the examinants. The
Lincolnshire figures are based on the 6 per cent of male and 11 per cent of

Table 5.2. *Distance from place of birth or from home to place of farm service*

County	Mean distance (km)	s	N
Hertfordshire, eighteenth century	4.12	3.91	13
Suffolk, eighteenth century	8.42	8.48	18
Lincolnshire, 1767–85			
Male	12.46	7.43	46
Female	10.31	6.86	74

Source: SE Coll., HRO and SRO; LAO, Holland QS D2.

female servants who were recorded at the Spalding hiring sessions as having come to the sessions 'from home', or from a household headed by someone sharing their surname. The mean distance in Lincolnshire is higher, but all distances from home in Table 5.2 are similar to the corresponding distances between successive hirings by county in Tables 4.7 and 4.8 above.

Some servants returned home for a year or two in the middle of their career as servants. Several explanations for this are possible. The most likely is that the death of a family member or the acquisition of a larger holding suddenly required more family help.[9] One elaborate instance of this can be traced in Cambridgeshire records. Thomas Bond, a labourer, was examined by the settlement authorities in Cambridge in October 1784. He reported that he had lived with his father in Hardwick until he was twenty-two, that he then went into service in Barton for one year and eleven months, returned home to his mother, stayed a year, and later married. The Hardwick parish registers provide the missing demographic details. Thomas's father, Reuben, was a farmer; he married Thomas's mother, Elizabeth, in 1736 (she was his second wife – the first was buried in 1735); Thomas was born in 1751; Reuben was buried in August 1774. All this is consistent with Thomas's having stayed in service until his father died, and with his then having gone home (from Barton) in August, one month before the traditional date of expiration of the servant contract at Michaelmas.[10] Home was also a refuge to which servants unable to find places returned.

What initiated the move from home into farm service? In Chapter 2 we saw that many factors, which might be called environmental, supported the existence of the institution of service, and some of these can be applied to this question. Nuclear families dispersed their children before marriage, and service in husbandry provided a place for them to learn and save. It was a site of preparation for independence, similar in some respects to school or apprenticeship, but with the difference that farm service allowed servants to save, rather than simply engage in 'human capital formation'.

The high age at marriage may have been a sufficient cause for the departure from home. Macfarlane has stated the argument in its most explicit form:

> we might well have expected that such a delay [in marrying] would lead to sexual competition within families. Incestuous temptations, however, would be minimized by the virtual absence of more than two co-residing adults of the same family. Another source of tension, the changes in patterns of authority as the children approached adulthood, would also be diminished.[11]

Puberty, then, was the initiator of the move from home, and the incest taboo the ultimate cause. Servants in husbandry, however, were hired only when old enough to be useful farm hands. Thus an apparent motive of avoiding incest, deduced from the age at which farm servants left home, may have been no more than a reflection of the age of the youngest servants farmers would have been willing to hire. Farm service, and service to craftsmen and tradesmen, differed in this respect from schools and apprenticeship. In the latter, parents paid the schools and masters to take their children. Macfarlane's explanation of the timing of the departure of apprentices and students seems more necessary in these cases.

It is probable that the high age at marriage influenced departures from home. The longer the delay before marriage, the higher was the chance that one or both of the parents would have died before their children married. Hervé le Bras has estimated that only 34 per cent of French twenty-five-year-olds in the eighteenth century would not have lost one parent; 17 per cent would have lost both parents.[12] There are no comparable English estimates. The increasing probability of what Laslett termed 'parental deprivation' is shown in Figure 5.2, a reworking of le Bras's estimates.[13] Three explanations for exit from home can be inferred from it. First, the death of a parent could cause the household to collapse, dispersing its surviving members. Second, the remarriage of a widowed parent often caused open conflict between children and stepparents. More records exist of this tension than of the necessarily hidden sexual tension posited by Macfarlane. Settlement examinations sometimes note, for example, that the death of a parent or the remarriage of the survivor had occasioned the entry into farm service.[14] Three of the very small number of servants in husbandry whose lives have been remembered in autobiographies and biographies had lost at least one parent before entering service.[15] None, however, entered service immediately upon the death of his parents. Charles Varley was six when his mother died, and spent the next eight years as the subject of arguments between his father and stepmother over the wisdom of spending money on his schooling, before running away into service. Bettesworth's parents both died when he was young; he was

Proportion
of children

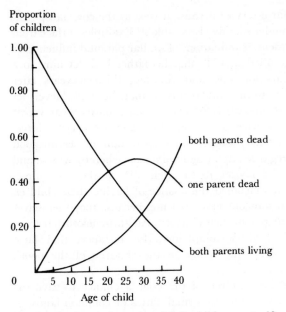

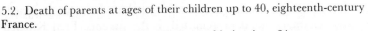

5.2. Death of parents at ages of their children up to 40, eighteenth-century France.
Source: Le Bras, 'Parents, grands-parents, bisaieux', p. 34.

rescued from the workhouse by an uncle, and escaped into farm service at twelve. Fred Kitchen was orphaned at eleven, but could not legally leave school until he was thirteen; he then worked for half a year as a day-labourer before being placed into service by his widowed mother. The death of parents cannot be the direct explanation of all entries into service, however, since the probable number of orphans is too small to account for all servants. A more general reason for the departure from home may have been the likelihood that one or both parents would die before their children married. Sending them from home would have lessened the psychological and economic disruption attending the unpredictable event.

Farm servants also left home for reasons more contingent upon their economic position. Children were sent out to spare their parents the expense in keeping them, to learn farming techniques, and to save for their eventual marriage. Smallholders, cottagers, and labourers sent their children into service as soon as a farmer would accept them. The children were, as Varley put it, 'of no use, but rather a burden' to the parents.[16] Fred Kitchen travelled to the Doncaster hiring fair in 1905 in a cart with a married cowman and his thirteen-year-old son, who was being sent into farm service because it was, as the cowman put it, 'time he put his feet under som'dy else's table'.[17] Examples surface from time to time in settlement examinations of similar parental influence. A Hertfordshire man testified in 1782 that his father had 'let him' to a farmer for three years for food and clothing; thirteen years later another Hertfordshire examinant reported that he had 'never let himself, nor been led by his father, for a year, to any master whatever'.[18] Macfarlane interprets service as a means by which the servant-hirers exploited their poorer neighbours: 'The institution of servanthood might, therefore, be regarded as a disguised means whereby wealth and labour flowed from the poorer to the richer.'[19] At the same time, however, husbandmen welcomed the chance of having their children fed and maintained at someone else's expense, because they themselves had no employment to give to their children. An anti-enclosure tract of the mid seventeenth century complained, for instance, that farm service to arable farmers, 'the refuge of the children of the poor', declined with enclosure.[20]

Farm service gave the children of the poor a chance to save the wages they received in order to stock small farms or common lands, or simply to furnish the cottage they would inhabit when they married. Alternatively, wages could be remitted to the parents. Fred Kitchen took his wages to his mother when he was fourteen; there is an indirect suggestion in the account book of a farm in Tetney, Lincolnshire, that younger servants sent their wages home.[21] Poor children could also learn the farming techniques that would make them skilled day-labourers. Charles Varley once agreed to serve a master only after he had been promised to be taught to break and swingle flax.[22] A Leicestershire labourer told his settlement examiner in 1780 that when he was twenty he wanted to learn to mow, but his master, having no mowing needing to be done, agreed to let the servant leave for a month with a hay-mowing team in return for the wages the servant received on the team.[23]

Farmers also sent their children out to be servants in husbandry. Dunbabin, Davies, Hoskins, and Williams all observed that many of the farm servants they discovered in their studies of widely varying places and times were the sons and daughters of farmers, waiting until they could marry, saving to stock farms, and training themselves in farm operations.[24] Children of craftsmen and tradesmen also became farm servants.[25]

Larger farmers as well as small sent their sons and daughters into farm service. Economic necessity was not their immediate motive, because they hired servants to take their places in the economic life of the household. Servants were psychologically easier to discipline than the farmer's own children. They made no claims upon the farmer other than their maintenance and wages, and, most importantly, the practice left the farmer free to compose his labour force to his best advantage.[26] Pinchbeck and Hewitt called service 'training unalloyed by the sentiment of family'.[27] Marshall remarked that the large farmers of the Midland counties sent their sons into farm service 'as PUPILS, with superior farmers, at some distance from their father's residence'.[28] William Fleetwood cautioned all servants against 'eye-service', idleness, and sloth, which made them 'incapable of answering the design of their parents or friends, in putting them to trades and callings'.[29]

It seems likely, from the foregoing discussion, that more labourers sent their children into service in husbandry than farmers did. They had all the reasons to do so that farmers had, and the push of economic necessity as well. The listings that form the basis of Table 5.1 indicate the tendency. The distribution of the youthful populations of the three parishes, by household and status, is shown in Figure 5.3. In each parish, the proportion who were children of labourers, resident at home, declined with age more rapidly than did the proportion of resident children of farmers.

We cannot know, however, what proportion of early modern servants in husbandry were children of labourers and what proportion were children of farmers. This is, to say the least, unfortunate. Our interpretation of the institution would be radically different if service

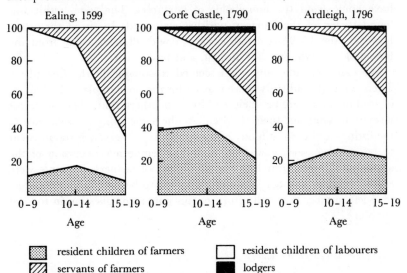

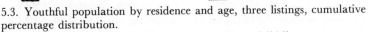

5.3. Youthful population by residence and age, three listings, cumulative percentage distribution.
Source: CG, Parish Listings Collection, Dorset, Essex, Middlesex.

were only, as Macfarlane suggested, a means by which the rich exploited the children of the poor, in which 'half the parish hired the other half'.[30] Parish listings do not reveal the household of origin of servants. Settlement examination of paupers are strongly biased against representing the children of farmers.

The best, and very crude, statistical approach to the question can be made by using parish listings. It must be posited, first, that the listed parishes were not *net* importers or exporters of servants to or from the unlisted neighbouring parishes; second, that a constant proportion (0.75) of servants in the parishes were aged 15 to 24; third, that 15–24-year-olds constituted a fixed proportion (0.175) of the population of the parishes; and finally, that the 15–24-year-olds came from households distributed by occupation as were the existing households in the parish.[31] By multiplying the observed proportion of servants in each population by 0.75, and dividing the product by 0.175, an estimate is yielded of the proportion of all 15–24-year-olds who were servants at the time the listing was made. This estimate can then be compared with the proportion of households headed by labourers, farmers, and craftsmen. In Carlton Rode, Norfolk, for example, 0.107 of the population were servants, 0.75 ×0.107 or 0.080 of the population were servants aged 15 to 24; 0.080/0.175 or 0.459 of 15–24-year-olds were servants. Since labourers in Carlton Rode headed only 0.33 of the households, the crude method indicates that all the servants could not have come from the households of labourers. The same result was found in ten of the fourteen parishes examined. In six of these ten, however, the 15–24-year-old servants could all have come from the households of labourers, craftsmen, and tradesmen.

We can conclude only what seemed reasonable in the first place. There were undoubtedly more reasons for the poor to place the burden of feeding and lodging their children on others than there were for farmers to send out their children. At the same time, the evidence of the listings and the testimony of contemporary observers is too insistent to be ignored: service was not simply a temporary extension of the agricultural proletariat into the household of farmers. Servants were not all children of poor labourers, destined to become labourers when they left service. We shall return to this important question in the last chapter.

Exit from service in husbandry

At term's end, not all servants moved on to new masters or renewed their contracts with the old. Just as some being hired were being hired for the first time, some leaving a place were leaving service behind. Most servants eventually sought an adult status.

A few remained unmarried servants for life. Bachelor servants in southwest Wales too old and stiff to be ploughmen became cowmen.[32] Various late-eighteenth-century agricultural societies gave prizes for long service to the same master, and one discovered, 'to their great astonishment', that some servants had stayed on for more than fifty years.[33] Still fewer remained in service after their marriage. Loudon thought the combination of a resident married cattlekeeper and dairymaid ideal, provided they had no children.[34] Googe referred to the 'baily and his wife' who looked after his model farm and farmhouse.[35] The agent of the Duke of Buccleuch, who had written to his employer to explain that good single servants were hard to find in mid-term, continued: 'a man and his wife both properly qualified would be more readily procured, and would with less reluctance quit their station'.[36]

Most servants finally left, and established their own households.[37] The movement of individuals from service to householding is as difficult to observe as is the movement into service. It involved a change of status, usually from servant to householder (or wife), and it is hard to trace the path across status lines. From the little information that can be gleaned from settlement examinations, exit from service often involved longer moves than had been made during service.

The greater distances were the result of migration to towns and cities, which were necessarily farther away than was the next farm or village. Former farm servants examined in Bury St Edmunds, for example, had travelled an average of 14.6 km from their place of birth to Bury ($n = 54$, $s = 14.2$ km), while those examined in the villages of Clare, Debden, and Wickhambrook in Suffolk had travelled an average only of 7.9 km ($n = 64$, $s = 11.6$ km).[38] The militia transported former servants over far greater distances.[39]

The age at exit can also be gleaned from settlement examinations, but, as was the case with ages at entry, the estimates are not representative of all servants. Whatever future the examinants had anticipated when entering service, they were, by and large, poor labourers when they left it. The median age at their exit in 265 cases was twenty, but 20 per cent remained in service until they were at least twenty-five.[40] The ages are low, compared to the figures of Table 5.1, but the discrepancy should not surprise us. Early exit ensured low savings, which in turn helped ensure an eventual settlement examination. The total number of years served could be calculated in eighty-one cases, and in them no central tendency emerges. The median number was six years, but almost one-quarter had served at least ten years before exiting, and eleven per cent served at least fourteen years.[41]

Farm servants left service to marry, and to establish independent households. Male servants, especially, could escape the patriarchal domination of a master in his household by establishing domination over their own households. Female servants, similarly, could escape the authority of the household's mistress by coming to occupy that status themselves, but their escape would not have seemed as complete, to the extent that they simply exchanged, in leaving service, one master for another. As Tusser rhymed it:

> I serve for a daie, for a week, for a yere,
> For life-time, forever, while men dwelleth here.[42]

Given both the motives of marriage and of independence, servants still had cause not to rush from service. Ex-servants had to support themselves, and in areas where small farms were scarce and rural manufacturing non-existent, exit entailed becoming an agricultural labourer. The attraction of a labouring life was not strong, and the farm servant lucky enough to have year-round employment might well have been tempted to put off the time when he would be 'metamorphosed into a labourer by marrying and setting up his cottage, finding himself and receiving weekly instead of yearly wages'.[43] The labourer 'finding himself' would be subject to all the vagaries of work, weather, and ill health that made day-labouring so risky an occupation.[44] Daily wage rates were consistently higher than prorated yearly rates not only because the labourer had greater expenses than the servant, but also, as Minchinton pointed out, because of seasonal unemployment: labourers did not earn the day rates every day of the working year.[45]

Leaving service may also have entailed a clear loss of status. Horsekeeping was the best job a male worker could have, and in some regions, only farm servants were horsekeepers. To leave service to become a labourer, therefore, meant to become a lesser worker. The Board of Agriculture report on Worcestershire implied this,[46] and Jenkins was explicit about the relative statuses in southwest Wales. Young unmarried servants did the 'highest work'. The hierarchy of farmworkers ran from the farmer's sons down to servants and finally to labourers.[47] Such a hierarchy could exist wherever only servants were ploughmen and carters, but it would have been strengthened in regions of small farms where servants could hope to become farmers. To be a servant was to be a potential farmer, but to be a labourer was to be a realized failure.

Thus there were reasons not to rush from service. But we know that most servants eventually left. What else had they saved for, than to form 'the foundation of independence'[48] from service? How else could they marry? Most servants left, but what they then became was dependent both on the opportunities for independence provided them and on the resources they commanded.

Many farm servants expected to become farmers themselves. This would obviously have been true of the sons of farmers for whom service was a farming apprenticeship; it was the hope of others. Kebble reported that the small farm was to farming servants in the north 'the *ne plus ultra* of their hopes'.[49] Some servants inherited farms, others had land settled on them at their marriage. Where small farms were available a servant could probably have saved enough in a normal span of service to rent and stock it. Arthur Young dedicated a chapter of his *Farmer's Guide* 'to the service of the servant, labourer, or other poor men' who wished to become farmers; the *Farmer's Letters* described the little one-plough farm 'which those labourers, servants, and others in general take when possessed of money enough to begin business'.[50] Young estimated that an intelligently stocked farm of twelve acres, all in grass, would cost £65.5.0 the first year, including rent, tithe, and rates at £21, implements at £10, and stock of one horse, four cows, and one sow at £29. A farm of sixteen acres, half arable and half grass, would cost £91 the first year, the extra expense being largely for plough-horses and tackle.[51] Davies reported that Cheshire servants and labourers in the late eighteenth century applied to their landlords for six- to twelve-cow farms.[52]

Estimates of the amounts that servants could save vary. Fifteen years after Young made his estimates, the *Political Enquiry* stated that an industrious young man could 'scrape up' £20 to £30 'in the course of a few years' service' and that a young woman could be 'possessed with nearly an equal sum'; Howlett's tract on enclosures repeated these estimates four years later.[53] William Pitt thought servants could reasonably save as much as two-thirds of their wages, although he feared that most wages went for ale.[54] Assuming that one-half to two-thirds of wages were saved, we may use the wages recorded at the Spalding hiring sessions to estimate possible late-eighteenth-century savings. The results are shown in Table 5.3. It is conceivable that a male and female servant could have pooled their savings and stocked a small farm on their combined savings alone, if they both served at least ten years (note that far lower totals were available to be saved by women). Some contemporary writers expressed concern about the viability of small farms, however. Young found them inefficient, and greatly favoured a somewhat larger, two-plough farm; he called small farmers 'a set of very miserable men'.[55] The *Commercial and Agricultural Magazine* railed

Table 5.3. *Possible pooled savings of a male and a female servant (based on mean male and female wages, Spalding, 1767–85)*

Years in service of each servant	Total wages (£)		Amount savable by both servants (£)	
	Male	Female	1/2 saved	2/3 saved
2	12.5	5.5	9.0	12.0
4	25.1	11.0	18.1	24.1
6	37.6	16.6	27.1	36.1
8	50.2	22.1	36.2	48.2
10	62.7	27.6	45.2	60.2

Source: LAO, Holland QS D2.

against the failed farmers who were not content to be respectable labourers.[56] Occasional settlement examinations testify to the risks. Robert Bush, a pauper of Addlethorpe, Lincolnshire, in 1811, had been hired at fourteen, served eleven years, and had rented a £40 farm when he left service; a Belchford man had rented a large farm with two others (his share had been £62.10.0) but was six years later being questioned about his settlement as a labourer.[57]

The *Political Enquiry* of 1785 expected its industrious servants to become prosperous cottagers, not small farmers: 'they . . . find a cottage near the common; they then stock their cottage with cows, calves, sheep, hogs, poultry, etc., as much as their little fortunes will admit of'.[58] The husband would work as a day-labourer while the wife looked after the livestock. For some servants, as long as commons remained unenclosed, this must have been the most hopeful expectation.[59] Hitt argued in 1760 that servants married as soon as they could find a cottage and land enough for 'a cow or two, and a garden for potatoes, beans, etc.'.[60] The improvident servant, or any servant in a region of enclosed wastes, could not expect to attain even the modest independence from constant wage-labouring that such cottagers enjoyed. The savings were needed only to rent and furnish a cottage, and the only checks to marriage and exit were the availability of cottages and the rival attraction of remaining in service.

Most farm servants remained in agriculture when they left service, as farmers, cottagers, or full-time agricultural labourers. But some also left agriculture. A Suffolk servant to a 'considerable farmer' left service to be apprenticed to a wheelwright in 1759.[61] Other servants could take advantage of burgeoning rural industries by applying their savings to the purchase of necessary tools. The city drew others away. The *Museum Rusticum et Commerciale* complained about 'the allurements of greater

gain and better fare [that] draw them from the plough and flail'; it
continued, graphically:

> A lad who used to be content with the plain and homely diet of the
> farmhouse, and five or six pounds a year wages, now pants after the
> life of idleness and luxury, a laced livery, high wages, and card
> money: and as soon as he has raised three or four guineas, in the
> country, to get inoculated, away he flies to London, or some other
> seat of great opulence.[62]

It is impossible to calculate the proportions of farm servants who
entered adulthood through farming, labouring, occupying cottages,
and so forth. Settlement examinations are more biased in this respect
than any other. Nearly every examinant was at best a labourer, at
worst a vagrant or pauper. Parish listings can be used only if large
assumptions are made, allowing cross-sectional lists to stand proxy for
longitudinal histories of cohorts, and even then insurmountable problems arise: if two-thirds of twenty-year-olds are servants, and one-
third of twenty-five-year-olds farmers, which servants became farmers?
The estimate could range from half to none of them.

Those leaving service typically married. The *Museum Rusticum et
Commerciale* referred to service as a 'covenanted state of celibacy',[63]
and just as servants were assumed to be single, former servants were
assumed to be married. Hitt and Arbuthnot both assumed all labourers
to be married, and all servants single, when they made their estimates
of the costs and benefits of agricultural improvements.[64] The metamor-
phosis of servants into labourers spoken of by Howitt was accomplished
by their marrying.[65]

Marriage and exit from service were most often nearly coincident
events. The time elapsed between the two can be measured from
settlement examinations, and is shown in Table 5.4. More than half of
the ninety-six former servants had married before or immediatetly after
their departure from service, and two-thirds had married within a
year. The coincidence of marriage and exit from service was not
accidental. The two events were in several obvious and not-so-obvious
ways tied together. Servants who married usually had to leave service
and find another occupation, unless the marriage could be concealed.
Table 5.4 shows that eleven of the ninety-six servants had married
within their last term of service. The pregnancy of the wife-to-be
probably caused many combined departures from service and marriages.[66] Marriage did not follow the departure from service as in-
exorably as departure followed marriage, but there was a strong
tendency for this to occur. Male servants had saved in order to become
householders, either farmers or cottagers, and householders needed

Table 5.4. *Time elapsed between date of exit and date of marriage, from settlement examinations, eighteenth and early nineteenth centuries*

Timing of marriage	*N*	Percentage of total
Married while still in service	11	11
Married immediately upon leaving	40	42
Married within one year	11	11
Married within two years	4	4
Married within three years	12	13
Married within four years	4	4
Married within five years	3	3
Married within six years	3	3
Married within seven years	3	3
Married within eight or more years	5	5
Total	96	99

Source: SE Coll., ERO, HRO, LAO, LRO, Northants RO, NRO, SRO(B).

housekeepers, who could either be hired or married. All but four of thirty-six Ardleigh, Essex, farmers in 1796 were either married or widowed (with resident children): three of those four kept at least one female servant. All the labourers in the listing were married or widowed.[67]

A few niches existed to which servants who did not wish to set up a household could go. Some servants became lodgers in a house other than their master's.[68] Others returned home, to become lodgers in their own families, as Gillis called them.[69] For most servants, however, leaving service meant establishing an independent household.

The exit from farm service in early modern England comprised mobility in status, from dependent servant to married householder or wife, and mobility in occupation, from farm servant to labourer or farmer. Service was not so much a check to early marriage as an opportunity for not marrying. As Macfarlane put it, 'the system of farming out the children, which permitted them a moderate freedom without forcing them to resort to marriage, allowed them to marry late'.[70] Service was the link between the high age at marriage and adult independence as a farmer or cottager. Young people became and remained farm servants in order to save to stock farms or commons, and regions with small farms and commons were, as was argued in Chapter 2, the regions in which servants were preferred to labourers by farmers.

The link was weakened as small farms and commons disappeared.

Young people had less reason to save, and therefore less reason to become servants, when their future consisted of wage-labouring, and larger farmers demanded relatively fewer servants. The decision to marry became dependent upon the availability of housing and a calculation of their likely earnings as labourers. Labouring required only the labourer and a place for him to eat and sleep; maintaining a cottage and commons required help. Arthur Young, reporting on farming in the later eighteenth century, assumed that in the north of England, where service was strong and small farms prevailed, only one-tenth of labourers were unmarried, but that in the south, with larger farms and relatively fewer servants, one-quarter of labourers were unmarried.[71]

Diachronicity has finally introduced itself into this synchronic attempt to understand the workings of the institution of farm service. Times changed, and the patterns governing entry into and exit from service changed with them. Part III of this study will be concerned with the changing environment of service in husbandry and the abandonment of the institution.

Coda: Joseph Mayett

Much of Part II has been aggregative. Observations of many thousands of servants and masters, in many times and places, were drawn together to expose regularities in the practice of service. A look at the life of one servant in husbandry should provide a refreshing change from statistical anonymity, a fitting conclusion to this discussion of form, and an apt introduction to the notion of change. We owe this rare glimpse to the existence of a literate servant in husbandry at the turn of the nineteenth century.

His name was Joseph Mayett.[72] He was born in March 1783 in Quainton, Buckinghamshire, near the border with Oxfordshire, the son of Methodist parents. His father was an agricultural labourer. Of these mundane facts, none was more important to him than religion, for it was Methodism, Baptists, election, damnation, morality, hypocrisy, and Providence that informed his recollections and moved him to record his erratic progress from childhood piety through youthful lapse to rather pragmatic Baptism. So much of the manuscript is concerned with the mechanics of Dissent (the licensing of his parents' house as a Methodist meeting-place in 1789, the coming of a Baptist preacher, the conversion of the Mayetts, the slow growth of the Baptist congregation, and often interrupted building of the Chapel), Mayett's view of religious practices (his one Catholic master, 'a very odd man', who, to

Mayett's relief, did not require his attendance at mass, his seduction by the 'pomp and music' of the church in Buckingham, through which the devil led him in a slide from hymns to martial music to love songs to 'paltry and filthy' songs, and thence to enlistment in the Royal Buckinghamshire militia), and in seeing the hand of God everywhere (and the voice of God, mistakenly, in the grunts of a pig in a thunderstorm), that we are fortunate that the vehicle for his interpretation of nature and man is often his description of tasks, masters, and fellow servants. We probably would not have been told, for example, that among his jobs at one farm was the milking of eight cows, had not he dreamed one night of the coming of the devil to snatch him from the distant cowshed, and of his rescue by the intervention of a flying figure garbed in white.

What does he tell us of his farm service? First, the great frequency of his movement: from 1795 to 1802, he moved from place to place eleven times (see Table 5.5), although never more than 15 km from his home in Quainton (see Figure 5.4). Second, the annual nature of the contract: in nine of the twelve hirings he entered service at Michaelmas, and the other hirings were under special circumstances (he entered service for the first time in the Spring, and twice was hired in mid-year after leaving another service in mid-term); in each of these latter instances, he left the new place at Michaelmas. Third, his progression from home, where he had assisted at lacemaking from the age of nine, into service, 'sent out' by his parents at twelve to the farm in Quainton where his father was employed as a labourer. Fourth, his continuing contacts with his parents. Fifth, the largely tacit nature of the institution. Only once did he explain why he left at Michaelmas to find a new place, but each time the contract was broken in mid-year, twice by him and once by his master, he was at pains to understand why. He expected to be a servant in husbandry, hired by the year; his parents expected it. Only when the expectations went unmet was he driven to reflection. He recorded his wages and living conditions, for example, only when he was forced to work as a day-labourer. To Mayett, the only noteworthy variation within service was the character of his master and mistress, ranging from the two 'good scholars' who encouraged his reading to the hypocritical Baptist mistress and the foul-tempered drunkard who beat his servants with a walking-stick.

His first master was the drunkard, Mayett's father's employer; Joseph returned to him at fourteen for his fourth hiring. During the latter term, one of his less agricultural tasks was to go to the alehouse to see his drunken master safely home. Sent on this task one evening by his mistress, for sixpence, he replied that '6d. was worth a hiding'; he

Table 5.5. *Joseph Mayett's farm service*

Hiring	Time of hiring	Time of departure	Place	Length of service	Age at hiring
1.	Spring 1795	Michaelmas 1795	Quainton	c. six months	12
2.	Michaelmas 1795	Michaelmas 1796	Quainton	one year	12
3.	Michaelmas 1796	Michaelmas 1797	Quainton	one year	13
4.	Michaelmas 1797	Michaelmas 1798	Quainton	one year	14
5.	Michaelmas 1798	Michaelmas 1799	Quainton	one year	15
6.	Michaelmas 1799	Michaelmas 1799	Wingrave	three days	16
7.	Michaelmas 1799	Michaelmas 1800	Ludgershall	one year less three days	16
8.	Michaelmas 1800	November 1800	Godington, Oxon	one month	17
9.	February 1801	Michaelmas 1801	Quainton	eight months	17
10.	Michaelmas 1801	February 1802	Waddesdon Hill	five months	18
11.	Spring 1802	Michaelmas 1802	Quainton	c. six months	19
12.	Michaelmas 1802	February 1803	Buckingham	c. four months	19

Source: Bucks. RO, D/x 371.

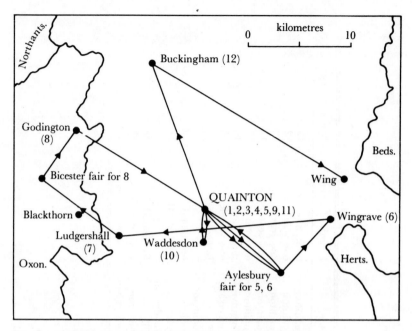

5.4. Joseph Mayett's mobility, 1795–1802 (order of hiring).

was reproved by her for being saucy (a charge that was to be made again). When the master had made his own way home, he pulled Mayett from bed and threatened to turn him out naked; Mayett, in turn, grabbed 'a working tool that was in the room', and threatened to beat the master's brains out. The master retreated, telling Mayett he was forbidden the house, and Mayett dressed and went home. There, his rudely awakened father persuaded him to return, saying that if the master, also the senior Mayett's employer, refused, he would 'mocke him smart for it'. Mayett was taken back, and served out the rest of his term. He had three fellow male servants on this farm, two of whom enticed him to the alehouse. They soon grew tired of paying for Mayett's ale, however: he 'had no money'. This episode provides the strongest grounds in the memoir for presuming that he remitted his wages to his parents. If he did, he literally did not find it remarkable.

Between these hirings, he served, first, a master and mistress, 'good in temporal things although carnal' (i.e., not religious), and second, because the prior master had given up his farm at Michaelmas, another master in Quainton, 'and here was under no kind of restraint whatever so that I gave myself entirely to vice and folly as far as my age and knowledge would admit at that time of life'. He was thirteen, and the nature of the vice and folly is left unspoken. His movement from this second to third master is the only normal Michaelmas movement that is explained.

These years were not the happiest of Mayett's memory: he was caught between the taunting of those who called him 'methodist . . . tubthumper' and the reproof of his Methodist parents for swearing (one, doubtless, of his vices and follies; he answered that it didn't matter, either he was elected or not, and swearing would make no difference). When he left his drunken master at Michaelmas 1798, it was to go at fifteen to the Aylesbury hiring fair with his father; there Mayett was hired by still another farmer of Quainton, and his father arranged with the farmer for Joseph to be employed in the garden of the lone farm in the spring evenings, when the others went to the cricket matches. Here there was only one other servant, a fellow Methodist, and Mayett was sometimes allowed by the master to read books 'of a religious nature . . . as we sat by the fireside in the weekday evenings'. He was compelled by his mistress to attend church or meeting once a week. It was to this lone farm and 'very moral woman' that he returned in the Spring of 1802; by that age (nineteen) he was grateful that the combination of her compulsion and his dissent meant that he could spend Thursday evenings at the Baptist meeting in Quainton and Sunday at the meeting in Waddesdon Hill 'without control', as he succinctly put it.

At Michaelmas 1799 he went again, apparently on his own, to the Aylesbury fair, and was hired by a farmer of Wingrave who proved to be 'like a madman', swearing incessantly at his servants, and Mayett and two other servants left within three days. On the Wednesday that they departed, Mayett found a new place, another lone farmhouse, Sharp's Hill, in Ludgershall. Here, his master was another 'good scholar'. Mayett found it a 'very good place', his master was at pains to teach him to read, and in the spring, Mayett's fourteen-year-old brother joined him in service. This was the farm with the distant cowshed of the dream of salvation.

The next Michaelmas he ventured further, to the Bicester (Oxfordshire) fair, and was hired by Mr Thomas Tompkins (the only master's name noted) of Godington, Oxfordshire, the 'Roman Catholick'. Within a month, Mr Tompkins came to him in the stable, paid him a month's wages, told him that he didn't suit and that he should take his clothes and leave. This was in November 1800: bread prices were higher than they had ever been before, and Mayett did not find another place easily. He returned to his parents in Quainton, applied to the overseer for work, and was sent out for the week at 8d a

day, first to one farmer, and the next week to a second. The second
farmer sent his son out to Mayett while he was working, and asked him
to stay on, but not as a servant. He was offered work going with the
team and milking morning and night at 6d more a week and occasional dinners, but he was to board and lodge himself. 'I was not
very fond of it but it being winter and provisions dear and many
servants out of place I could not extracate myself.' A month after
Christmas, in early 1801, he learned that the farmer intended to
continue to employ him, but, because of the price of provisions, 'would
not hire me servant so long as he could have me at four shillings and
six pence a week'. Mayett knew, however, that the farmer needed a
carter, and hatched a plot: 'I began to be a little political.' He
discussed the plan with his father, and then put it into action. His
Sundays were his own, and one Sunday he walked to a large farm in
Blackthorn, Oxfordshire that he had heard of. He knew that the
farmer's name was Garner, but 'knew him not nor nothing about him'.
He had told the head cowman of his recalcitrant employer that he had
heard that Mr Garner wanted a carter: 'this thought struck my mind
at this time that if I beat out after a place and my master knew of it he
would soon hire me or I should get a place somewhere else'. The
surprised Mr Garner told Mayett that he wanted a servant girl, not a
carter, and that a Mr King wanted a shepherd; meanwhile, however,
the obliging head cowman was remarking to the subject of Mayett's
scheme, 'I wonder whether Joe will be hired today or not?' The next
day, while Mayett was ploughing, the master came to him in the field,
and Mayett moved in on Thursday. It had taken him three months of
that famine winter to get the place as servant that he thought to be his
own, and these were three months in which he abruptly descended
from the standard of living of a farmer to that of a poor labourer. The
contrast was greatly heightened by the high grain prices; his new diet
was barley bread and hog peas. This was not his only complaint about
his placeless situation. He was seventeen when thrown out of service by
Mr Tompkins, and did not enjoy returning to live under the strict
discipline of his parents after five and a half years away from home. He
found them especially unhappy at his swearing: 'I was grown to the
stature a man and did not fear correction at their hands yet I knew it
would displease them.'

For most of the rest of the year 1800–1, he lived instead 'in vice and
prodigality' with his conquered master. All his companions tried to
reform him, but to no avail. It took, instead, three occurrences to turn
him back towards righteousness. He was ill for a fortnight in May, and
'somewhat came to [his] senses'. In the summer, returning to the farm

after staying with a girl he had met in hay harvest until after midnight, he paused to rob a pear tree. He returned another night for a second attempt at the pears, but he and a fellow thief were frightened off by a bigger set of villains intent on the same theft, and seeing the pears he had collected being carried off, he resolved to give up this new career. Finally, in a violent temper, he broke the rib of a restive cow with a milking-stool. He set the broken bone the next day before the farmer noticed, and his conversion was complete. Now he castigated his reform-minded companions, telling them that *he* was elect, and *they* damned. The action was, he noted, unpopular, but by this time Michaelmas was approaching, 'and I have never seen some of them since'.

Mayett moved on to a farm near Waddesdon Hill, and again did not last the year. That same October his parents joined the new Baptist Congregation at Waddesdon Hill; he also attended the services, as did his Baptist mistress. In January 1802, the mistress discovered that he had 'formed a correspondence with a young woman', another member of the church. The mistress disapproved, Mayett recalled, because he was not a Baptist, and told the minister, who rebuked him from the pulpit. This occasioned a period of thoughtful questioning of the nature of religious belief and its relation to morality. A month later, a servant girl in the household, joining in the family practice of gossip, told her mistress that Mayett had sworn at the eleven-year-old daughter of the house. Mayett answered indignantly that he had not done so; he had not told her to 'go to hell and be damned', but to 'go to 'Enley upon Thames' (a major reform in his manners, had she but known). Mayett had had enough of the household, and quit. His mistress threatened to 'blast his character so that he should not get another place within five miles', but she had overestimated her range. Immediately upon returning home he met a man drumming up labourers for his master at eight shillings a week, was hired, and for the next eight weeks lived at home. During the eight weeks Mayett's father's employer, the drunkard of hirings one and four, sent word home with the father that Mayett could have a place there, but his father, recalling the beatings, his son's temper and nineteen-year-old strength, advised against it. It was after these eight weeks that Mayett met another former master, the good scholar with the very moral wife, and he was hired by him to hoe beans; after a day's work, he was taken in as servant for the rest of the year.

His years as farm servant were by this time moving quickly towards their end. That summer, while carting hay, he and a fellow carter were pressed by the farmer to get the hay loaded before the skies opened, and in the oppressive heat before the storm, he found himself at odds with the other servant. Once again, his temper ruled his fate. In exasperation, he declared that he would go and be a soldier; instead, he went off to do the evening milking. On his return to the farmhouse, the farmer's thirteen-year-old son, seeing him still a civilian, called him a coward for not going, and he set off for Buckingham, only to discover that the recruiting party had left. He met an acquaintance there, a sergeant in the militia, who stood him a pint and kindly sent him back to the farm, to which he returned in time for the morning's work, after sleeping in a hayfield and catching cold.

He stayed the rest of the hiring year, and then moved to a farm in Lenborough, within Buckingham. There he was compelled to attend the Anglican Church, seduced, as noted earlier, by the pomp and music; he was also struck by the uniforms of the soldiers he saw in the church, 'sergeants and corporals and musick men and all very clean'. Led on by Satan, as he remembered it, he enlisted, and was sworn in at Wing in February 1803. His parents were upset: 'would one shilling buy him off?' They still had not understood, in any case, why he had left their fellow congregationalist's employ a year earlier.

Mayett was never again a farm servant; his mobility now took on a geographical component that most farm service lacked. For thirteen years he was marched from one shore of England to the next; his only overseas service during the Napoleonic Wars and War of 1812 was a tour in Ireland. In May 1815, in Portsmouth, the regiment was disbanded, and he went home. So did the rest of the armed forces, and after six months' steady employment carting building materials for the new Baptist Chapel, he found himself, during the hard winter 1815–16, selling rags, tapes, and laces. In December he married a woman who had recently joined the Waddesdon Hill Congregation, and gave up ragpicking the next winter for more settled employment as a labourer.

Mayett was, in many senses, not a typical servant in husbandry. He was a Methodist, reflective, literate. His time of service, the very late eighteenth century, was also in some ways different from other times. He did not leave service to marry, but to enlist; this means of exit must have been common during the Napoleonic Wars, as well as during the other labour-intensive wars of the second half of the eighteenth century.

Mayett was atypical, but the institution he entered was not. The distinctions between servants and labourers were sharply drawn; he was, as servant, an unmarried youth, hired on annual Michaelmas contracts, maintained in the farmhouse. He gave us a glimpse, on four occasions, of the power of a determined servant to counteract the abuse of power by his master. He showed us variations in practice possible within the institution, especially the variety of hiring practices, ranging from hiring fairs to chance encounters.

Two facets of his experience were not those described within the last three chapters. His frequency of movement was extraordinary: twelve different hirings in seven years. The influence upon service in husbandry of the disruptions caused by war, population growth, and high grain prices at the end of the eighteenth century will be returned to in Chapter 7. In no instance, however, did Mayett suggest that faithful adherence to annual departures from places was to him unusual. If the inexplicable firing by Thomas Tompkins in 1800 and the baiting by the Baptist mistress in 1802 had at their root a fear that Quainton would be supplanted as Mayett's legal place of settlement if he finished the year, the perceptive Mayett, so quick to respond to wrongs done him, did not realize it. That he found himself, on two occasions, without a place as a servant, was certainly a position in which many youths found themselves in the later eighteenth and nineteenth centuries. His experience was part, in that sense, of the slide into near extinction of service in husbandry in the south and east of England. As we shall see in the next chapter, however, changes in the incidence of service were not unique to the turn of the nineteenth century. A century and a half before Mayett lived, youths would have found themselves unemployed as servants, ensnared, as Mayett put it, 'by the cares of the world'. Cycles in the incidence of farm service were known to early modern England, with this difference: in the earlier cycles, the form of the institution remained intact. When Mayett entered service in 1795, he entered into an institution practised much as it had been in Buckinghamshire in 1595 and 1695, and as it would still be in the north and west in 1895. The incidence varied, but the form remained rigid.

PART III

Change

6   Cycles: 1540–1790

The incidence of service in husbandry did not remain fixed, but rose and fell in two major cycles from c. 1450 to c. 1900. Only the first phase of the second cycle, the abandonment of service in the late eighteenth and early nineteenth centuries, has been generally noted by modern historians. Board of Agriculture reports, Parliamentary Papers, and the 1851 census all strongly attest to this collapse, at least in the south and east. Before that, however, the incidence of service had declined from a probable high point in the fifteenth century[1] to a trough in the mid seventeenth century, and then rose sharply to a second peak in the mid eighteenth century. After the mid nineteenth century, in the north and west, the incidence rose once again.

Changes after 1790 can be directly observed and will be considered in the next chapter. Before 1790, the evidence is indirect. The parish listings of Chapter 2, which do not contradict the argument of cyclical motion, are too few and too scattered to bear the weight of a cyclical interpretation. The measure that reveals the cycles is the proportion of marriages celebrated in October in the rural south and east, where Michaelmas was the date at which servants' contracts began and ended. We have seen that service was for most a stage in life between childhood and married adulthood. When servants chose to leave this stage in order to marry, and thus put an end to their status as servants, Michaelmas would have been the logical time to leave service behind, and October the first month in which they were likely to marry. Thus, changes in the frequency of marriages occurring in October should reflect changes in the proportions of youths who entered marriage via farm service.

The changing incidence of post-Michaelmas marriages, 1539–1840, in fifty-six agricultural parishes in the south and east is shown in Figure 6.1.[2] Marriages in the month following the frenzied activities of the grain harvest are common in this arable country over the whole period. The low point of 160 at 1652–3 in the twenty-five-year moving average indicates that October marriages were 1.6 times the proportion that would have been expected had marriages been evenly distributed throughout the year. The trough is exaggerated by the virtual absence of October marriages in 1653; the Commonwealth's new Marriage Act

97

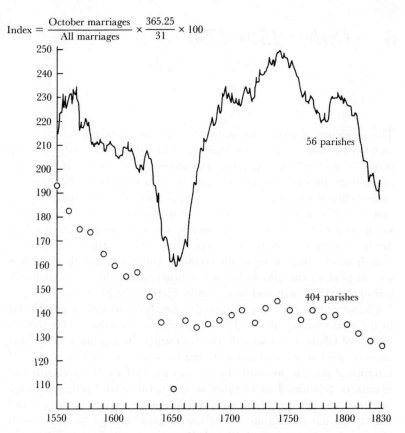

$$\text{Index} = \frac{\text{October marriages}}{\text{All marriages}} \times \frac{365.25}{31} \times 100$$

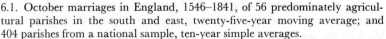

6.1. October marriages in England, 1546–1841, of 56 predominately agricultural parishes in the south and east, twenty-five-year moving average; and 404 parishes from a national sample, ten-year simple averages.

required all marriages to be performed before Justices of the Peace after 29 September 1653.[3] At the start of the series, more than 2.3 times more marriages were celebrated in October than a random distribution would predict, and in the 1740s, the index reached 250. Figure 6.1 exposes all of the first cycle in incidence, and half of the second.

The proposition that the cycle of post-Michaelmas marriages reflects the changing incidence of service in husbandry is strongly supported by the close matching of the marriage-cycle to the three factors most likely to have influenced the incidence of service: population growth, the cost of living, and relative prices. These three were interrelated, but each had its distinctive effect on the keeping of farm servants.

The growth of the English population, 1541–1841, is shown in

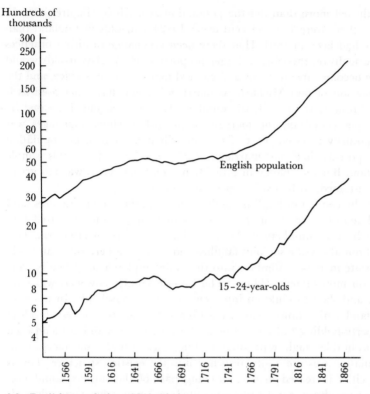

6.2. English population, 1541–1841.
Source: Wrigley and Schofield, *Population History of England*, tables 7.8 and
A.3.1.

Figure 6.2.[4] Both turning points in the series are precisely correlated
with the turning points in post-Michaelmas marriages. Until the
middle of the seventeenth century, population grew and post-
Michaelmas marriages declined; after 1656, population at first declined, to 1685, and then grew so slowly and inconsistently that by
1735 the population was only 3.2 per cent larger than it had been in
1656. During this period, post-Michaelmas marriages increased. In
1741, population began the exponential growth that continued into the
nineteenth century, and post-Michaelmas marriages declined.

The simplest connection between population growth and the incidence of service in husbandry was the changing age-composition of
the population. Most servants in husbandry were youths. The decline
in population after 1656, according to Wrigley and Schofield, was
principally caused by a drop in fertility, and the absolute number of

youths fell more than did the population as a whole (Figure 6.2).[5] In 1681, there were 16.6 per cent fewer 15–24-year-olds in England than there had been in 1661. Had there been no change in hiring practices in agriculture, therefore, a larger proportion of 15–24-year-olds would have become farm servants and entered marriage from service, and the proportion of post-Michaelmas marriages would have increased as it did. From 1701 to 1721, the number of 15–24-year-olds increased by 20.9 per cent, and the increase in post-Michaelmas marriages was temporarily arrested. Part of the coincident movement of population and post-Michaelmas marriages can be explained by this simple relation. But the change in post-Michaelmas marriages was too great, too sustained, to be explained by this alone.

In the context of English family structure, inheritance practices, and land tenure, growth in the numbers of people translated itself into growth in the numbers of placeless adults, propertyless labourers. This need not always be so: joint families and partible inheritance can easily translate increased numbers into the underemployment of family workers on morcellated holdings. The English family, however, was nuclear, and shed its children into new, separate households. In much of England, inheritance was impartible, even at the lowest level of property-holding.[6] Much of English farming practice did not lend itself to profitable, high rent smallholding. Accordingly, an increase in population was not easily absorbed into the existing structure. Towns and cities increased in size, drawing part of the surplus population from agriculture, rural crafts expanded, and new crops were adopted, better suited to profitable spade-labour and smallholding, but none of these changes was an automatic response to population growth. The ability of the early modern economy to find places for all its people was limited.

The effect of population growth on the composition of the hired labour force was to create a mass of poor adult labourers in need of wage-work. In such a setting, farmers need not have hired servants. Desperation, not annual contracts, would have ensured the attendance of workers when they were needed. Wages need have been paid only for work done, and annual contracts, which served as insurance against the everyday risk of finding no workers willing to work, were unnecessary. Such was the situation in England in the later sixteenth and the first half of the seventeenth centuries; it was to be repeated in the later eighteenth and nineteenth centuries in the south and east.

During the second half of the seventeenth century conditions reversed. London continued to grow rapidly, increasing in numbers by 44 per cent from 1650 to 1700.[7] Rural crafts, organized to serve the national, London-centred market, continued to flourish. Population, meanwhile, declined. In a relatively short period, the surplus of labour diminished. In this new setting, in all probability previously seen in England only in the later fourteenth and fifteenth centuries, servants in husbandry appeared indispensable. The new problem faced by farmers was the necessity of ensuring that they would have labour when they needed it. Their valuable investments in draught animals, fat and breeding stock, sheep and dairy herds needed constant attention. The solution, suggested by Timothy Nourse in 1700, was simple:

> Whether it be better for a House-keeper to have his Work Manag'd by Day-Labourers, or by Domesticks, is a Point likewise of some Consideration in the Oeconomy of a Family. Domesticks may be a greater Charge, because we are obliged to pay and provide for them, even when they do us no Service, as in case of Sickness, or of unseasonable Weather, or of wanting full Employment: In all such cases, Day-Labourers ly more easilie upon us, as being paid no longer than they work; But for all this, 'tis better to have Work wanting for our Servants than Servants for our Work.[8]

Farmers made certain of their labour forces by binding youths to annual contracts and by keeping them on the farm. Skilled and seasonal work continued to be done by day-labourers: when Nourse and Defoe sought descriptions of poor labouring men in the midst of the century of increasing farm service, they called them hedgers, threshers, ditchers.[9] During the late seventeenth and early eighteenth centuries, farmers found it necessary to keep servants, as farmers had not in the early seventeenth century, and would not in the nineteenth century.

Changes in the cost of living (Figure 6.3), which were themselves strongly correlated with population movements, directly affected the keeping of servants in husbandry.[10] A good proportion of a servant's cost to a farmer was the food, drink, and lodging provided in the farmhouse. When the cost of living rose, the proportion grew. Money wages tended to be 'sticky', that is, they tended neither to rise nor fall as rapidly as the cost of living rose or fell. Inflation thus had the effect of making the cost of hiring day-labourers, who were paid a far smaller part of their wages in real goods, fall relative to the cost of hiring farm servants.

The cost of living rose sharply until the 1590s, then rose more slowly until the mid seventeenth century when it fell, recovering somewhat in the 1690s, and then remained trendless until the mid eighteenth century, when the rise leading to the extraordinary inflation of the Napoleonic Wars began. It was during this last period that Joseph

Index
1451–75 = 100

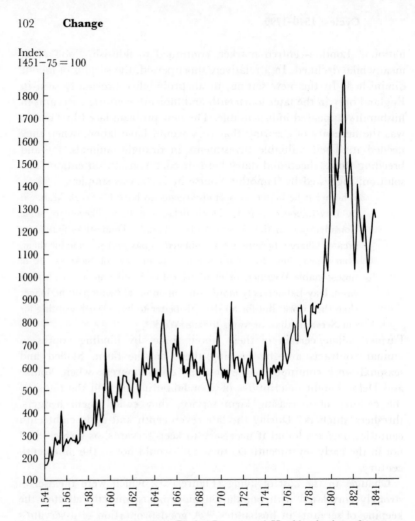

6.3. Cost of living, 1541–1841. Phelps Brown and Hopkins basket of consumables 1451–75 = 100.

Mayett's employer, and many others, temporarily threw the burden of hyper-inflation onto their unfortunate employees. In 1776, after thirty years of steady increase in the cost of living, William Marshall warned farmers:

> Perhaps the Farmer who keeps no accounts imagines he saves money by boarding his servants in the house: but I am confident, that if he keeps them in the luxurious style which farming-servants in this country *expect* to be kept in, he is mistaken ... Feeding farming servants in the house lessens the quantity, and of course enhances the price, of provisions.[11]

The first period of increase, the sixteenth to mid seventeenth century, also saw farmers attempt to cut costs by hiring labourers. Robert Loder, a Berkshire farmer, decided in 1613 that his servants were too dear and put his carter on board wages, paying him an additional money wage in place of the board and lodging Loder had grown loath to provide.[12] Poor Loder. His reading of long cycles in the English economy was correct: for over a century, prices had risen and the trend would continue to mid century. His sense of the short run, however, was deficient. He chose the only period in the entire Phelps Brown and Hopkins series, 1321–1901, in which the cost of living fell for seven consecutive years. His experiment failed: the cost of keeping the carter at board wages was greater than the cost of boarding him had been.

What neither Loder nor Marshall tells us directly is that the precondition for throwing servants onto board wages, or for hiring no servants at all, was that the labour market be glutted enough that youths had no choice but to accept the changed terms of employment. The decisions of Loder and Marshall were based on relative costs; they took the ready availability of willing labourers for granted as Nourse could not in 1700.

The rise in real wages after 1650 may have further reinforced the demand for farm servants by restricting the reliable supply of day-labourers. The increase in the purchasing power of a labourer's wages made it possible for him to work fewer days in the year while still purchasing the same quantity of goods. The 'consumerism' of the modern economy, coupled with inflexible wage-contracts, has modified this response to increasing real wages, eliminating the backward bend in the supply curve of labour. In the seventeenth century, however, de Vries has argued that the fires of consumerism in the general population had only begun to be kindled by the increased range of domestic and imported goods,[13] and the contracts under which agricultural day-labourers were hired were extremely short in duration. If this were so, periods of increases in real wages would have seen labourers taking advantage of their position by 'consuming' more leisure, and farmers increasingly unable to rely upon the continuous offer of labour from day-labourers. The annual contracts of farm servants took the decision to enjoy more leisure out of the worker's hands, and guaranteed farmers a continuous supply of labour during the contractual year.

The last of the three determining cycles is the relative price of grain and animal products (Figure 6.4).[14] The index, the variation of which is largely determined by trends in wheat prices, rose sharply to the mid sixteenth century, slowed its upward progress to the 1630s, rose rapidly again until the early 1650s, and then dramatically reversed, dropping precipitously, with few interruptions, until 1740, when the series

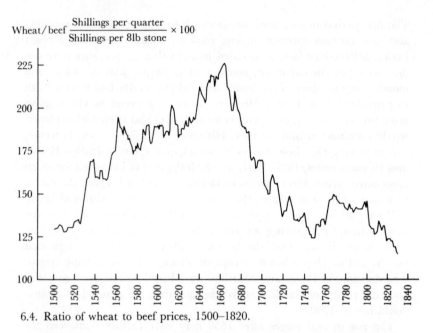

$$\text{Wheat/beef} \; \frac{\text{Shillings per quarter}}{\text{Shillings per 8lb stone}} \times 100$$

6.4. Ratio of wheat to beef prices, 1500–1820.

reversed again. Wheat prices then rose strongly against beef prices for twenty years; the (smoothed) index then fell gently, interrupted by the high wheat prices at the turn of the century; finally, the depressed wheat prices that followed the Napoleonic Wars pulled the index down further. Until the late eighteenth century, Figure 6.4 is a near-precise mirror image of the cycle of post-Michaelmas marriages (Figure 6.1). The explanation is simple: animals require constant attention, fields of wheat do not. The trend of relative prices was a signal to farmers to alter the composition of their output, and with it, the composition of their hired labour force. Grain production, *ceteris paribus*, was associated with the hiring of relatively more temporary workers, that is, day-labourers, than permanent workers, servants in husbandry, and animal husbandry was associated with the hiring of relatively more servants. The strong shift in relative prices in the mid seventeenth century encouraged a shift away from cereal production. More farm servants were hired to care for the increased flocks and herds, and more youths entered marriage from farm service. The encouragement to grain production after the 1740s reversed the process, and fewer youths were hired as servants. In the later eighteenth century, the close inverse relation between the smoothed trend of relative prices and the season-ality of marriage was broken. Post-Michaelmas marriages, after 1790, declined in the south and east, while the wheat/beef price ratio rose briefly, and then also declined. Some of the reasons for the changed relation are structural, others contingent; none are cyclical. The incidence of service in the south and east had stopped moving cyclically: the process by then was one of decay and extinction.

The cycle in the incidence of service in husbandry before 1800 can only be shown through the combined impact of the course of post-Michaelmas marriages and the compelling logical reasons why service should have fluctuated as the marriage index did. Loder and Marshall complaining about the high cost of servants, and Nourse about a shortage of available labour, are perfectly consonant with the cyclical interpretation, but their works hardly provide the basis on which to build an argument for major fluctuations. The index of marriages was initially calculated only for the period after 1701, in an attempt to pin down the timing of the near-disappearance of service in husbandry from the thoroughly agricultural parts of the south and east. The discovery that the index did not simply fall, but rose from 1701 to mid century, was felicitous; curiosity led to the calculation of the index for earlier centuries, and thus to the revelation of the cycles, which are not apparent in the whole sample of 404 English parishes (Figure 6.1). Only in the south and east did Michaelmas marriages move in the two long cycles from 1539 to 1829. The discovery of the correlation of the cycles and their logical connection with long swings in population, cost of living, and relative prices, was pleasing. Service in husbandry did not remain fixed in its incidence in early modern England.

The variation in the incidence of service was not the only message conveyed by the seasonality of marriage. The path that post-Michaelmas marriages traced from 1650 to 1750 is in one respect curious. While the path is in thorough agreement with the hypothesis that anything that encouraged the keeping of servants should have increased the clustering of marriages, the path is not the one we should expect to have followed from the strong incentive which grain prices gave farmers to switch to pastoral farming. Arable husbandry has one hectic season, the harvest, followed abruptly by a slack period in October and November, when leases were taken up, servants hired, marriages celebrated. Pastoral husbandry, when mixed with some arable, shows the same autumnal peak, but adds a springtime peak, the lambing and calving season. Wholly pastoral regions experience only the extra activity of the early spring. The large sample of 404 parishes can be subdivided into the categories given by Joan Thirsk in her survey of farming regions;[15] the seasonality of marriage in three of those regions, 1601–1720, is shown in Table 6.1. The peculiarity of Figure 6.1, then, is that autumnal marriages in the southern and

Table 6.1. *Seasonality of marriage, three agricultural regions, 1601–1720*

	Spring		Autumn		
Region	May	June	Oct.	Nov.	No. of parishes
Clay vales; mixed	60	85	350	393	117
Down, wolds, breckland; mixed	46	31	677	169	65
Stock rearing and fattening	357	143	107	71	28

Source: CG, Aggregative parish register file (404 parishes).

$$\text{index} = \frac{\text{marriages in month}}{\text{marriages in year}} \times \frac{365.25}{\text{days in month}} \times 100$$

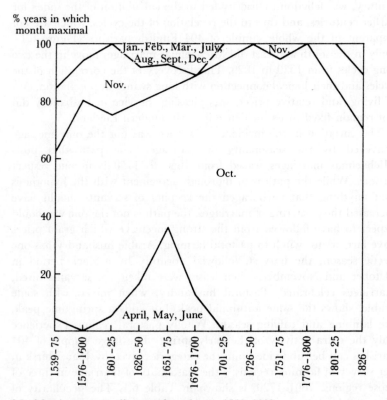

% years in which
month maximal

6.5. Marriage seasonality, south and east, 1539–1839.

eastern counties do not yield to springtime marriages when farmers were given the strong incentive to adopt pastoral husbandry. This is not, as it turns out, a dilemma, but a question whose answer tells more than the question implied. Figure 6.5 is a cumulative frequency distribution of the number of years in which springtime (April, May, June) and autumnal (October and November) marriages were maximal in each twenty-five-year period, 1539–1840, in the fifty-six southern and eastern parishes of Figure 6.1. From the first quarter through the third quarter of the seventeenth century, springtime marriages increased relative to autumnal marriages; from the last quarter of the seventeenth century through the last quarter of the eighteenth, springtime marriages declined, and autumnal marriages crowded into October. In the periods 1726–50 and 1776–1800, no month but October was maximal. What we see in Figure 6.5, I believe, is the timing and nature of the agricultural revolution. In relation to the course of population movements (Figure 6.2) and relative prices (Figure 6.4), three phases of agricultural change can be discerned.

The first phase, ending in the mid seventeenth century, comprises the somewhat tentative experimentation with new seeds and new practices that characterized late Elizabethan and early Stuart England. Cereal prices softened somewhat during the late sixteenth and early seventeenth centuries, and the combination of moderately threatened returns to cereal production, a glutted labour supply, the growth of industrial and urban demand, and the importation from the Low Countries of new techniques and seeds evoked a series of responses, some old, others new. Many farmers retained traditional cereal rotations. Cereal prices, after all, only softened in relation to those of other farm products. On some heavy lands, less well-suited to cereal production, the other traditional response to change, a shift to open pasture, occurred.[16] Near cities, and especially near London, labour-intensive market gardening spread.[17] New arable crops were introduced, including industrial dye-stuffs and fodder crops such as sainfoin, lucerne and clover. Of all these responses it is probable that the traditional were most common.[18] The decline of October seasonality to 1650 is thus a result both of the increasing proportion of youths who worked as day-labourers in arable and spade culture, and of the increase in pastoral agriculture.

The softening of cereal prices before 1650 was no more than a gentle hint that profits might be made from producing something else. During the third quarter of the seventeenth century, the abrupt fall in wheat prices served as a clear warning that adhering to traditional cereal rotations meant the possibility of failure. Figure 6.5 indicates the presence of one traditional response to deteriorating cereal prices, the adoption of open pasture. Where this occurred there was an increase in springtime seasonality of marriage.

What might be termed the 'panic' response occurred in some parts, and arable yielded to pasture. Springtime marriages continued to increase, and now, with them, October marriages, as the shortage of labour prompted farmers to hire servants. By the last quarter of the seventeenth century a third phase had been ushered in. Increasingly, the response to depressed wheat prices was not a simple shift to pasture, but the adoption of mixed farming, the New Husbandry.[19] Wheat continued to be grown, and thus the wheat harvest regained its preeminence as the year's busiest season in the south and east, but the wheat was grown far more efficiently, thanks to the incentive farmers were given to keep livestock, and thanks to the livestock contributing dung to the corn lands. Seen in one light, water meadows, the Norfolk four-course turnip rotation, up-and-down husbandry, the cultivation of lucerne and sainfoin, sheep folds and cow closes are a remarkable technological and aesthetic triumph, the blending of pastoral and arable techniques to increase the productivity of land.[20] Seen from a lesser height, all are either ways for wheat growers to avoid disaster, by incorporating high-profit livestock into their low-profit arable farms, raising their profits in both activities, or ways for pastoral farmers to keep more livestock than open pasture permits. In both instances, high animal prices and a shortage of labour resulted in harvest-dominated seasonality, and in the October marriages of servants in husbandry who had been hired to manage the ploughing, carting and harrowing, to care for the sheep, cows and cattle, and to provide a core of labour for the summer and autumn harvests.

In areas that were more traditionally pastoral it is not possible to demonstrate the changing incidence of service in husbandry by observing marriage seasonality. Figure 6.6 is constructed on the same principle as Figure 6.5, but covers twenty-three parishes in four western counties: Cheshire, Shropshire, Staffordshire, and Herefordshire. There are subtle similarities between the two figures up to the middle of the seventeenth century, despite the very different shape of the distributions. In both the 'arable' south and east and the 'pastoral' west, harvest seasonality initially predominated and increased up to the end of the sixteenth century, relative to pastoral seasonality. Then, in both regions, pastoral seasonality grew relative to arable seasonality. In the west, however, the pastoral pattern continued to dominate the series, while the arable pattern recovered in the south and east after 1675.

% years in which
month maximal

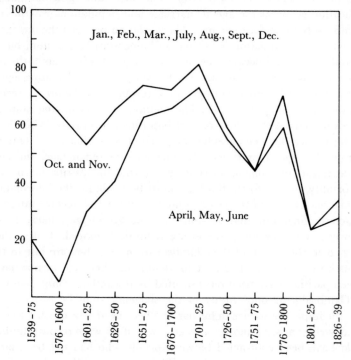

6.6. Marriage seasonality, west, 1539–1839.

Figures 6.5 and 6.6, taken together, can be said to illustrate the strong tendency towards regional specialization after 1660.[21] Nothing of the incidence of service in husbandry in the west can be deduced from Figure 6.6 because the principal influence on the changing seasonality of marriage was the changing seasonality of agriculture. Logic would suggest that the incidence of service relative to day-labouring rose. The number of cattle, cows and sheep increased, and so did alternatives to day-labouring. The regional specialization of the English economy was not simply a matter of making the south and east the principal arable region and the north and west principally pastoral. During the seventeenth century, rural industry increasingly concentrated itself in the north and west, followed in the eighteenth and nineteenth centuries by the growth of the industrial cities and towns of the north.[22] Both drew labour from agriculture; both forced farmers to hire servants on annual contracts to be assured of continuous labour.

Two major implications emerge from the existence of change in the incidence of service in husbandry. The first and most tantalizing implication concerns the age at marriage and population growth. It is tantalizing both because the most likely relation between the incidence of service and population is not one of homeostatic regulation, but of destabilization, and because the probable effect of service upon the age at marriage is so difficult to observe. The only way of calculating age at marriage in early modern England is through the laborious reconstitution of parish populations. The method involves linking nominal records of marriages with records of baptisms and burials. When links can be made, the demographic histories of individuals and families emerge: the age at marriage, the incidence of remarriage, the age-specific fertility of women, the spacing of births, the distribution by age of mortality, and so forth. But links must be made for the information to emerge. The problem is less that the process of reconstitution is time-consuming, but that servants are the group least likely to be reconstitutable. Servants, almost by definition, moved. Unless they returned to the parish of their baptism to marry, they are lost to the reconstituter, at least in respect to identifying their age at marriage. Sixteen parishes have been reconstituted by researchers connected with the Cambridge Group. Many of the sixteen cannot be expected to show the impact of service in husbandry, because they are either towns, or industrial parishes; most marriages, even if all were reconstitutable, would have been contracted between people who had not been farm servants. The age at marriage from 1600–49 to 1800–49 in three of the least complicated agricultural parishes is shown in Figure 6.7, which conveys an intriguing message. Aldenham is in Hertfordshire, close to London; Willingham is in the Cambridgeshire fens;[23] Bottesford is in the Vale of Belvoir, in Leicestershire. If service in husbandry had been a major determinant of the age at first marriage, we should expect the age at marriage to show the same cyclical pattern traced by post-Michaelmas marriages. The age at marriage should at first rise from 1600–49 to 1700–49, and then fall, because during the first period, more youths entered marriage from farm service, whereas during the second, fewer did. The median ages at marriage of all but the women of Aldenham rise and fall as predicted. The pattern is especially clear in Bottesford, a parish in the shadow of Belvoir Castle, closely controlled by its principal landlord, the Duke of Rutland. Bottesford would be expected to display the cycle with the most clarity, for the Dukes ensured that it would be uncontaminated by the early marriages of rural craftsmen.[24] That the age at marriage of men born in Bottesford drops sharply in the nineteenth century while the age at marriage of Bottesford women does not may well indicate a decline in

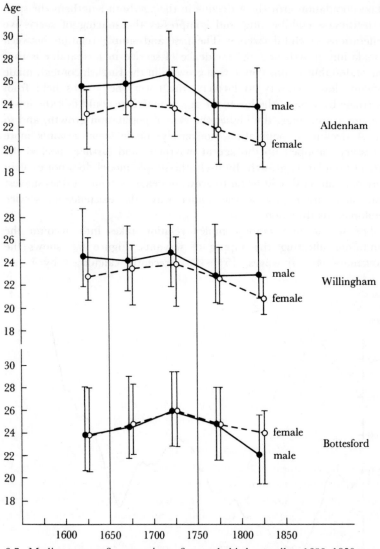

6.7. Median age at first marriage, first and third quartiles, 1600–1850.

the hiring of male, settlement-gaining, servants and a continuation of
the hiring of dairymaids, busy making Stilton cheese. The other wholly
agricultural southern parish in the sample of sixteen, Terling, in Essex,
shows no cycle, but only a downward trend over the two centuries.
This also is what we should predict of a village that early became
proletarianized.[25]

Changes in the age at marriage of females can have profound effects upon population growth. A decline in the age both lengthens the span of legitimate childbearing and compresses the spacing of successive generations of childbearers.[26] The first and simple relation between population growth and the incidence of service in husbandry is thus one of destabilization. Population growth, in the English context, made servants less necessary to farmers; the fewer the youths held from marriage by service, the lower the age at marriage could fall; the lower the age at marriage, the higher the rate of population growth, and so on. A decline in population, conversely, made farm servants more necessary, propped up the age at marriage, and further checked the rate of population growth. By itself, the simple model does not explain why population should begin to grow, or cease growing; it does suggest that once either process was under way, the existence of service reinforced its direction.

The second and more complex relation takes into account the conditions affecting the supply of servants. Figure 6.8 shows the movement of real wages, 1541–1881, recently calculated by E. A.

Index
1451–75 = 1000

6.8. Real wages, 1541–1881, twenty-five-year moving average.
Source: Wrigley and Schofield, *Population History of England*, table A.9.2.

Wrigley.[27] It is likely that changes in real wages affected the supply of servants, and that this effect modified the destabilizing tendencies of the simple model. To the extent that servants were supplied from families 'to get their feet under som'dy else's table', a rise in real wages received by the supplying families should have weakened the urge to throw the cost of maintaining the servants on someone else. The rise in real wages from 1650 to 1750, which is correlated with the falling cost of living, stable population, and rising relative prices of animal products, should thus have checked the tendency of youths to become servants, for their economic necessity diminished, just as farmers were finding them cheaper to maintain. The cost of establishing a separate household also declined as real wages rose. The doubled effect of an increase in real wages was thus to make it easier for youths to remain at home, and easier for them to establish their own households when they left home.[28] An increase in real wages should thus have depressed the supply of servants.

It is likely, however, that the stabilizing effect of real wages on the supply of servants was less marked than was the destabilizing effect of population growth on the supply of day-labourers. In the first place, as argued above, increased real wages were widely believed to depress the supply of all labour, because fewer days of work purchased an unchanged amount of goods.[29] Anything that made labourers indifferent to constant employment made the guaranteed labour of farm servants attractive, and strengthened the will of farmers to seek youths and put them under contract, probably offering them an improved diet (more meat, more ale) as an inducement to become and remain servants. In the second place, economic necessity was not the only reason youths became servants. The comparison of the marginal costs of maintaining children at home with the changing revenue of the family was not the deciding factor in all cases. Adolescent rebellion at puberty and a desire to be educated in a variety of farming practices were not functions of real wages. Finally, it is unlikely that the modifying effect of real wages was as strong in periods of declining real wages. The supply of servants offered by ever-poorer households should then have increased, but there was little reason for farmers to have been induced to hire servants, especially because their total wages had a built-in floor, the cost of maintaining them in the farmhouse for the year.

The destabilizing relationship between farm service and population growth in the later eighteenth century has been suggested by Redford, Krause, Habakkuk and Chambers.[30] 'H' wrote to the *Farmer's Magazine* in 1800 to explain the results of an amalgamation of three farms in 1735. Before the amalgamation, there were three farmers, six cottagers, and thirty-three horses; in 1793, one farmer, fourteen cottagers, and sixteen horses. In 1735,

> the increase [in population] from the married servants [who would have been called labourers in the south] was not sufficient to keep up the numbers of unmarried servants, . . . [while] at the present period, the increase from the married servants does much more than supply the population necessary. The sons and daughters are therefore sent to supply the neighbouring towns, or to the smaller farms in the neighbourhood which cannot supply themselves.[31]

Arthur Young praised large farmers for keeping few servants, for 'it is not the employment of single hands that promotes population, but that of men who have families'.[32]

The relationship can first be observed directly in the 1851 census. Agricultural districts[33] with relatively few servants and many day-labourers were also those with low proportions of unmarried males and females aged twenty and older (Figure 6.9).[34] Both male and female correlations exhibit a significant relation between proportions un-married and the composition of the labour force: 25.6 per cent of the variation in proportions of unmarried males is accounted for by variations in the composition of the labour force, and 31.9 per cent of the variation in proportions of unmarried females.[35]

In order to assign to the decline in farm service a major role in the population increase after 1740, we should require better pre-census data than is ever likely to become available. Krause coupled a declining age at marriage with increases in fertility to explain the increase in population, and found both to be associated with better economic conditions. Habakkuk argued that a probable decline in the age at marriage led to the increase in population both by increasing fertility and by diminishing the gap between successive generations.[36] Their arguments must contend with those of Helleiner, Razzell, Eversley, Appleby, Philpot, *et al.*, that either an exogenous or en-dogenous decline in mortality caused population to increase,[37] and with those of Wrigley, Schofield, and Tucker, that increased fertility was the cause.[38]

What seems probable is that while the decline in the practice of service in husbandry from 1750 to 1790 contributed in some incalcul-able measure to the mid century upturn in population, the rapid abandonment of service after 1790 in the south and east, which will be dealt with in the final chapter, had a substantial effect on population increase in that region.[39] The regional breakdown of population growth given by Deane and Cole is shown in Table 6.2 (their 'south' is our south and east). Until 1780, the rate of natural increase in the south

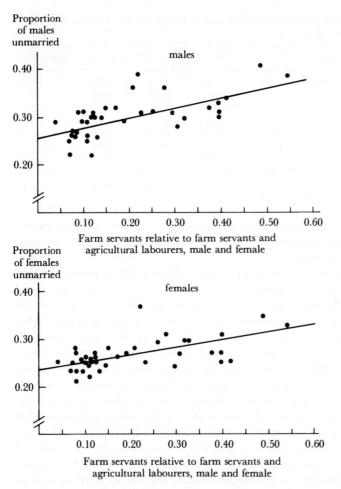

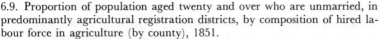

6.9. Proportion of population aged twenty and over who are unmarried, in predominantly agricultural registration districts, by composition of hired labour force in agriculture (by county), 1851.

rises, but remains considerably lower than the rates of increase in the north and northwest. In the latter regions, rural industry was driving down the age at marriage.[40] After 1780, however, the rate of natural increase in the only region that was rapidly shedding servants, the south, rises abruptly, until by 1801–30 it is the highest regional rate. All this simply brings us back to the much maligned Malthus, as both Hajnal and Habakkuk have suggested.[41] A high age at marriage was his great prudential, preventive, check to population increase, and it was

Table 6.2. *Average annual rates of natural increase, England and Wales, 1701–1830, by region (per cent)*

Region	1701–50	1751–80	1781–1800	1801–30
Northwest	0.56	1.29	1.28	1.58
North	0.41	0.82	0.98	1.43
London	−1.08	−0.48	0.27	0.82
South	0.22	0.76	1.12	1.65
England and Wales	0.11	0.68	0.98	1.43

Source: Phyllis Deane and W. A. Cole, *British Economic Growth, 1688–1959: Trends and Structure*, 2nd edn (Cambridge: University Press, 1967), p. 115.

to the rise in improvident marriages, which farm service had helped prevent, that Malthus assigned the cause of late-eighteenth-century population increase.

The other most significant feature of the cycle in service in husbandry is its relationship to the course of change in agricultural practices. As has often been observed, the effect of many of the improvements in agriculture in the sixteenth, seventeenth, and eighteenth centuries was to increase the need for hired labour.[42] Investment in agriculture often took its most direct form, the literal diversion of labour from immediate production (ploughing) to the creation of capital goods (ditching). Enclosure was both a change in the shape, size, and control of holdings, and a labour-using process, involving the creation and maintenance of the hedges and fences that separated newly enclosed holdings, and turned commons and waste into farms.[43] New crops, and new ways of growing old crops, created more jobs for workers in hoeing, weeding, and harvesting.[44] Increases in the size of farms on the whole increased the ratio of hired workers to farmers.[45]

When the new practices were adopted in times of an abundance of poor labourers, they tended to increase the demand for labourers relative to servants. Many of the new tasks were discontinuous, better suited to day-labourers. Others required, for short periods, highly skilled workers, and were better suited, for example, to travelling plashers, hired by a succession of farmers to create and repair the densely interwoven living fences. The increase in the size of farms increased the labour requirements of each farmer. Larger numbers of day-labourers did not mean that farmers needed to increase the living-space for the workers, nor that farmers needed to hire more ancillary servants, cooks and housemaids, to manage the enlarged household.

Larger farms grew at the expense of smaller ones, and of commons and waste; village populations were polarized into large farmers and day-labourers. The social distance between employers and their servants increased, discouraging farmers from welcoming the sons and daughters of labourers into their more prosperous families. In the sixteenth, early seventeenth, and later eighteenth centuries, it is likely that agricultural improvements changed the composition of the labour force by increasing the demand for day-labourers.

There is reason to suspect that these processes of improvement intensified in the later seventeenth and early eighteenth centuries. There may be better incentives to adopt new practices than the threat that old practices might fail, but the reality of failure, in an age of landlords and tenants, rewarded innovators with survival and with the ability to accumulate holdings, and weeded out those slower to change. The diffusion of new practices was thus the combined effect of the learning of new techniques and the success of those who learned. The end to the glut of labour that early-seventeenth-century farmers enjoyed did not mean the end to the adoption of labour-using techniques, because the increase in the productivity of land that the new techniques made possible was more than enough to bear the cost of the labour needed to introduce them. The composition of the hired labour force changed. Farmers who, like Nourse, would have preferred to hire day-labourers, for all the reasons suggested in the last paragraph, found themselves hiring servants, and found themselves using servants in some of the discontinuous tasks to which they were not well suited.

Barley found that in the later seventeenth century a new style of farmhouse began to become common.[46] Separate rooms were provided for servants; often the new houses were divided into servant-space and family-space, each with its own staircase, with no space common to both, and no connection between the two but the kitchen. Barley inferred from this that the number of servants in the economy was increasing, but the implications are more profound. More servants in husbandry and more ancillary servants were being hired by each prosperous housebuilding farmer, and the traditional farmers' families comprising wives, children, and servants were being sundered by the walls placed between the modern, private families and their servants. These were farmers who, given the choice, would rather not have had the expense of the servant-rooms, the walls, the ancillary servants, and the unpleasing presence of boisterous, grimy youths within the house, if they could be sure that their tasks would be reliably performed by day-labourers. When given the choice in the later eighteenth century, and especially after 1815, they put their preferences into practice.

Rather than rushing from this observation into a discussion of the extinction of service, we should take stock of what this account of two and a half centuries of service in husbandry signified. In order to explain changes in the incidence of service, the emphasis has been placed, in these last pages, on the tendencies of farmers and servants to respond to changed conditions. On the whole, however, these tendencies revealed themselves against a background of inertia and unresponsiveness. How could farmers assess the changing relative costs of servants and labourers, especially with reference to the different forms their labour took? Account books were not commonly kept. The *Commercial and Agricultural Magazine* exhorted farmers to keep careful records of costs and revenue in 1800; Marshall assumed in 1776 that so many farmers kept servants because they kept no accounts.[47] Even the meticulous recording of costs was only a partial answer. Robert Loder could only add up his household's annual expenditure, divide by eight (himself, wife, child, and five servants), and then add the resulting *per capita* cost to the money wages of his servants to arrive at their real cost to him.[48] A Shropshire farmer complained to *Annals of Agriculture* in 1785 that he could do no better than calculate the annual cost of housekeeping at £25 for himself, his wife, two children, two men servants, a boy servant, two maidservants, two boarded harvesters, and day-labourers' beer. Moreover, the £25 included only the purchases made, not the imputed costs of housekeeping labour and the farm's own supply of food and drink.[49] A Kentish farmer found he had difficulty in distinguishing between wages paid for farming, for improvements, and for sundry work.[50]

Until the later eighteenth century, commentaries on agriculture offered little advice to farmers on the use of their labour. John Houghten, for example, published two long questionnaires in 1681 and 1683, asking farmers everything about their farming practices except how they deployed their workers.[51] In 1776 the *Farmer's Magazine* complained about the dearth of writing on servants and labourers.[52] Even in the later eighteenth century, Marshall could only suggest the keeping of accounts, Young his estimates of relative costs on various farms, and Trusler and the *Commercial and Agricultural Magazine* the use of prevailing board wages as proxies for the real cost of servants.[53]

It is overwhelmingly likely that most farmers did not respond instantaneously to the signals given to them by changing relative prices, wages, and so on, and that some responded more slowly, and others not at all. Their inertia made the existence of the cycle in the incidence of service possible. The reaction to rising population, rising cost of living, and rising relative returns to arable production was not so great as to cause all sixteenth- and seventeenth-century farmers to rid their houses of servants. Service in husbandry was practised without intermission from the sixteenth to the nineteenth century. When conditions changed and favoured the hiring of servants, farmers and youths still knew the rules of the institution, its form and practice. It could, therefore, simply increase in incidence and did not have to be reinvented.

Very few changes in the form of the institution can be discerned in these centuries. It is possible that the increase in specialization in the English economy increased the evening hours of leisure of farmers and their servants, eliminating the odd chores that Markham described them occupied by in the early seventeenth century.[54] Pehr Kalm expressed his surprise in 1748 in finding that farm servants in Essex did nothing but eat, sit, and talk when they returned from the fields, and that agricultural implements were bought from, and repaired by, specialists.[55] The change in living conditions brought about by the new style of farmhouse, where they were built, implied a change in the meaning of service in husbandry to farmers and servants, but not yet a change in its form.

The inertia continued into the eighteenth century. By no means did all farmers respond to the changed conditions after 1750 by rushing to rid their houses of servants in husbandry. They were still hired in numbers large enough to abound in the militia lists of the 1760s, in Arthur Young's tours in the early 1770s, in William Marshall's farm-house, and in the Buckinghamshire Posse Comitatus of 1798. It took the conjunction of the structural changes of enclosure, the growth in the size of farms, and new agricultural techniques with hyperinflation, the Poor Law, and Napoleon's exile to Elba, to cause the rush towards extinction to begin.

7 *Extinction*

It seemed like a revival of the good old times, but it was really a continuance of them, the practice had never been intermitted ...
Modern habits of society are, however, unhappily incompatible with this beneficial intercourse, and the practice is dying out.[1]

But Don, still a young man, does not consider it to be a dying trade. He continued: 'It is a specialised trade but it isn't a dying trade. It is only dying in respect of people not coming into it – the trade is still there.'[2]

Individuals decay and die; species become extinct. Servants in husbandry were creatures of the early modern economy; the institution of service was imbedded in a matrix of agricultural practices and social organization. They were agents in the growth in the size of farms and in a revolution in agricultural practices at a time when the supply of full-time adult labourers was unreliable, and were victims of the growth they helped procure. Service flourished in most of early modern England, but by the mid nineteenth century it had been nearly extinguished in the south and east.

The conditions for the extinction had been laid down in the century before 1750. What began simply as a second cycle in the incidence of service, twin to the decline of the early seventeenth century, became, by 1815, a rout.

The new cyclical downturn was set off by the rise in population, the cost of living, and grain prices at mid century. By the 1770s and 1780s, a generation of farmers had been given the opportunity to discover the implications of these changes, and commentators noted, in ink they had earlier spared in considering agricultural labour, clear distinctions in the conditions governing the employment of servants and labourers:[3]

The occupation of a common field farm is generally managed by servants hired into a farmer's house, ... as there are no quicksets to plash, weed, or mould up, trees to preserve, wheat, peas, or beans to drill, or in many instances no considerable quantity of turnips or beans to hoe; labourers on these accounts are unnecessary.[4]

Their message was concise. Progressive farmers with large enclosed holdings hired (or should hire) day-labourers;[5] only small, inefficient farmers hired (or should hire) servants.[6] The range of occupations better suited to the short contracts of labourers was greater on a large improved arable farm; large numbers of workers could not easily be lodged in the farmhouse and stable; the rising cost of the provisions fed to hearty young ploughmen and dairymaids was a growing burden on the household's accounts.[7]

Regions of newly enlarged farms were also regions of many new day-labourers, only recently freed from the incumbrance that smallholdings and commons had thrown between them and constant wage-employment.[8] Mavor, in his report on Berkshire in 1808, suggested that enclosure and consolidation further eroded the institution of service because

> good servants every year become more scarce and difficult to be found. The best domestics used to be found among the sons and daughters of little farmers; they were brought up in good principles, and in habits of industry; but since that valuable order of men has been so greatly reduced in every county, and almost annihilated in some, servants are of necessity taken from a lower description of persons, and the consequences are felt in most families.[9]

Where farms remained small and wastes unenclosed, farmers retained their need for servants, and servants their hope for adult independence from constant wage-labour in agriculture. There, the social gap between servant-hiring and servant-supplying families had not widened.

In general, the region of newly enclosed larger farms was the south and east, and that of smaller farms the north and west. In the latter, topography made both the profitable growing of grains and the economical consolidation of farms difficult.[10] There, too, the proliferation of rural and later urban manufacturing created ample opportunities for work other than agricultural day-labour. Servants continued to be hired in the north and west in the latter half of the eighteenth century, but were increasingly not hired in the south and east.[11]

The tendency for service in husbandry to decline in the south and east strengthened after 1790. Rapid population growth, astronomical grain prices, and the Poor Law combined to shout a message that the cyclical changes at mid century had only whispered: stop hiring farm servants. The cost of living had risen persistently in the second half of the eighteenth century, but the inflationary period before 1790 must have seemed, by 1810, to have been a Golden Age of the consumer. Command purchases of foodstuffs during the Napoleonic Wars and a sequence of poor harvests propelled food prices, especially wheat prices, to unprecedented levels. The variation in prices after 1794 was great, but until 1815 the range within which they varied could have been described as between 'very high' and 'very much higher than that'.

The first servant-displacing effect of the inflation was the pronounced shift to wheat production, even on the fells of the north and sheep downs of the south.[12] The elegant multi-course rotations of the New Husbandry were temporarily altered in the rush to profit from wheat.[13] The cultivation of wheat required constant labour in horse-keeping for the drawing of ploughs, harrows, and carts, but none of the constant labour required in maintaining other livestock. The inflation thus tipped the balance of demand for labour towards day-labourers.

The shift to wheat production, however, was subtle in its effect on farm service, compared to the direct impact of the rising cost of living on the consciousness of servant-hiring farmers. Complaints about the cost of feeding servants flooded the second set of county reports to the Board of Agriculture (1804 to 1813) as they had not the first (1794 to 1797).[14] The same reports, interestingly, do not demonstrate unequivocally that servants were becoming more expensive than labourers in this period. From 1794–7 to 1804–13, the weekly wages of day-labourers rose at an average annual rate of 3.0 per cent; the cost of living also rose by 3.0 per cent, but the yearly wages of farm servants rose by only 1.1 per cent.[15] It is likely, however, that decisions to expel servants in this unsettled period were not so much based on calculations of the cost of feeding servants and paying their money wages versus the money wages and perquisites of labourers and savings in laying them off in slack times, as on an aversion to the risk posed by wildly fluctuating food costs. Money wages did not respond instantaneously to increases in grain prices, and farmers may have wanted to throw the short-run risk of changing costs onto their workers. In the short period from 1794 to 1801, for example, the cost of living rose by 79 per cent. It was in the winter of 1800–1 that the eighteen-year-old Joseph Mayett was thrown out of his post as farm servant and forced to subsist for two months on a diet of cow peas.[16]

The nervousness created by unpredictable prices was compounded by the prevailing forms of poor relief. Parishes were responsible for the relief of their own poor; their own poor were those legally settled in the parish; and one year's service was sufficient to establish a settlement, and to bestow upon the parish of service life-long responsibility for the former servant. During the Napoleonic Wars, the seasonality of wheat production and periods of extremely low real wages combined to increase the burden on poor rates. Relief took many forms, but all forms shared one feature: the poor rates were never used to subsidize employed servants, whose care was the responsibility of the master who kept them.[17]

Two strands of response to the poor law can be discerned. Both undermined the demand for farm servants. The first was to hire labourers, especially married labourers, in the place of servants. When labourers had work, they posed less of a burden on the rates; unemployed youths might return home, as Joseph Mayett did, and if home was not in the same parish, they would become a burden on someone else's parish. All ratepayers subsidized paupers, and they may have resented hiring unsubsidized workers. A 'Country Clergyman' expressed this concern to *Annals of Agriculture* in 1801:

> Day labourers are in effect the servants of farmers, but they are distinguished from those who usually bear that name by this circumstance – that they are never lodged and seldom boarded by the farmer: it therefore becomes the interest of the farmer who lives under that form of administration [of poor rates] to keep few, if any, men servants in his house, and even to diminish as much as possible the amount of women servants by employing boys and day women about the house, who are paid the same low scale of wages; the deficiency in which wages comes afterwards to be made up to them in the same manner in which it is made up to the ploughman, the hedger, the thresher, and others, i.e., by the overseer of the parish under the different denominations of rent, hiring, clothing, and occasional relief.[18]

The other response might be called the ratepayer's preventive check. Farmers acted individually and collectively to deny new settlements in the parishes by refusing to keep servants for the year.[19] Servants were dismissed days before the end of the year, their wages were docked for days of absence within the year, explicit hirings were made for half a year, and for the notorious fifty-one weeks. Occasionally, servants were bribed to move on to a new parish; more often, servants were simply not hired. Probably more effective than this were collective actions. Farmers compacted to hire no servants, or no male servants, since females would lose their own settlement at marriage, and put up bonds with the overseers to ensure the adherence of all to the compact. Landlords stipulated in their leases that tenants hire no servants.

None of these actions was unknown earlier in the eighteenth century. Pockets of surplus labour or of progressive landlords and farmers produced occasional attempts to prevent the attaining of new settlements.[20] But just as the changes in prices and population after 1750 failed to move most farmers to respond until their efffect had been magnified by the inflation of the wars, so the manipulation of the work force to prevent settlements did not begin to become widespread until the turn of the nineteenth century. The tenants of Sir Gregory Page Turner in Battlesden, Bedfordshire, for example, were required in the leases of 1802 to discharge servants before settlements had been gained; they had not been so required in the leases of 1794.[21]

Until 1815, however, farmers were thwarted in their desire to rid their houses of budget-threatening, settlement-gaining servants by the temporary labour shortages of the period. The Napoleonic Wars saw increasing numbers of potential agricultural labourers in uniform, dying in Portugal and France, or being marched, as Joseph Mayett was, from one temporary station to the next within Great Britain. Mayett's history illuminates both the divergent interests of farmers and servants and the bargaining power of servants during the labour shortage. Mayett was thrown out of service in the winter of 1802–2, and was forced, with many other youths, to accept weekly work. His job, however, was to aid the elderly carter of his employer, and he had only to threaten to leave the farmer without an able carter to be hired into the farmhouse as a servant. A year later he contributed to the labour shortage by enlisting and found himself in Kent, helping to bring in the harvest with his fellow Buckinghamshire militiamen.[22]

Temporary expedients abounded. The use of threshing machines increased;[23] great interest was shown in them in the second series of Board of Agriculture reports. Several of the house plans suggested by the Board at the turn of the century were late Georgian versions of the late-seventeenth-century farmhouses described by Barley, with segregated living quarters for servants and for the private family of farmer, wife, and children, houses for farmers who would rather not have had servants in their families, but who could not yet do without them.[24] An increase in the use of board wages was generally observed.[25] Some Board of Agriculture reports suggested the minimum numbers of servants that could be kept on each farm.[26]

Instead of the disappearance of farm service desired by so many farmers, the Napoleonic Wars saw an increase in the resentment of both farmers and servants as the practice of service continued in an ever more attenuated form. The frequency of mobility within service increased.[27] The Board of Agriculture reports ring with alarm over the 'rude manners' of servants and the 'growing detachment' between masters and servants.[28] Youths found their expectations of steady employment and ample diet crushed by continuing experiments at doing without servants and by the use of board wages. Middleton recorded the pleas of servants to be taken back into the farmhouse, so meagre was the diet provided by the housekeepers with which they were boarded.[29] Mayett's meals of cow peas are a good step down from the bread and cheese that Marshall had pictured his labourers eating contentedly in 1777.

The resentment survived the end of the wars; service in husbandry, as a major form of agricultural labour in all of England, did not. Mayett and hundreds of thousands more were discharged in 1815. The last set of conditions needed for the drive to extinction of the institution was the glut of labour that swamped the agricultural south and east and the agricultural crises that came with peace.[30] The pent-up desire to rid farmhouses of their servants was released. Farm incomes were more threatened in the intermittent depression than they had been in the inflation, and farmers trimmed their labour costs by hiring labour only when it was needed. The underemployment of servants was replaced by the unemployment of labourers.

Poor rates per capita, following Blaug's calculations, were higher in 1821 than in 1802 in every county but one.[31] Farmers had the incentive, as ratepayers, to reduce the rates by hiring no further settlement-gaining servants, and now had the means to replace them with day-labourers made reliable by their desperation. Significantly, the poor rates per capita in 1821 were lower than they had been in 1812 in thirty-six counties. The difference in the impact of the Poor Law was that, by 1821, farmers could do without servants, as many could do, whether forced by unrest or not, without labour-saving threshing machines.

Keith Snell's extensive study of settlement examinations of paupers clearly reveals the difference between the checked desire before 1815 and its fulfilment after 1815.[32] He calculated the number of hirings that were for periods of less than a full year, by date of hiring. From the middle of the eighteenth century, the percentage of hirings that were for a week, month, three months or six months rose somewhat from a low of approximately one per cent of all hirings of servants in 1741–50 to approximately 11 per cent in 1801–10; the percentage then dipped slightly in 1811–20, and then increased to approximately 25 per cent in 1831–40. The path traced by fifty-one week hirings, which were pure attempts at preventing settlements, is even more striking. Until the decade 1811–20, these hirings were never more than 3 per cent of the total, but in the next decade, they shot up to approximately 23 per cent. Before 1821–30, the percentage of hirings that were for the full fifty-two weeks never fell below approximately 87 per cent, but by the next decade they had dropped to only 66 per cent of hirings.

It is maddening that no systematic national measure of the incidence of farm service is possible before 1851. One can sense, from the second series of Board of Agriculture county reports, a partitioning of England between the low service south, such as Bedfordshire, Berkshire, Middlesex, and Sussex, where servants were reported to have been inessential, and the high service north, such as the East Riding of Yorkshire, where servants were reported to have been responsible for the 'principal part' of work.[33] The division continued in the Parliamentary Reports on the Depressed State of Agriculture (1822) and on Agriculture (1833). That 'the labourers no longer live in the farmhouses' or 'fewer farming servants are hired' was noted in Norfolk, Suffolk, Sussex, North-amptonshire, Hampshire, Wiltshire, and Somerset, while many servants were still noted as being hired in Nottinghamshire, Cumberland, Westmorland, Shropshire, and the North Riding of Yorkshire.[34] The witness for Somerset remarked with disdain that the farmer of fifty to sixty acres still lived with his servants, but that such a farmer was 'like a servant himself'. He added that it was 'not very pleasant to have too many servants in the house'.[35]

The 1831 census did not provide separate estimates of the numbers of servants and labourers, but it is possible to manipulate its categories to yield an approximation of the composition of the agricultural labour force (see Appendix 8). The results are shown in Figure 7.1. The partition between the north (and west) and the south is clear. It is likely, moreover, that the approximation used conceals the absolute differences between the north and south. The estimate of 'servants' drawn from the census includes unmarried male labourers over twenty and excludes male servants twenty and under and all female servants. The estimate of servants would therefore be too low where servants were important components of the labour force, and too high where servants had been transformed into placeless unmarried labourers. The *ranking* of counties by this measure is not apt to have been destroyed by the error, however, and that ranking is highly correlated with the rank-ordering of counties on the basis of poor law expenditures per capita in 1831, as reported by Blaug.[36] Counties with few servants relative to labourers had high poor law expenditures. The causation between the two measures is logically reflexive. The higher the poor rates, the greater was the incentive to hire no servants; the fewer youths hired as servants, the greater was the proportion of the labour force subjected, by farmers, to the blows of seasonal and cyclical unemployment and low real wages. Surplus labour, further, influenced both measures by making servants unnecessary and labourers un-employable.

The 1834 Poor Law Report is tantalizingly close to being a systematic national survey of the decline of service in husbandry. The first version of Question 38 was: 'Is it less common than formerly for labourers to live under their employers' roofs? To what do you

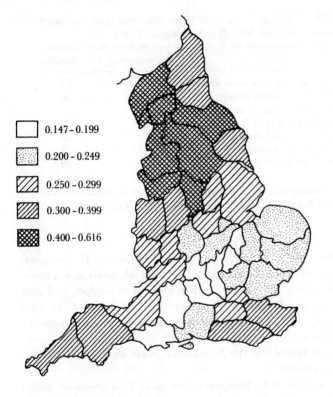

0.147 – 0.199

0.200 – 0.249

0.250 – 0.299

0.300 – 0.399

0.400 – 0.616

7.1. 1831 census: composition of the hired agricultural labour force (servant/all hired workers).
Source: Appendix 8.

attribute the change? Is it more common for labourers to change their service?'[37] The third version, however, which was distributed to many respondents, omitted the first questions and asked only about the frequency of change. The phrasing and order of the questions undoubtedly evoked the kinds of answers that the commissioners wanted to hear. By the time the respondents had waded through the first thirty-seven questions, it is not surprising that so many answered that it was a fear of creating new settlements which kept farmers from bringing servants under their roofs, and which increased the mobility of the remaining servants by moving them on after fifty-one weeks.[38] More revealing is the wealth of responses in which the decline in service was not simply attributed to the Poor Law. Table 7.1 presents a statistical synopsis of the types of response.[39] More than one-quarter of the answers were the expected ones: farmers wanted to prevent new

Table 7.1. *'Why are labourers no longer under their employers' roofs?'*
Responses to Question 38 of Poor Law Report of 1834

	Percentage	Number
Fear of creating new settlements	28	67
Surplus of labourers available	21	50
Need to cut farming costs	20	47
Elevated manners of farmers	10	25
New manners of labourers	7	16
Lower age at marriage	2	5
General, unattributed	12	29
Total	100	239

Source: PP 1834, XXXIII, Appendix B, Part IV.

settlements. But the most common type of response (41 per cent) referred to some combination of a glut of willing labourers and a desire to cut costs by hiring workers only when they were needed, and only when they were fit. A further seventeen per cent were of the kind provided in Rolvenden, Kent: 'The master cares not one straw for the man, nor the man for the master.'

The impact on farmers of the Napoleonic Wars was vividly recalled by several respondents:

> It is less common for labourers to live under their employers' roof. I consider this change to be in great measure owing to the improved condition of the farmers during the high prices of agricultural produce. Their families were unwilling to associate with the labourers; and a second table was out of the question.
>
> Oddington, Oxon

> The change is to be attributed to the alteration of manners and habits of the employers, not entirely caused, but much accelerated, by their prosperous circumstances during the high prices.
>
> Great Milton, Oxon

> Since farmers lived in parlours, labourers were no more found in kitchens.
> Rougham, Suffolk

Many blamed the 'caprice' of the young, their dislike of confinement and restraint. A few, however, with greater insight, recognized that the 'intractability' of workers and the elevated positions of farmers were but aspects of one process, the decline of service itself. In Great Marlow, Buckinghamshire, the 'old fashion, regularity, and confidence' of masters and workers had been destroyed when farmers and servants ceased to eat together. The 'growing disposition' of labourers to change employments was attributed in Great Farington, Buckinghamshire, to the ill-service done them by farmers when hirings for fifty-one weeks prevailed. Most perspicacious was the rector of Westmill, Hertfordshire, Henry Pepys:

> The farmers say they [move more frequently]. The reason I believe to be the discontinuance of the once (I believe) universal practice of receiving the unmarried labourer to board in the farmers houses. They say this is caused by the altered character of the labourers, but I think they mistake the effect for the cause.

Regional differences are reflected in the responses. Only in Cheshire, Cumberland, Durham, Huntingdonshire, Kent, Leicestershire, Lincolnshire, Northumberland, Rutland, Warwickshire, Westmorland, and the North and West Ridings of Yorkshire were parishes found in which there had been little decline in the hiring of servants.

Once the glut of labour was swept back to England by the peace of 1815, then service in husbandry was consumed, in most of the south and east, in a great self-fuelling fire. Farmers did not want to give annual contracts to servants, did not want to live with them, and ceased hiring them. They thus ceased to know any of their workers as companions, their sense of social position was reinforced, and they became even less willing to live with mere labourers. To take labouring youths into their families was to raise the youths, temporarily and unnaturally, above their class.

The lessons were not lost on their workers. Farmers, singly and collectively, had destroyed the niche where youths could be placed, relieving their parents of the expense of maintaining them. The right, under the Law of Settlement, of servants to choose their place of legal settlement by serving their last year in their chosen parish had been denied them before 1834, not by law, but by the actions of farmers. The annual contracts at the Spalding hirings fairs began, in the 1830s, to include provisions for servants paying for their own 'medical attending', and explicitly to permit the termination of the contract with 'a month's wage or a month's warning'.[40]

By the 1830s, the abandonment of service in husbandry had become sufficiently pervasive to alter categories of analysis and language.[41] The 1831 census was the first to remove servants from the families that employed them, and the first that distinguished farmers from their employees. The category 'Families in Agriculture' was preserved from earlier censuses, but separate calculations were provided of occupiers employing labour, occupiers employing no labour, and agricultural labourers. The category of 'agricultural labourers' explicitly included both day-labourers and farm servants. The Poor Law Report of 1834 confirms the change in categories, in speaking of the 'labourers' who once lived in the farmers' houses. Joseph Mayett had recalled the winter of 1801–2, when many *servants* were unemployed; such a conception was impossible thirty years later. It had been grounded in the common experience of youths as servants; a youth without work as a servant was only temporarily placeless, an unemployed servant. By 1830, in the south and east, servants were youthful labourers who had exceptionally been taken into the farmer's house.

When William Howitt wrote with nostalgia in 1838 of the 'old oak table' around which had once sat the farmer and his family of wife, children, and servants, and added that it persisted 'in many an obscure district of merry England yet', he grasped the extent of the decline of service, but underestimated the extent of its survival in the north.[42] His 'obscure districts' covered more than half of England. This is shown with clarity in the 1851 census, which finally provided separate totals of farm servants and agricultural labourers. Figure 7.2 is drawn from that census. It is based on the tables of employment of males twenty and over in each of England's 544 registration districts.[43] Farm service survived wherever the combination of small farms, rugged terrain, and manufacturing did. Figure 7.3 shows the relation between farm size and the hiring of servants directly. As farmers in the south and east hired more workers, they did so by hiring not more servants, but more labourers. In the north, however, mines, textile mills, iron mills, and other industrial opportunities all drew labour away from agriculture, and increased the need for servants made reliable, at least for the year, by their contracts.[44] The marked persistence of a wage differential between the north and south reflected the differences in opportunities and weakness of interregional migration,[45] and encouraged northern farmers to economize by paying a substantial part of wages in the board and lodging provided to servants. A Northamptonshire respondent to the Poor Law Report of 1834 had groped towards an expression of this relation in recalling that servants had earlier been hired, 'when the population was thinner'.[46]

Pockets dominated by labourers existed in the north in 1851, notably on the large farms of Northumberland, and pockets in which servants were still hired in substantial numbers still existed in the south, especially in parts of Kent[47] and the Sussex wolds, but on the whole, England had been divided between the low-service agricultural south and the high-service industrial north and west. Of England's 277,887 male and female farm servants, 74 per cent lived to the north of Dorset,

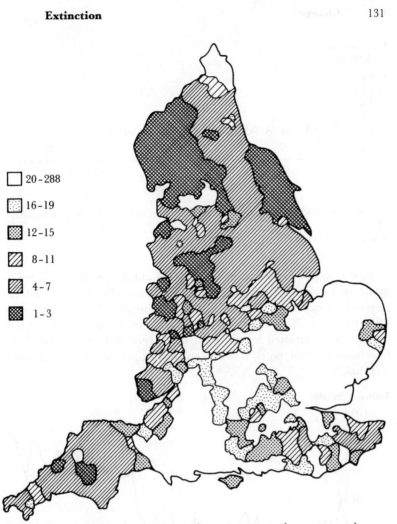

	20-288
	16-19
	12-15
	8-11
	4-7
	1-3

7.2. Agricultural labourers relative to farm servants, males twenty and over, England 1851, by registration districts.
Source: 1851 census.

Wiltshire, Oxfordshire, Northamptonshire, Cambridgeshire and Norfolk. The remaining 26 per cent were thinly spread over the most intensively agricultural region of England, the south.

After 1851, as Dunbabin has shown, the incidence of service continued to decline in the south. By 1871, in Suffolk, the ratio of male farm servants to male labourers was 1 to 194.5; in Essex, the ratio was 1 to 440.[48] In much of the north, however, the incidence increased from 1851 to 1871. It is likely that the increase represents a muted

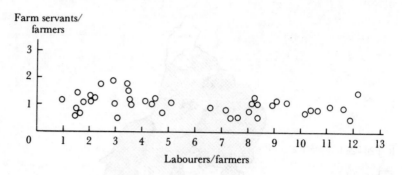

Farm servants/
farmers

Labourers/farmers

7.3. Servants and labourers, each relative to farmers, by county, England 1851.
Source: 1851 census.

cyclical response to the rise in the prices of animal products relative to grains that followed the repeal of the Corn Laws (Figure 7.4). Pastoral farming became more profitable, and the continuous labour of servants more necessary. But the process of extinction in the south and east was beyond being arrested by the relative recovery of animal prices. New farmhouses, Kebble noted in 1870, were built without accommodations for servants.[49]

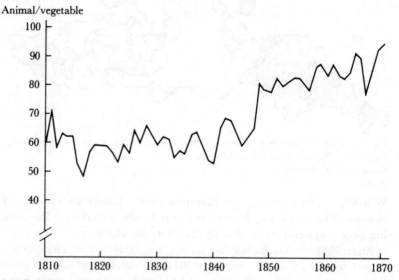

Animal/vegetable

7.4. Relative prices, animal and vegetable products, 1810–70.
Source: Rousseaux Price Indices, Mitchell and Deane, *Abstract of British Historical Statistics*, pp. 471–2.

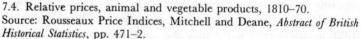

Humans create institutions. Once institutions have been created, however, they more resemble small-brained animals than the humans whose creative capacity made them possible. They are the means by which humans adapt to an environment, by freeing those who enter them from the need to struggle with that environment. They remove the need for thought and action, by requiring humans to fill roles, to behave in accordance with tacit rules. Farm servants could be mobile, for example, because the roles of servant and farmer were well established, and individuals interchangeable within them.

Variations within institutions are possible. Servants could remain in service well beyond the customary age of exit, and a few did. Some servants moved every year, others stayed for many years in one service. Neither choice was so environmentally favoured as to become universal, nor so unsuitable as to be impossible. Gross variations, however, were fatal. A farmer who hired enough annual servants to harvest his autumn crop would have failed; a father who offered his infant child as servant would have found no takers. It might be argued that fifty-one week hirings, the payment of board wages, and refusals to pay medical expenses so weakened the institution that they hastened its extinction.

On the whole, however, the process of abandoning service in husbandry was more akin to wholesale extinction, caused by the deterioration of its environment, than it was to the decay of the form of the institution. Service had been nurtured by an agrarian environment of small farms, labour shortage, and a high age at marriage; it had been enmeshed in a web of social and economic relations. When the environment changed, servants ceased being hired. The essential stability of form can be glimpsed in the 1851 census (Fig. 7.5). The median age of farm servants, an indicator of the tacit rule that servants be youths and young adults, did not vary as a function of the degree to which the institution had been abandoned. Instead, it varied randomly around a mean of 19.8. The median age of labourers, by contrast, was strongly correlated with the presence or absence of large numbers of youthful servants. Where many youths were hired as servants, few could be young labourers. Even where the institution was being driven into extinction, however, the surviving remnants, by this measure, were similar to their fellows in the north and west.

Most species have not evolved into new species. They have become extinct, and their habitat occupied by coeval species better suited to the environment. Service in husbandry did not evolve into a new form of labour. It collapsed. The increase in the size of farms and of the social position of farmers, the decline in the opportunities of the poor to

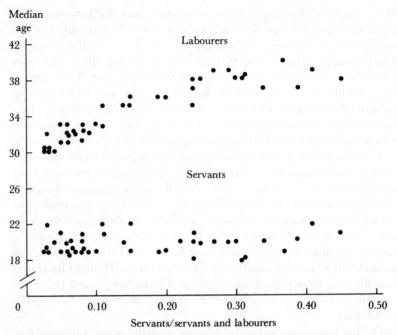

7.5. Median ages, male servants and labourers, England 1851, by county.
Source: 1851 census.

be anything but wage labourers, and population increase all led to the near total substitution of the coeval institution, day-labouring. Farm service is one of the large reptiles of economic history, extraordinarily successful in its time, and driven rapidly to extinction when times changed.

Twentieth-century change has nearly eradicated service from modern England. The deferential character of the relationship between master and servant was incompatible with the notion of equality. The spread of tractors eliminated the need for horsekeepers, and that of automatic milkers the need for dairymaids. Mandatory education removed youths from service. Remnants of the institution survived, but only in niches more rare than Howitt's 'obscure districts'. Williams described the working of the old institution in western Cumberland in 1952–3,[50] and even today the occasional advertisement appears in the *Cambridge Evening News* for single persons to tend a farm's livestock, in return for wages, board, a private room, and television.

Appendix 1 'Servants' and 'labourers' in early modern English

> Servants and labourers are of two sorts, Domestick and such as live by the year, or such as we commonly call Day-Labourers, whether carpenters, masons, etc., or other poor men which we employ about our husbandry.[1]

Despite the wide generic and the variant uses of 'servant' and the very occasional variant uses of 'labourer', farm servants were normally differentiated from day-labourers by the words 'servant' and 'labourer'. The words connoted two clusters of attributes. A 'servant' was hired by the year, lived with his or her master, and was unmarried; a 'labourer' was hired by the day, week, or by the task, had his or her own residence, and was either married or still living with his or her parents.

It will be simplest to present the evidence for this contention in the form of a table. The date and place of each usage will be given, and an indication of its consistency with four standard meanings will be given:

1. *Term*: servants are hired for the year and/or labourers are hired for the day, week, harvest month, or by the task.
2. *Master*: a servant, and only a servant, has one master.
3. *Residency*: a servant, and only a servant, resides with the master.
4. *Marital status*: servants are unmarried.

The exceptions to these standards are noted, and the sources of the usages are given at the foot of the table.

The table is not presented primarily as a contribution to the debate between Peter Laslett and C. B. Macpherson over the question of whom the Levellers had in mind when they excluded 'servants and almstakers' from their model franchise of 1647.[2] Both readings are consistent with seventeenth-century usage: 'servant' could have a general meaning, as Macpherson argued the Levellers intended, or a specific one, as Laslett contended. The debate can be continued only on the ground of political theory and not on that of semantics.

Table A1.1. *The usage of 'servant' and 'labourer', 1360–1850*

+: the source confirms the standard meaning
0: the source contradicts the standard meaning
—: the source gives no indication of the meaning

Date	Place	Term	Master	Residence	Marital status	Source
1360–1		+[1]	—	—	—	34 Ed. III, c. 10
1388		0[2]	—	—	—	12 Ric. II, c. 4
1402		+	—	—	—	4 Hen. IV, c. 14
1427		+	—	—	—	6 Hen. VI, c. 3
1444–5		+	—	—	—	23 Hen. VI, c. 12
1495		—	—	—	—	11 Hen. VII, c. 22
1512		+	—	+	—	4 Hen. VIII, c. 19
1514–15		—	—	—	—	6 Hen. VIII, c. 3
1514–15		+	—	+[3]	—	6 Hen. VIII, c. 3
1534		—	—	+	—	Fitzherbert, *Boke of Husbandry*, p. 59
1549–50		—	—	—	+	3 & 4 Ed. VI, c. 22
1562–3	Kent	+	—	—	0[4]	5 Eliz. I, c. 4
1563		—	—	—	—	Putnam, 'Lambard's "Eirenarcha"', pp. 270–3
1563	Kent	+	—	—	0[5]	H & L, II, 215–18
1563	New Windsor	0	—	—	—	H & L, II, 219
1563	Lincs.	+	—	—	—	H & L, II, 221–3
1563	York	+	—	—	—	H & L, II, 223–4
1563	Rutland	+	—	—	—	H & L, II, 212–14
1565	Kent	0[6]	—	—	—	H & L, II, 212–14
1566	Northants	+	—	—	—	H & L, II, 285–7
1566–95	Essex	+	—	—	—	H & L, II, 283–4; III, 18–19, 143–4

Date	Place					Reference
1570	Hull	+	—	—	—	H & L, II, 337–9
1575–97	Chester	0	—	0[7]	—	H & L, II, 393
1576	Canterbury	+	—	—	—	H & L, II, 405–7
1580		+	—	+	+	Tusser, *Five Hundred Points*, fols. 11, 67
1583	Colchester	+	—	—	—	H & L, II, 499–500
1589	Kent	+	—	—	—	H & L, III, 36–8
1591–2	Herts.	+	—	—	—	*Notes and Extracts*, pp. 8–12
1593	E. Riding	+	—	—	—	JETR, VI, 686–9
1594	Canterbury	+	—	—	—	H & L, III, 138–41
1595	Herts.	+	—	—	—	H & L, III, 145–6
1595	Devons.	+	—	—	—	H & L, III, 150–1
1595	New Sarum	+	—	—	—	H & L, III, 147–8
1595	Lancs.	+	—	—	—	H & L, III, 149–50
1603	Wilts.	+	—	—	—	HMC, *Various*, I, 163–5
1606	Staffs.	+	—	—	—	*QS Rolls*, pp. 324–6
1610	Rutland	+	—	—	—	JETR, VI, 691–3
1612	Essex	+	—	—	—	ERO, Q/AA 1
1621	Lincs.	+	—	—	—	HMC, *Rutland*, I, 460–1
1628	Herts.	0[8]	—	—	—	*Calender to the Sessions Books* (1928), p. 107
1630	Suffolk	+	—	—	—	Camb. U. L., Add. Ms. 22, no. 76, fol. 72–4
1632	Herefords.	+	—	—	—	HMC, *Portland*, III, 31
	Gloucs.	+	—	—	—	JETR, VI, 694
1633	Dorset	+	—	—	—	Roberts, *Social History*, pp. 207ff.
1634–48	Derby.	+	—	—	—	Cox, *Three Centuries*, Vol. II, pp. 239–42
1642–9	Sussex	+	—	—	—	*Quarter Sessions Order Book*, p. xii.
1647–8	Somerset	+	—	—	—	*QS Records, Somerset* (1907), III, 40, 66, 121, 151, 177, 236, 263

Table A1.1. (cont.)

Date	Place	Term	Master	Residence	Marital status	Source
1649		−	−	+	+	Chamberlayne, *Angliae Notitia*, pp. 441–5
1651		−	−	+	−	Firth and Rait, *Interregnum*, Vol. II, 13 Aug. 1651
1651–61	Essex	+				JETR, VI, 694–8
1655–85	Wilts.	+				Cunningham, *Wiltshire*, pp. 290–2
1658	N. Riding	+				*QS Records, North Riding*, VI, 3–5
1662		0[9]				14 Car. II, c. 6
1663	Worcs.	+				HMC, *Various*, I, 323
1665	Herefords.	+				Hereford RO, QSO fols. 27B, 28A
1673	Lancs.	+				Hardwick, *Preston*, pp. 405–6
1677–91		−			0[10]	29 & 30 Car. II. c. 1; 1 Wm and Mary, c. 13; 2 Wm and Mary, c. 2 *Notes and Extracts*, p. 292
1678	Herts.	0[11]				JETR, VI, 698–9
1682	Suffolk	+	0[12]			JETR, VI, 699–700
1684	Warwicks.	+				HMC, *Seventh Report, Appendix*, 698–9
1685	Somerset	+				
1687	Herts.	+		0[13]		*Calendar to the Sessions Books* (1930), pp. 400–1
1687	Bucks.	+				Co. of Buckingham, *Calendar* (1933), pp. 227–9
1693		−		+		Mayo, *Present for Servants*, pp. 3, 39–40
1694		−		+	+	6 & 7 Wm and Mary, c. 6
1696–7		−		−		8 & 9 Wm III, c. 17

Date	Location					Reference
1697–8		—	—		0 [14]	9 Wm III, c. 38
1698		—	—	+	—	Yarranton, *England's Improvement*, vol. I, p. 171
1700	W. Riding	+	—	+	+	Nourse, *Campania Foelix*, p. 208
1703	Warwicks.	+	—	—	—	JETR, VII, 610–14
1710–65	Notts.	+	—	—	—	VCH Warwicks, II, 180–1
1723–4		+	—	—	—	Meaby, *Nottinghamshire*, p. 232
1724			—	+	+	[Tancred], *Scheme*, p. v
1724		+	—	—	—	Waterman, 'Some New Evidence', pp. 405–8
1732	Salop	0 [15]	—	—	—	Orders of Shropshire QS, II, 79
1736	Wilts.	+	—	—	—	Wiltshire QS, p. 37
1746–57		0, + [16]	—	—	—	20 George II, c. 19
1755	Westmorland	0 [17]	—	—	—	Burn, *Justice of the Peace*, p. 213
1757			—	—	—	31 George II, c. 11
1765		+	—	+	—	Blackstone, *Commentaries*, vol. I, pp. 411–14
1766		—	—	—	+	*Museum Rusticum* (London), VI (1766), 138
1770	N. England	—	—	+	+	Young, *Northern Tour*, passim.
1772	S. England	—	—	—	+	Young, *Southern Tour*, pp. 316–17
1773		—	—	+	+	Arbuthnot, *Present Price of Provisions*, p. 26
1776		—	—	+	—	*Farmer's Magazine* (London), I (1776), 270–1
1776		+	—	0 [18]	—	Smith, *Wealth of Nations*, vol. I, p. 98
1779			—	0 [19]	—	*Farmer's Magazine, General Dictionary*, 'labourer'
1780	Lincs.	+	—	+	—	LAO, Misc. Dep. 161
1793	Hunts.	0	0 [20]	—	—	Maxwell, *GV Hunts*, p. 12
1794	Norfolk	—	—	+	—	Kent, *GV Norfolk*, p. 46

Table A1.1. (cont.)

Date	Place	Term	Master	Residence	Marital status	Source
1794	N. Riding	—	O[21]	—	—	Tuke, *GV North Riding*, p. 81
1794	Cumberland	—	—	+	—	Bailey and Culley, *GV Cumberland*, p. 37
1794	Isle of Man	—	—	+	—	Quayle, *GV Isle of Man*, p. 15
1794	W. Riding	—	—	+	+	Rennie, *GV West Riding*, p. 25
1794	Herefords.	O	O[22]	—	—	Clark, *GV Hereford*, p. 29
1795	Essex	O	O[23]	—	—	Vancouver, *GV Essex*, p. 196
1795	Herts.	+	—	+	—	Walker, *GV Hertford*, p. 83
1797	Sussex	—	O[24]	—	—	*Annals of Agriculture*, no. 29 (1797), 602
1799	Scotland	—	—	—	O[25]	Douglas, *GV Roxburgh and Selkirk*, pp. 190–1
1799	W. Riding	—	—	—	O[26]	Brown, *GV West Riding*, p. 208
1800	Northumberland	—	—	O	O[27]	*Annals of Agriculture*, XXV (1800), 218–19
1801			+	+	—	*Ibid.*, XXXVII (1801), 103
1803	Salop	O[28]	—	—	—	Plymley, *GV Shropshire*, p. 138
1804	Kent	—	O	—	O[29]	*Annals of Agriculture*, XLII (1804), 136–7
1805	Westmorland	+	—	O	O[30]	Pringle, *GV Westmorland*, p. 333
1806–8	Kent, Norfolk	—	O	—	O[31]	*Annals of Agriculture* no. 44 (1806), 91; no. 45 (1807), 98–9; no. 46 (1808), 427–8

Year	Place					Source
1808	Beds.	+	+	+	—	Batchelor, *GV Bedford*, in Marshall, *Review and Abstract*, p. 589
1808	Scotland	—	—	—	0[32]	Robertson, *GV Inverness*, p. 270
1809	Scotland	—	—	—	0[33]	Kerr, *GV Berwick*, p. 413
1810	Worcs.	—	0[34]	—	—	Pitt, *GV Worcs.*, p. 254
1810	Durham	—	—	0, +	0, +[35]	Bailey, *GV Durham*, p. 68
1812	Scotland	—	—	+	0[36]	Henderson, *GV Caithness*, pp. 225–32
1812	Isle of Man	—	—	0, +	0	Quayle, *GV Isle of Man*, p. 124
1813	Staffs.	0	—	—	+	Pitt, *GV Stafford*, p. 217
1813	Surrey	—	0[37]	—	—	Stevenson, *GV Surrey*, p. 542
1813	Sussex	—	—	+	—	Young, *GV Sussex*, p. 404
1813	Gloucs.	—	—	—	0[38]	Rudge, *GV Gloucs.*, p. 329
1825		+	—	—	+	Loudon, *Encyclopaedia*, pp. 419–20
1825		+	—	—	+	*Ibid.*, p. 726
1827		—	—	+	+	PP 1826 (V), I, 381
1833	Cumberland and Westmorland	—	—	0, +[39]	—	PP 1833 (V), I, 326
1838		—	—	+	+	Howitt, *Rural Life*, vol. II, p. 163
1850	Lincs.	—	—	+	—	LAO, Dixon 21/5/6/3

Sources: For full sources, see abbreviations to Notes and Bibliography.
Notes to table are on page 142.

Notes:

1. Labourers, but not servants, are not to take wages on festival days.
2. All wages in assessment are annual ones.
3. Hours of work are specified only for labourers.
4. Married people are compelled to serve by the year.
5. Married servants and labourers are hired by the year.
6. Men servants in husbandry or labourers by the day are also quoted day-wages.
7. Women servants by day or year; servants have choice of meat and drink or none.
8. Labourer hired for yearly wages.
9. Parish to hire yearly labourers.
10. Children of servants in husbandry exempt from tax.
11. Labourers annual.
12. 'Best hired servants ... for harvest ...'
13. Meat and drink choice of servants and labourers.
14. Children of servants in husbandry.
15. Current servant by the week.
16. Each meaning used.
17. Servant in husbandry hired for less than a year.
18. Wear and tear of free servant is at his own expense.
19. Servants in tied cottage.
20. Constant labourers.
21. 'Farmers' own labourers.'
22. Labourer hired by the year.
23. Constant labourer.
24. Prize for labourer in same service for longest time.
25. Married servants.
26. Married servants.
27. Married servants.
28. Constant labourers.
29. Married servants; labourers in constant employ.
30. Tied cottages.
31. Labourers in constant employ, married bailiffs and waggoners.
32. Married servants.
33. Married servants.
34. Labourers in constant employ.
35. Married servants.
36. Married servants.
37. Servant by year or week with or without board.
38. Cottages for farm servants.
39. 'Labourers' live with farmers; domestic farm servants.

Appendix 2   Age and sex

Correcting for age and sex to produce a uniform measure of the composition of the labour force is possible, but requires so many assumptions about the samples that would be subjected to these corrections that it was decided to present the uncorrected totals.

The standard method involves, first, constructing a series of deflators to convert women's labour, children's labour, etc., into men's labour. Cho and Gill have done this in their studies of South Korea and India, using the wages of women and children relative to those of men as the deflators.[1] But early modern wage data are scarce, and usually intractable. Wages actually paid to individuals can be gathered from a few account books, from presentments at Quarter Sessions, and from settlement examinations, but unless we know the age of the servant or labourer receiving these wages, we cannot know which were the wages of adults and which were those of children, and we are back where we started. Wage assessments made at Quarter Sessions are no guide.

Female wages as a proportion of male
wages, highest and lowest paid male
and female farm servants

A2.1. Female wages as a proportion of male wages, sixteen Quarter Sessions assessments, 1564–1724.

They are highly formalized, never more so than in the wages assigned to men and women. In none of the assessments examined were the wages of the meanest man servant lower than those of the most important woman servant. Men and women were assigned tasks according to their sex, and wages were thus paid on the basis of sex. In a random selection of thirty assessments,[2] the ratios of highest female to highest male wages and lowest adult female to lowest adult male wages ranged from 0.30 to 0.83 (see Figure A2.1): the median was 0.57, the mean 0.61 ($s = 0.132$). The range could be ignored and a deflator of 0.57 or 0.61 used; this is approximately the deflator chosen by Cho, but less than the 0.75 used by Gill.[3]

It is equally difficult to find a deflator, or series of deflators, to correct for the presence of young servants. Each Quarter Session appears to have had its own idea of the productiveness of children. Figure A2.2 shows the distribution of male wages for three ages (twenty, sixteen and fourteen), as a proportion of adult male wages; Figure A2.3 shows the distribution of ages for which the maximum wage was allowed. Twenty can be taken as the modal adult age, but this is higher than the ages used by Cho and Gill (fifteen and sixteen), and once again reflects a measurement of status, not of productivity. Male youths between sixteen and nineteen could be assigned deflators of 0.65 on the basis of Figure A2.2 and males under sixteen arbitrarily assigned a deflator of 0.55, the median for males aged fourteen.

Since the ages of the servants are not shown in the records, assumptions will then have to be made about the distribution of ages so that the deflators can be applied. Three parish listings included the ages of all farm servants. If the three lists are combined, the age distribution on Table A2.1 results.

All this has yielded three sets of correction factors which must be simultaneously applied to the observed numbers of male and female servants to convert them into adult male equivalents. There is, first, the age-distributor (a), which breaks down the aggregate observation into likely age categories. To each of these categories must then be applied the appropriate age-deflator (d), which converts youthful labour into adult equivalents. Finally, in the case of women, the whole deflated result must be multiplied by 0.6, the sex-deflator:

If F = number of female servants

        M = number of male servants

        a_i = age-distributor for categories $i = 1(> 16)$, $2(16–19)$, and $3(20+)$

        d_i = age-deflators for the same three categories

        A = adult male equivalents

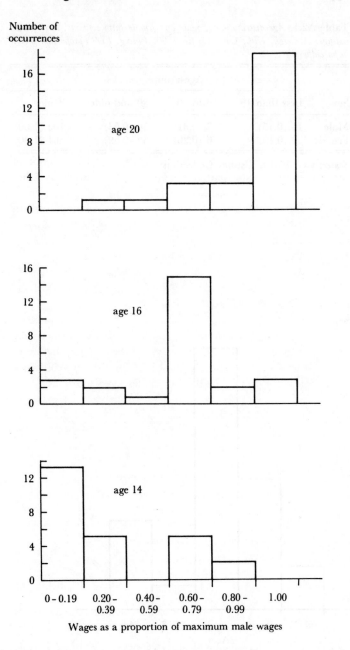

A2.2. Male wages at ages fourteen, sixteen and twenty as proportions of maximum adult male wages, twenty-six Quarter Sessions assessments, 1563–1724.

Table A2.1. *Age distribution of male and female farm servants, three parish listings: Ardleigh, 1796; Corfe Castle, 1790; Ealing, 1599 (proportion shown in parentheses)*

	Age groups			
Sex	Less than 16	16 to 19	20 and older	Total
Male	16 (0.15)	33 (0.31)	56 (0.53)	105 (1.00)
Female	9 (0.15)	16 (0.26)	36 (0.59)	61 (1.00)

Source: CG, Parish Listings Collection.

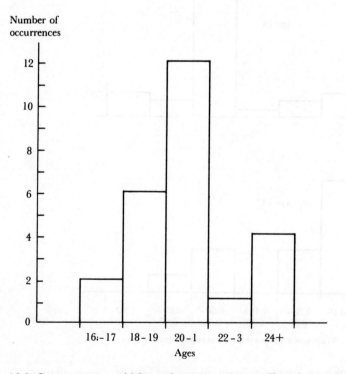

A2.3. Lowest ages at which maximum wages were allowed, twenty-six Quarter Sessions assessments, 1563–1724.

then $\quad A \quad = \sum_{i=1}^{3} Ma_i d_i + 0.6 \sum_{i=1}^{3} Fa_i d_i$

and $\quad A \quad = 0.53M + 0.31(0.65)M + 0.15(0.55)M + 0.6[(0.59)F +$
$\qquad\qquad (0.26)0.65F + (0.15)0.55F]$
$\qquad = M[0.53 + 0.31(0.65) + 0.15(0.55)] +$
$\qquad\quad 0.6F[0.59 + 0.26(0.65) + 0.15(0.55)]$
$\qquad = 0.81M + 0.50F$

According to this method, deflated adult equivalents are calculated by multiplying observed male totals by 0.81 and observed female totals by 0.50. I hope the patient reader will agree that too many assumptions have to be made for this method of correction to carry much conviction; it should be noted that no correction has yet been made for older and weaker labourers. All data therefore have been presented in uncorrected form.

Appendix 3   Legal control of mobility

Farm servants were mobile. No possession of land, household goods, or dependants inhibited their movement, and they were bound to stay in one place only by yearly contracts. Occasionally this mobility was a cause of concern to society. At times of extreme scarcity of labour, there was no assurance that the places of departing servants would easily be filled with newcomers. Masters could also be wary of hiring strangers: were they to be trusted? Had they run away from another master? Statutes were drawn up to deal with both aspects of the problem of mobility, and the Statute of Artificers represents a compilation of earlier solutions. Servants departing from the parish in which they had served were required by it to take with them letters of testimonial, sealed by the parish constable and registered with the vicar. The letters were to state that the servant had been licensed to depart the last master, and that he or she was at liberty to serve elsewhere. Earlier statutes anticipated this legislation. The Statute of Labourers simply forbade servants to leave the county in which they lived. Just as the Statute of 1388 (12 Ric. II, c. 4) had attempted to make the wage regulation of the Statute of Labourers workable, so did another statute of the same year (12 Ric. II, c. 3) with respect to restricting mobility. In it, travel outside the hundred, rape, or wapentake was forbidden unless the traveller had a letter patent, a copy of which was on deposit in the parish. A servant was free to leave at the end of the term only if he or she had a new master to go to. This statute was repeated with force in 1414 (2 Hen. V, st.1, c. 4). The Statute of 1444–5 represented a new development. Under it, a servant was required, before his or her departure, to make a new covenant with the next master and to give warning of his or her departure, and if both conditions were not met, the new covenant was to be declared void, and the servant was to continue with the old master for another year.[1] In 1549–50, the minimum time of warning a master of a forthcoming departure was set at three months (3 & 4 Ed. VI, c. 22).

The Statute of Artificers narrowed the possible range of mobility without a letter patent, or testimonial, to the parish itself. It seems to have been only sporadically enforced. There are presentments of masters in several Quarter Sessions for receiving servants without

148

testimonials and of servants for failing to carry testimonials.[2] A possibly unique and certainly rare parish register of testimonials from Heydon parish in Essex for 1563 to 1585 has survived.[3] It is entitled 'The Register for Servants departing from their Masters According to the Statute', and is of the form prescribed in the Statute of Artificers. Complaints were made that the practice of giving testimonials was not common and that the law was therefore useless. A petition of Sir Richard Titchborne argued that 'by reason that no officer has been appointed for making those testimonials, the same are neglected'.[4] Christopher Tancred suggested in 1724 that personal registers, signed by each successive master, be required to be kept by every servant. Nothing came of it.[5]

The Law of Settlement, which was one strand in the web of poverty measures of Stuart England, has been mistakenly interpreted as constituting a check on the mobility of servants.[6] The first explicit form of the law appeared in 1662, and like the Elizabethan and Stuart statutes discussed above, it was an attempt to rectify earlier practice. Parishes were bound to relieve only those who had a legal settlement in the parish; Justices of the Peace could send newcomers away to the parish in which they legally settled, but forty days' residence was sufficient to establish a new legal settlement.[7] The minimum period was raised in 1691 to one year for unmarried persons in service (3 Wm and Mary, c. 11). Each new year of service established a new place of residence, and nullified the earlier legal settlement. Parishes thus had every reason to encourage servants to leave at the end of their terms. In the long run, the attempt would prove to be futile: the final year of service established the final place of settlement for a man servant or woman servant who remained unmarried (women took on their husband's place of settlement), and there had to be a final year of service for every servant.

Appendix 4   Statute Sessions and hiring fairs in England, sixteenth to nineteenth centuries

The following table shows the Statute Sessions and fairs that were encountered in the course of this research. The list is regionally unbalanced, being far richer for the east than the west of England. This result was predictable. The best sources of information are local; newspapers such as the *Norwich Mercury* and the *Suffolk Mercury* announced the dates of the forthcoming sessions, and settlement examinations sporadically noted that the hiring had been done at a particular sessions or fair.

The table gives the place, year, and date of the session. Where the date was specified as a weekday near a saint's day, such as 'the Friday before Michaelmas', only Michaelmas has been indicated in the list.

Table A4.1. *Statute Sessions and hiring fairs*

Place	Year	Date	Source
Bedfordshire			
Ampthill	1770	nd	BRO, DDP 1/13/4
Bedford	1794	Mich OS	BRO, P5/13/4
Biggleswade	1784	nd	BRO, P35/13/4
Bletsoe	1800	nd	BRO, P5/13/4
Clophill	c. 1710	Mich	BRO, QSR 5 1738/36
Deadman Cross	1781	nd	BRO, P35/13/4
Dropshort	1781	nd	BRO, DDP 1/13/4
Lidlington	1761	nd	BRO, DDP 1/13/4
Luton	1780	nd	BRO, DDP 1/13/4
Markgate Street	1825	nd	BRO, P35/13/4
Thurleigh	1772	nd	BRO, DDP 1/13/4
Willington	1755	nd	BRO, DDP 1/13/4
general	1858		Chester, *Statute Fairs*, p. 3
Berkshire			
Abingdon	1815	nd	Berks. RO, 34/13/3
	1792	Mich OS	PP 1888, LIII
Aldermaston	1810,		
	1822	nd	Berks. RO, 132/13/1/1
Bracknell	1760	nd	Berks. RO, 141/13/3
	1783	nd	Bucks. RO, PR 115/13/4
Farringdon	c. 1760	Mich	Wilts. RO, 1189/66
	1792	Mich OS	PP 1888, LIII
	1805	Mich OS	Owen, *Book of Fairs*

Table A4.1. *Statute Sessions and hiring fairs*

Place	Year	Date	Source
Hungerford	1805	Mich	*Ibid.*
Ilsley	1812,		
	1826	nd	Berks. RO, 132/13/1/1
Maidenhead	1805	Mich	Owen, *Book of Fairs*
Newbury	1798	nd	Berks. RO, 34/13/3
Reading	1830	nd	Berks. RO, 130/13/1
Thatcham	1823	nd	Berks. RO, 132/13/1/1
Wallingford	1769	nd	Berks. RO, 143/13/5
	1805	Mich	Owen, *Book of Fairs*
	1792	Mich OS	PP 1888, LIII
Wantage	1745	nd	Berks. RO, 143/13/5
	1792	Mich	PP 1888, LIII
	1805	Mich OS	Owen, *Book of Fairs*
Buckinghamshire			
Amersham	1720	nd	Bucks. RO, PR 44/13
Aylesbury	1766, etc.	nd	Bucks. RO, PR 169/13/2
Buckingham	1769	nd	Bucks. RO, PR 223/13
	1805	Mich OS	Owen, *Book of Fairs*
Burnham	1792	2 Oct.	PP 1888, LIII
	1805	2 Oct.	Owen, *Book of Fairs*
Chesham	1804	nd	Bucks. RO, PR 36/13/6
Stony Stratford	1792	Mich OS	PP 1888, LIII
Winslow	1738	nd	Bucks. RO, PR 51/16/1
	1766	nd	Bucks. RO, PR 169/13/2
	1792	Mich OS	PP 1888, LIII
	1805	Mich OS	Owen, *Book of Fairs*
Wycombe	1792	Mich NS	PP 1888, LIII
	1805	Mich NS	Owen, *Book of Fairs*
Cambridgeshire			
Sturbridge	1821	nd	CRO, P/25/13/6
Cumberland			
Carlisle	1956	nd	Williams, *Gosforth*, p. 41n
Cockermouth	1673	Whit and Mart	Brome, *Britannia*, p. 70
	1956	nd	Williams, *Gosforth*, p. 41n
Penrith	1673	Whit and Mart	Brome, *Britannia*, p. 70
Derbyshire			
Alfreton	1792	Mart OS	PP 1888, LIII
Bretby	1815	Mich	Farey, *GV Derbys.*, vol. III, p. 184
Devonshire			
general	nd	nd	Wright, *Calendar*, vol. III, p. 167
general	1796	None	Marshall, *Rural Economy West of England*, vol. I, p. 108
Dorset			
Dorchester	nd	Candlemas	Wright, *Calendar*, vol. III, p. 167
general	1812	None	Stevensen, *GV Dorset*, p. 269
Essex			
Barking	1574	8 Mar.	ERO, Cal. Sess. V, 175

Table A4.1. (*cont.*)

Place	Year	Date	Source
Chardwell Ward	1574	nd	ERO, Cal. Sess. V, 187
Chigwell	1792	Mich NS	PP 1888, LIII
	1805	Mich NS	Owen, *Book of Fairs*
Colchester	1575	23 Mar.	ERO, Cal. Sess. V, 247
Dagenham	1574	8 Mar.	ERO, Cal. Sess. V, 184
East Ham	1574	8 Mar.	ERO, Cal. Sess. V, 180
Epping	1792	Mich OS	PP 1888, LIII
Fordham	1578	17 Mar.	ERO, Cal. Sess. VIII, 52
Great Dunmow	1577	1 April	ERO, Cal. Sess. VII, 105
Helion			
Bumstead	1574	28 Sept.	ERO, Cal. Sess. VI, 20
Hempstead	1574	28 Sept.	ERO, Cal. Sess. VI, 20
High Roothing	1577	1 April	ERO, Cal. Sess. VII, 104
Ilford Ward	1574	8 Mar.	ERO, Cal. Sess. V, 187
Leyton	1574	8 Mar.	ERO, Cal. Sess. V, 182
Manningtree	1578	27 June	ERO, Cal. Sess. VIII, 96
Ongar	1792	Mich OS	PP 1888, LIII
	1805	Mich OS, Easter Tues.	Owen, *Book of Fairs*
Plaistow Ward	1574	8 Mar.	ERO, Cal. Sess. V, 179
Ripell Ward	1574	8 Mar.	ERO, Cal. Sess. V, 186
Stanway	1574	26 Mar.	ERO, Cal. Sess. V, 151
Stratford	1574	8 Mar.	ERO, Cal. Sess. V, 177
Waltham Abbey	1805	14 May Mich NS	Owen, *Book of Fairs*
Walthamstow	1574	8 Mar.	ERO, Cal. Sess. V, 181
Wanstead	1574	8 Mar.	ERO, Cal. Sess. V, 183
Woodford	1574	8 Mar.	ERO, Cal. Sess. V, 183
Gloucestershire			
Cheltenham	1812	Mich OS	CSE, 15 Sept. 1815
	1727		Gloucs. RO,
	1762		P 76 OV 3/4,
	1783	Mich	P 46 OV 3/4,
	1784		P 31 OV 3/4
	1807		
Chipping Camden	1745		
	1749		
	1750		
	1758		Gloucs. RO,
	1759	Mich	P 81 OV 3/4,
	1760		P 52 OV 3/4/1
	1778		
	1782		
	1790		
Chipping Sodbury	1825	Mich	Wilts. RO, 796/51

Table A4.1. (*cont.*)

Place	Year	Date	Source
Cirencester	1763 ⎫		
	1769 ⎪		
	1770 ⎪		
	1772 ⎪		
	1773 ⎪		Gloucs. RO,
	1779 ⎪		P 44 OV 3/4/1,
	1782 ⎬ Mich		P 76 OV 3/4,
	1790 ⎪		P 71 OV 3/4/1–2,
	1791 ⎪		P 189a OV 3/4,
	1794 ⎪		P 170 OV 3/4
	1798 ⎪		
	1801 ⎪		
	1804 ⎭		
	1792	Mich OS	PP 1888, LIII
	1760 ⎫		Wilts. RO,
	1777 ⎬ Mich		59/1, 1189/66
	1789 ⎭		
	1787	Mich	Worcs. RO, 850 Bredon 6256/4/ii
	1805	Mich OS	Owen, *Book of Fairs*
	1819	Mich OS	CSE, no. 431
Fairford	1790	Mich	Gloucs. RO, P 189a OV 3/4
Gloucester	1785 ⎫		Gloucs. RO,
	1797 ⎬ Mich		P 76 OV 3/4,
	1806 ⎭		P 228 OV 3/4/1–2, P 31 OV 3/4
	1612	nd	Deloney, *Thomas of Reading*, p. 87
	1813	nd	CSE, 17 Dec. 1816
Northleach	1787 ⎫		Gloucs. RO,
	1807 ⎪		P 44 OV 3/4/1,
	1812 ⎬ Mich		P 76 OV 3/4,
	1813 ⎭		P 47 OV 3/4/1–2
	1786	Mich	Worcs. RO, 850 Claines 2683/12
Stow	1747	nd	OXRO, PC/vi/iii
	1813	nd	CSE, no. 175
Tetbury	1760 ⎫		Gloucs. RO, P 29 OV 3/3, P 47
	1765 ⎬ Mich		OV 3/4/1–2, P170 OV 3/4,
	1809 ⎭		P 328a OV 3/4/1
	1763 ⎫		Wilts. RO, 59/1
	1777 ⎬ Mich		1149/6
	1794 ⎭		
	1811	nd	CSE, no. 649
Tewkesbury	1813	nd	CSE, 10 Oct. 1815
	1787	Mich	Gloucs. RO, P 112 OV 3/4
	1757 ⎫		
	1780 ⎪		Worcs. RO, 850 Bredon
	1783 ⎬ Mich		6256/4/ii
	1793 ⎪		
	1795 ⎭		

Table A4.1. *(cont.)*

Place	Year	Date	Source
Winchcomb	1795	Mich	Gloucs. RO, P 46 OV 3/4
	1796	Mich	Worcs. RO, 850 Bredon 6256/4/ii
	1809	nd	CSE, no. 494
Thornbury	1888	25 Mar.	PP 1888, LIII
Westerleigh	1888	19 Sept.	*Ibid.*
general	nd	25 March	Wright, *Calendar*, vol. II, p. 167
Hampshire			
Basingstoke	1799	nd	Hants RO, 19 M 76
	1792	Mich OS	PP 1888, LIII
	1805	Mich OS	Owen, *Book of Fairs*
	1896	nd	Bourne, *Memoirs*, p. 18
Kingsclere	1789	nd	Berks. RO, 130/13/1
Titchfield	1792	25 Sept.	PP 1888, LIII
Hereford			
Bromyard	1888	25 Mar.	PP 1888, LIII
	1797	Mayday	Hereford RO, A9 207/269
Knighton	1778	Mayday	Hereford RO, F 71/71
Wigmore	1806	Mayday	Hereford RO, A9 207/269
Hertfordshire			
Berkhamstead	1792	Mich NS	PP 1888, LIII
	1805	Mich OS	Owen, *Book of Fairs*
		Mich NS	
Bramfield	1798	26 Sept.	Johnson, *Memorandums*, p. 33
Buntingford	1750	Mich	HRO, D/P 107/13/2
Codicote	1798	20 Sept.	Johnson, *Memorandums*, p. 33
Dacorum and	1656	nd	*Notes and Extracts*, p. 116
Cashio			
Hartingfordbury	1804	13 Sept.	Johnson, *Memorandums*, p. 90
Hemel Hempsted	1792	3rd Mon. in Sept.	PP 1888, LIII
	1805	3rd Mon. in Sept.	Owen, *Book of Fairs*
Hemstead	1805	Whitsun	*Ibid.*
Hertford	1798	25 Sept.	Johnson, *Memorandums*, p. 33
Kimpton	1798	19 Sept.	*Ibid.*
	1801	nd	BRO, P35/13/4
Northall	1805	Mich NS	Owen, *Book of Fairs*
Northaw	1762	nd	HRO, D/P 29/13/5
Puckeridge	1805	19 Sept.	Owen, *Book of Fairs*
Rickmansworth	1792	Sat. before 3rd Mon. in Sept.	PP 1888, LIII
	1805	Sat. before 3rd Mon. in Sept.	Owen, *Book of Fairs*
St Albans	1805	25, 26 Mar., 10, 11 Oct.	*Ibid.*
Tring	1674	Mich	*Notes and Extracts*, pp. 245–6
	1792	Mich OS	PP 1888, LIII
	1805	Easter Tues. Mich OS	Owen, *Book of Fairs*

Table A4.1. (*cont.*)

Place	Year	Date	Source
Watford	1792	9 Sept.	PP 1888, LIII
	1805	9 Sept.	Owen, *Book of Fairs*
Welwyn	1798	24 Sept.	Johnson, *Memorandums*, p. 33
Whitwell	1798	26 Sept.	*Ibid.*
Wotton	1792	Mich	HRO, D/P 29/13/5
	1798	17 Sept.	Johnson, *Memorandums*, p. 33
Huntingdonshire			
Fenstanton	1760	Mich	SRO(B), EL 110/7/1
St Neots	1766	nd	BRO, P5/13/4
	1792	1 Aug.	PP 1888, LIII
	1805	1 Aug.	Owen, *Book of Fairs*
Kent			
Tunbridge	1792	Mich OS	PP 1888, LIII
	1805	Ash Weds., 5 July, Mich OS	Owen, *Book of Fairs*
Lancashire			
Ulverston	1888	Mart NS	PP 1888, LIII
Leicestershire			
general	1794	Mich	Monk, *GV Leics.*, p. 49
Loughborough	1799	Mart	LRO, DE 394/39
Sileby	1811	Mart	LRO, DE 308/4
Lincolnshire			
Baston	1811	Mayday	Brears, *Lincs.*, p. 71
Bourne	1811	Mayday	*Ibid.*
Caistor	1823	Mayday	LAO, SE Coll., Belchford
Candlesby	1811	Mayday	Brears, *Lincs.*, p. 71
Fleet		Mayday Mart	LAO, Holland QS D3
Folkingham	1811	Mayday	Brears, *Lincs.*, p. 71
Frieston	1811	Mayday	*Ibid.*
Grimsthorpe	1811	Mayday	*Ibid.*
Heighington	1811	Mayday	*Ibid.*
Holbeach		Mayday, Mart	LAO, Holland QS D3
Horncastle	1803	Mayday	LAO, SE Coll., Belchford
Ingoldmells & Addlethorpe	1588– 1596	Mart	LAO, MM 8/51, 52, 55
Kirton	1811	Mayday	Brears, *Lincs.*, p. 71
Leake	1811	Mayday	*Ibid.*
	1796	7 Nov.	LAO, Banks Coll., folder M 1796
Limber	1811	Mayday	Brears, *Lincs.*, p. 71
Long Sutton		Mayday, Mart	LAO, Holland QS D 3
Louth	1804	Mayday	LAO, SE Coll. Belchford
Partney	1811	Mayday	Brears, *Lincs.*, p. 71
Revesby	1811	Mayday	*Ibid.*
Spalding	1767– 1850	Mayday, Mart	LAO, Holland QS D3

Table A4.1. (*cont.*)

Place	Year	Date	Source
Spital	1811	Mayday	Brears, *Lincs.*, p. 71
Spittlegate	1811	Mayday	*Ibid.*
Sutterton	1811	Mayday	*Ibid.*
Swineshead	1833	Mayday	LAO, SE Coll., Algarkirk
Waltham	1808	Mayday	LAO, SE Coll., Saleby
West Deeping	1811	Mayday	Brears, *Lincs.*, p. 71
Whaplode	1811	Mayday	*Ibid.*
Middlesex			
Edmonton	1805	14, 15, 16 Sept.	Owen, *Book of Fairs*
Enfield	1792	23 Sept.	PP 1888, LIII
	1805	23 Sept.	Owen, *Book of Fairs*
Staines	1792	Mich NS	PP 1888, LIII
Uxbridge	1792	25 Mar., Mich NS	*Ibid.*
	1805	25 Mar. 31 July, Mich NS	Owen, *Book of Fairs*
	1805	nd	Bucks. RO, PR 115/13/4
	nd	Mich	Warwicks. RO, DR 458/44
Norfolk			
Acle	1762	28 Sept.	*Norwich Mercury*
Aylsham	1770	2 Oct.	*Ibid.*
Blofield	1763	3 Oct.	*Ibid.*
New Buckenham	1761	26 Sept.	*Ibid.*
Bungay	1758	2 wks before Mich OS	NRO, PD 136/73
Costessy	1753	25 Sept.	*Norwich Mercury*
Cromer	1770	6 Oct.	*Ibid.*
E. Dereham	1762	29 Sept.	*Ibid.*
Diss	1781	Mich	SRO(I), FC 84/G3
	1793	Mich	NRO, PD 78/72
Downham Market	1760	4, 18 Oct.	*Norwich Mercury*
Easton	1755	30 Sept.	*Ibid.*
Fakenham	1763	6 Oct.	*Ibid.*
Forncett St Peter	1761	17 Sept.	*Ibid.*
	1781	nd	NRO, PD 78/72
Frettenham	1755	30 Sept.	*Norwich Mercury*
Halesworth	1784	Mich OS	NRO, PD 136/73
Harleston	1775	Mich OS	NRO, PD 136/73
	1799	Mich	NRO, PD 119/114
	1814	Mich OS	SRO(I), FC 84/G3
Harling	1736	Mich	NRO, PD 108/95
	1776	Mich	SRO(B), N2/1/1
Market Harling	1769	26 Sept.	*Norwich Mercury*
Hingham	1802	Mich	NRO, PD 124/41
Holt	1762	2, 9 Oct.	*Norwich Mercury*
Kenninghall	1770	2 Oct.	*Ibid.*
	1799	Mich	NRO, PD 78/72
Litcham	1769	3 Oct.	*Norwich Mercury*

Table A4.1. (*cont.*)

Place	Year	Date	Source
Loddon	1762	14 Sept.	*Ibid.*
Lowestoft	1756	11 Oct.	*Ibid.*
Ludham	1760	2 Oct.	*Ibid.*
Mattishall	1755	6 Oct.	*Ibid.*
Mulbarton	1763	27 Sept.	*Ibid.*
Ostridge	1753	13 Sept.	*Ibid.*
Rackheath	1762	27 Sept.	*Ibid.*
Reepham	1762	27 Sept.	*Ibid.*
South Repps	1763	5 Oct.	*Ibid.*
E. Rudham	1767	3 Oct.	*Ibid.*
Shottesham	1770	27 Sept.	*Ibid.*
Somerleyton	1760	18 Sept.	*Ibid.*.
Sprowston	1760	25 Sept.	*Ibid.*
	1763	26 Sept.	*Ibid.*
Stoke	1762	7 Oct.	*Ibid.*
Stoke Ferry	1815	nd	NRO, PD 109/95
Swaffham	1761	26 Sept.	*Norwich Mercury*
	1763	24 Sept.	*Ibid.*
Swainsthorpe	1768	nd	*Ibid.*
Thetford	1763	17 Sept.	*Ibid.*
Tittleshall	1769	25 Sept.	*Ibid.*
N. Walsham	1762	4 Oct.	*Ibid.*
Walsingham	1755	3 Oct.	*Ibid.*
Watton	1761	16 Sept.	*Ibid.*
Wymondham	1761	23 Sept.	*Ibid.*
Northamptonshire			
Brackley	1743	nd	Bucks. RO, PR 169/13/2
	1805	Mich OS	Owen, *Book of Fairs*
	1813	Mich OS	Pitt, *GV Northants*, p. 237
Corby	1630	24 Sept.	*QS Records*, Northants, p. 60
Daventry	1781 ⎱	Mich	Warwicks. RO, DR 367/27,
	1785 ⎰		DR 583/52
Gillesborough	1630	28 Sept.	*QS Records*, Northants, p. 60
Haddon	1797	Mich	Warwicks. RO, DR 367/27
Kingsthorpe	1773	Mich	Warwicks. RO, DR 367/27
New Inn Road	1792	3 Oct.	PP 1888, LIII
	1805	3 Oct.	Owen, *Book of Fairs*
Norton	1630	23 Sept.	*QS Records*, Northants, p. 61
Oulde	1630	21 Sept.	*Ibid.*, p. 61
Thrapston	1630	20 Sept.	*Ibid.*, p. 62
	1630	27 Sept.	*Ibid.*, p. 60
Towcester	1630	25 Sept.	*Ibid.*, p. 61
	1792	Mich OS	PP 1888, LIII
	1805	Mich OS	Owen, *Book of Fairs*
Yarwell	1630	22 Sept.	*QS Records*, Northants, p. 62
Northumberland			
Alnwick	1805	12 May	*GV Northum.*, p. 172

Table A4.1. (*cont.*)

Place	Year	Date	Source
	1888	1st Sat. in Mar.	PP 1888, LIII
Belford	1888	1st Weds. in Mar.	*Ibid.*
Berwick	1873	7 Mar. 26 Nov.	Dunbabin, *Agri. Trades Unionism*, p. 121
	nd	5 Jan.	Wright, *Calendar*, vol. II, p. 78
Morpeth	1825	nd	Webb, *English Local Government*, vol. II, p. 499
Newcastle	1873	nd	Dunbabin, *Agri. Trades Unionism*, p. 121
Wooler	1805	4 May, Whit	*GV Northum.*, p. 172
Nottinghamshire			
Balderton	1814	1st wk Nov.	Notts. RO, PR 5773/8
	1822	1st wk Nov.	Notts. RO, PR 5773/11
Bingham	1888	1st, 3rd Thurs. Nov.	PP 1888, LIII
Eastwood	1888	1st Mon. Nov.	*Ibid.*
Tuxford	1726	28 Oct.	Notts. RO, PR Laxton
Oxfordshire			
Abingdon	1812	nd	CSE, no. 88
Banbury	1805	Thurs. after 1 Oct.	Owen, *Book of Fairs*
	1786 ⎱ 1785 ⎰	Mich	Warwicks. RO, DR O 114/267
Bicester	1718, etc.	nd	Bucks. RO, PR 169/13/2
	1805	Fri. after 10 Oct.	Owen, *Book of Fairs*
	nd	Fri. before and after Mich	Bridges, *Book of Fairs*, p. 13
Burford	1757 ⎱ 1766 ⎰	Mich	Gloucs. RO, P 44 OV 3/4/1
	1814	nd	CSE, 15 Sept. 1815
	nd	Sat. before Mich	Bridges, *Book of Fairs*, p. 13
Chipping Norton	1792	3 Oct.	PP 1888, LIII
	1805	3 Oct.	Owen, *Book of Fairs*
	1888	Weds. before and after 10 Oct.	PP 1888, LIII
	nd	Thurs. before and Weds. after Mich	Bridges, *Book of Fairs*, p. 13
Chipping Warden	1764	nd	OXRO, PC/vi/viii
Deddington	1792	Sat. after 10 Oct.	PP 1888, LIII
	1805	Sat. after 10 Oct.	Owen, *Book of Fairs*
Henley on Thames	1768	nd	Berks. RO, 141/13/3
Nettlebed	1785	nd	Berks. RO, 132/13/1/1
Thame	1715, 1769	nd	Bucks. RO, PR 169/13/2
	1805	10 Oct.	Owen, *Book of Fairs*

Table A4.1. (*cont.*)

Place	Year	Date	Source
	nd	Mich OS	Bridges, *Books of Fairs*, p. 13
Watlington	1767	nd	Ox. Bod, MSS DD Par. Garsington
	1805	Mich OS	Owen, *Book of Fairs*
Wheatley	1805	Mich NS	*Ibid.*
Whitney	nd	Mich	Bridges, *Book of Fairs*, p. 13
Witney	1766	nd	Ox. Bod, MSS DD Par. Stanton Harcourt
Woodstock	1735	nd	OXRO, PC/1x/ii
	nd	21, 28 Sept.	Bridges, *Book of Fairs*, p. 13
Shropshire			
Clun	1888	11 May	PP 1888, LIII
Worthen	1888	2 May	*Ibid.*
general	nd	Mayday	*Wright, Calendar* vol. II, p. 243
Suffolk			
Beyton	1800	Mich	SRO(B), TEM 529/4
	1757	Mich	SRO(B), N 2/1/1
Boyton	1780	nd	SRO(B), N 2/1/6
Bury	1727	14 Sept.	*Suffolk Mercury*
Coddenham	1755	Mich	SRO(I), FC 101/G 9
Hartest	1770	Mich OS	SRO(B), N 2/1/1
Horningsheath	1757	Mich	SRO(B), EL 47/7/2
Ixworth	1772	Mich OS	SRO(B), N2/1/1
Mildenhall	1768	Mich	SRO(B), EL 25/7/18
Palgrave	1745	9 Sept.	SRO(I), FB 161/I1/8
Satterly	1769	Mich OS	SRO(B), N2/1/1
Saxham	1756	Mich	SRO(B), EL 47/7/2
Little Saxham	1769	Mich OS	SRO(B), N2/1/1
Little Stonham	1642	20 Sept.	SRO(I), FB 19/I1/2
Stadbrooke	1600–39	20 Sept.	SRO(I), FC 85/I1/7, 36, 66, 90, 96
Stradbrooke	1804	2 Oct.	SRO(I), FC 85/G2
Thetford	1769	Midsummer	SRO(B), N2/1/6
Walsham	1770	Mich	SRO(B), TEM 529/4
Wetherden	1725	13 Sept.	*Suffolk Mercury*
	1803	Mich	SRO(B), EL 119/7
Sussex			
Ashington	1792	21 July	PP 1888, LIII
	1805	21 July	Owen, *Book of Fairs*
Warwickshire			
Alcester	1752	Mich	Warwicks. RO, DR 259/45
Aston Cantelow	1734	Mich	Warwicks. RO, DR 201/48,
	1814		DR 74/53–5
	1827	nd	Hone, *Table Book*, vol. I, col. 177
Atherstone	1888	Mich	PP 1888, LIII
	1739	Mich	Warwicks. RO, DR 198/111/1–113
Berkswell	1776	Mich	Warwicks. RO, DR 189/227
Brinklow	1800	Mich	Warwicks. RO, DR 250/49
Bulkington	1747	Mich	Warwicks. RO, DR 250/49,

Table A4.1. (*cont.*)

Place	Year	Date	Source
	1785		DR 19/433–93
	1803		
Claverdon	1788	Mich	Gloucs. RO, P353 OV 3/4
Coleshill	1774	Mich	Warwicks. RO, DR B 27/35/1–66
Corley Moor	1761	Mich	Warwicks. RO, DR 250/49
Dunchurch	1776	Mich	Warwicks. RO, DR 367/27
Fillongley	1800	Mich	Warwicks. RO, DR 250/49
Hampton in Arden	1795		Warwicks. RO, DR 250/49,
	1797 } Mich		DR 296/67
	1799		
Harwoods	1778		
	1780		Warwicks. RO, DR 452/37,
	1784		DR 296/67, DR 74/53–5,
	1792 } Mich		DR 75/8, DR 295/73,
	1795		DR 583/52
	1796		
Henley in Arden	1781 } Mich		Warwicks. RO, DR 166/26,
	1816		DR 360/12/83
	1827	29 Oct.	Hone, *Table Book*, vol. I, col. 176
Hillmorton	1782	Mich	Warwicks. RO, DR 367/27
Hockley Heath	1888	13 Oct.	PP 1888, LIII
Kenilworth	1778		
	1780		
	1781		
	1782		
	1783		Warwicks. RO, DR 452/37,
	1786		DR 572/11/1–37, DR 250/49,
	1791 } Mich		DR 296/67, DR 176/53,
	1795		DR 295/73, DR 468/39/1–20,
	1796		DR 613/164/1–143, DR 146/8
	1800		
	1801		
	1812		
Lousan Ford	1783		
	1785		
	1789		Warwicks. RO, DR 166/26,
	1796 } Mich		DR 296/67, DR 75/33,
	1806		DR 259/45
	1809		
	1814		
Middleton	1768	Mich	Warwicks. RO, DR B 27/35/1–66
Nether Whitacre	1770–1	Mich	Warwicks. RO, DR B 27/35/1–66
Pailton	1790		
	1793		
	1799 } Mich		Warwicks. RO, DR 155/56/1–22,
	1801		DR 367/27
	1809		

Table A4.1. (*cont.*)

Place	Year	Date	Source
Polesworth	1744 ⎱		Warwicks. RO, DR B 21/5,
	1760 ⎰ Mich		DR 48/55
	1791 ⎰		
	1773 ⎱		Staffs. RO, D 783/2/3/19,
	1778 ⎰ Mich		D 1059/3/4, D 34/A/PO/150–242
	1785 ⎰		
	1796	27 Sept.	Marshall *Rural Economy, Midland Counties*, vol. II, pp. 17–18
Shipston on Stour	1827	nd	Hone, *Table Book*, vol. I, col. 177
	1785	Mich	Warwicks. RO, DR 468/39/1–20
	1748		
	1749		
	1763		
	1764		Gloucs. RO, P 216 OV 3/4,
	1787	Mich	P 353 OV 3/4, P81 OV 3/4,
	1791		P 52 OV 3/4/1–2
	1792		
	1797		
	1805		
	1813		
Southam	1778	Mich	Staffs. RO, D114/A/PO/150–242
	1780		
	1782		
	1784		Warwicks. RO, DR 452/37,
	1798	Mich	DR 296/67, DR 43A/2/30–94,
	1799		DR 295/73, DR 583/52
	1801		
	1803		
	1813		
	1827	Mich OS	Hone, *Table Book*, vol. I, col. 176
	1888	Mich OS	PP 1888, LIII
Stratford	1805	Mich NS	Owen, *Book of Fairs*
	1810	Mich	Gloucs. RO, P216 OV 3/2
Studley	1818	Mich	Warwicks. RO, DR 360/12/83
	1827	Mich NS	Hone, *Table Book*, vol. I, col. 174
Warwick	1792	Mich OS	PP 1888, LIII
	1805	Mich OS	Owen, *Book of Fairs*
	1808 ⎱	Mich	Warwicks. RO, DR 452/37,
	1813 ⎰		N5/103
Wellesbourne	1781		
	1788	Mich	Warwicks. RO, N5/103,
	1800		DR 296/67
	1801		

Table A4.1. (*cont.*)

Place	Year	Date	Source
Western Heath	1775		
	1776		
	1784		Warwicks. RO, DR 250/49,
	1794	} Mich	DR 296/67, DR 613/164/1–143,
	1795		DR 146/8
	1796		
	1798		
Woolston	1799	} Mich	Warwicks. RO, DR 296/67,
	1803		DR 74/53–5
Westmorland			
Northleach	1755	Mart	Burn, *Justice of the Peace*, p. 213
Wiltshire			
Cricklade	1805	21 Sept.	Owen, *Book of Fairs*
Highworth	1802	Mich	CSE, no. 95
	1760s	Mich	Wilts. RO, 551/103
	1765	Mich	Gloucs. RO, P44 OV 3/4/1
Malmesbury	1813	Mich	Wilts. RO, 59/1
Marlborough	1780		Wilts. RO, 551/103,
	1809	} Mich	673/21
	1812		
Sherston	1775	Mich	Wilts. RO, 59/1
Worcestershire			
Alvechurch	1804	Mich	Warwicks. RO, N5/103
	nd	22 Sept.	Wright, *Calendar*, vol. III, pp. 78–9
Blockley	1792	Mich OS	PP 1888, LIII
	1805	Mich OS	Owen, *Book of Fairs*
Droitwich	1792	23 Sept.	PP 1888, LIII
	1805	23 Sept.	Owen, *Book of Fairs*
Evesham	1806	nd	CSE, no. 450
	1780	Mich	Worcs. RO, 850 Claines 2683/12
	1782	Mich	Warwicks. RO, DR 468/39/1–20
	1795	Mich	Gloucs. RO, P 353 OV 3/4
Feckenham	1740	Mich	Worcs. RO, 850 Claines 2683/12
Hanbury	1813	Mich	Worcs. RO, 850 Ombersley 3572
Pershore	1794	nd	CSE, no. 427
St John's	1781	Mich	CSE, no. 381
Upton	1800	Mich OS	CSE, no. 189
	1778		Worcs. RO, 850 Bredon
	1791	} Mich	6256/4/ii
	1792		
Yorkshire, East Riding			
Aldborough	1860	9 Nov.	Skinner, *Facts and Opinions*, p. 21
Beeford	1860	2 Nov.	*Ibid.*
Beverley	1789	Mart	ERRO, PR 500
Brandsburton	1776	Mart	ERRO, PR 500
	1860	7 Nov.	Skinner, *Facts and Opinions*, p. 21
Bridlington	1773	Mart	ERRO, PR 500
	1860	14 Nov.	Skinner, *Facts and Opinions*, p. 21

Table A4.1. (*cont.*)

Place	Year	Date	Source
Great Driffield	1860	12 Nov.	*Ibid.*
Doncaster	1900	Mart	Kitchen, *Brother to the Ox*, pp. 90–8
Fridaythorpe	1860	16 Nov.	Skinner, *Facts and Opinions*, p. 21
Hedon	1860	7 Nov.	*Ibid.*
Helmsley	1888	5 Nov.	PP 1888, LIII
Holme on South Moor	1860	15 Nov.	Skinner, *Facts and Opinions*, p. 22
Hornsea	1860	7 Nov.	*Ibid.*, p. 21
Howden	1860	15 Nov.	*Ibid.*, p. 22
Huggate	1860	29 Nov.	*Ibid.*
Hummanby	1860	26 Nov.	*Ibid.*, p. 21
Keyingham	1860	29 Nov.	*Ibid.*, p. 22
Killam	1641	All Souls	Best, *Rural Economy*, p. 135
Kirkburne	1641	Mart	*Ibid.*
Knaresborough	1792	Mart OS	PP 1888, LIII
Otley	1805	Mart OS	Owen, *Book of Fairs*
Patrington	1860	6 Dec.	Skinner, *Facts and Opinions*, p. 22
Pocklington	1860	20 Nov.	*Ibid.*
Selby	nd	nd	ERRO, DDBD/5/113
Sherburn	1860	14 Nov.	Skinner, *Facts and Opinions*, p. 21
Sledgmour	1641	All Souls	Best, *Rural Economy*, p. 135
South Cave	1860	8 Nov.	Skinner, *Facts and Opinions*, p. 22
Stamford Bridge	1860	16 Nov., 3 Dec.	*Ibid.*
Market Weighton	1860	14 Nov.	*Ibid.*
Wetherby	1792	Mart OS	PP 1888, LIII
	1805	Mart OS	Owen, *Book of Fairs*

Sources: For full sources, see abbreviations to Notes and Bibliography.

Dates

nd	no date indicated in source
Mich	Michaelmas (29 September)
Mich OS	10 October (after 1751)
Mich NS	29 September (after 1751)
Mart	Martinmas (11 November)
Mart OS	22 November (after 1751)
Mart NS	11 November (after 1751)
Whit	Whitsuntide

Appendix 5   The Holland, Lincolnshire, Statute Sessions

The survival of the records of the Statute Sessions in Holland, Lincolnshire, can be attributed to the administrative zeal of Holland JPs in the mid eighteenth century. My 'discovery' of them is owed to the efficiency of the Lincolnshire Archives Office and directly to Miss Judith Cripps.

I could not find the original order that led to the deposit of the constable's records of each Statute Session in central Quarter Sessions for Holland, but it was this that led to their preservation. The lists begin in 1767. At that date, Holland Quarter Sessions minutes contain many orders to proclaim assessed wages (Jan. 1766; April 1766; March 1767, etc.) but none to deposit the lists with Quarter Sessions. In January 1777, however, Quarter Sessions in Boston ordered:

> that the chief constable of the Wapentake of Elloe be allowed and paid by the Treasurer of the said Wapentake the sum of eight pounds and eight shillings for their attendance and holding the statutes within the Wapentake of Elloe for the last years ... And further that the Chief Constables for the Wapentake of Elloe be allowed the sum of two pounds and two shillings for their attending and holding every statute for the said Wapentake and that they do not for the future receive or take any other fee or gratuity whatsoever from any servant or master on account of the said statutes. And the said Chief Constables are ordered to enter fairly in a Book to be kept for that purpose the names of all Persons hired and deliver in every midsummer and Christmas sessions to the Clerk of the Peace for the said Parts of Holland a true copy of such entries.[1]

The same session made a similar order to the constables of the wapentake of Kirton, and established a fund to maintain a record office. In the Christmas sessions of 1780, the proceedings of the statutes in the wapentakes of Kirton and Skirbeck were ordered to be filed in the records of the Quarter Sessions.

The original books and copies (made on separate sheets) are contained in the Quarter Sessions deposit. The Elloe series is more complete than the ones for Kirton and Skirbeck. No form was prescribed by Quarter Sessions, and the records vary from wapentake to wapentake. All give the immediately obvious information of the name and residence of the master, the name of the servant, the term, the

164

wages, and any other special conditions. From this, the distances travelled to the fairs by masters can be calculated, and changes in wages paid can be observed. The Elloe constables were more thorough, and their thoroughness makes the records of the Spalding, Holbeach, Fleet, and Long Sutton Statute Sessions invaluable. They asked, further, what the name and residence of the last master was, and, if the servant came to the fair from home, where the home was. From this can be calculated the distance servants travelled to the fair, the distance between consecutive services, and the distance from home to the fairs; wages can also be correlated with distances travelled. Because the Elloe records are continuous, some servants can be followed from year to year. The increase in their wages can be noted, and their pattern of mobility measured.

These calculations form parts of Chapters 4 and 5. Comparable records from other areas would multiply the value of the Elloe set, but as far as I know, none has survived. Elloe was in many ways unusual. The greater part of the wapentake was, in the eighteenth and early nineteenth centuries, undrained fen and saltwater marsh. Part of the fen had been drained and enclosed by the Adventurers in the seventeenth century, but the drains fell into disrepair in the eighteenth century.[2] The rest was either unimproved or ineffectively drained. Until the mid nineteenth century the land was subject to flooding three of every four years.[3] Between the marsh and the fen, and elevated three to five feet above the marsh, ran a silt ridge, and it was on this ridge that most of the villages were located. Each long and narrow parish cut across marsh, ridge, and fen; the marsh and fen were parish commons. The wapentake lies at the southeastern shore of the Wash. To the north and east, the land angles out towards the North Sea. Mobility was thus constrained by water, salt, fresh, and brackish, by flooded fens, marsh, and the Wash.

The figures of mobility calculated from the Elloe session cannot, therefore, be taken as representative of a general pattern of mobility. Only a comparable set of records, from a more geographically open region, would permit an evaluation of the fenland figures.

Appendix 6   Compulsory service

The Statute of Labourers (1350–1) compelled all men and women, sound of body, free or bond, and younger than sixty, without craft, merchandise, living, land, or service, to serve in husbandry. No changes were made to the legislation until the Statute of Artificers in 1562–3, which added only a lower age limit, twelve. The legislation was repealed, along with the rest of the statute, in the second decade of the nineteenth century.

Compulsory service had two objectives. It attempted, in the first place, to force cottagers to become reliable, year-round workers when they were protected from this position by their rights to the use of common pasture, forest, and marsh. Of probable equal importance, the statute was the necessary sanction behind wage assessments. Not only were wages to be controlled, but men and women were to be compelled to accept employment at the controlled wages.

Many examples of the enforcement of this legislation from the sixteenth and seventeenth centuries exist. In October of 1661, single persons out of work in Cambridgeshire were ordered to place themselves in service within a week.[1] Single men and women out of service were frequently ordered by Essex Petty Sessions in the later sixteenth century to find masters.[2] Similar presentments and orders were made in Buckinghamshire, Hertfordshire, and the North and West Ridings of Yorkshire.[3] In Wiltshire in 1656 young men and women were ordered to go abroad into service, not to remain at home holding out for excessive wages.[4]

Compulsory apprenticeship in husbandry was distinct in its intentions from compulsory service. It was an element of parish poor relief; its legislative basis is found in statutes for relief of the poor, and not in the Statute of Artificers. In 1572, legislation was provided for the binding out by the parish of beggars' children to farmers and others.[5] By that statute, children five to fourteen were to be bound as parish apprentices to serve until they were twenty-four, in the case of men, and eighteen in the case of women. The terminal age for women was raised to twenty-one in 1597–8 (39 Eliz. I, c. 3); the legislation was further clarified in 1696–7 (8 & 9 Wm III, c. 30), 1780 (20 Geo. III, c. 36), and 1792 (32 Geo. III, c. 57); in 1777 the terminal age for men was lowered to twenty-one. The overseers of parish relief were ordered in 1802 to keep registers of parish apprentices (42 Geo. III, c. 46). In 1814, the minimum age was raised to nine (56 Geo. III, c. 139). Throughout the long years of enabling legislation, farmers and others were compelled to accept parish apprentices if so ordered by the parish; in 1844, this necessary compulsion was repealed (7 & 8 Vic., c. 101). Little notice of this legislation appears in Quarter Sessions.

Appendix 7 Speculations on the origin of the institution

The study is concerned with early modern England, a time and place where the institution of service in husbandry had already come into existence. Positing the existence of an institution, and then explaining its extinction (Chapter 7), invites us to consider why the institution had come into being by the sixteenth century. What follows is no more than a speculation on that question, and a suggestion as to why speculation may be the only possible approach to an answer.

The institution existed in medieval England, although it does not seem to have been as dominant as it was to become in early modern England.[1] The first speculative step is to explain why the institution gained in popularity from medieval to early modern times. The explanation is to be found, I would suggest, in the sharp drop in population caused by plague. The rapid change in man–land ratios elicited several responses. Land, especially marginal land, was deserted, but no estimate has suggested that the desertion was in proportion to the decrease in population. Miskimin suggested that landlords adjusted to the new relative shortage of labour by shifting to pastoral agriculture (given the higher income-elasticity of demand for meat and dairy products relative to that of grain), by enforcing labour services from tenants and by forcing labourers to work for low regulated wages, and by letting the demesne to tenants for low rents, exchanging direct exploitation for indirect.[2] Several of these responses would have favoured the increased employment of servants. Pastoral agriculture demanded full-time labour at a time when abundant land made reliable adult labourers hard to find; the growth in size of peasant holdings ensured that more holdings would be large enough to support additions to the family work force.

The second speculative stage concerns the origin of the institution of service: how did it come to be in existence in the thirteenth century? The use of the metaphor of evolutionary change suggests that the origin is to be found in the successful mutation of a pre-existing institution, just as an explanation of the decline of service will be found in the competition between the more successful species, labourer, and the less successful species, farm servants. The change to be sought, it appears to me, is not a mutation of one sort of early medieval labour

168

(slaves, *famuli*, serfs, etc.) into a new sort of labour (servants). It is, rather, the mutation of the biologically related family to the contractual and variable family containing servants, and I confess my ignorance about this as an historical process, while suggesting that it is not a medieval invention. The existence of nuclear or stem families seems to present the 'farming-out' of adolescents as so obvious a solution to the developmental cycle of the family that all that would have to be posited would be nuclear or stem families, small family land holdings, and intelligent observers, for service in husbandry to result.

Service, in this sense, did not evolve from slavery, labour services, or the *famulus*. It was the functional successor to these institutions, occupying the same ecological niche at a later time. Similarly, day-labouring did not evolve from farm service. Labouring, a coexisting institution, displaced farm service from its habitat, causing its extinction. I stressed at several points that while the institution of married servants of Northumberland in the nineteenth century was similar in form and function to the institution of tied cottagers in the south, the evolutionary path that brought the institutions to this simultaneity were different. The cottagers of Northumberland were the remnants of a once-successful species of medieval England, the *famuli*, who survived because an entire evolutionary process had been arrested there; the tied cottagers of the south arose from the extinction of farm service: farmers found it necessary to ensure constant labour to their farms, and invented a new institution.

Appendix 8   The 1831 census

The map of Figure 7.2 uses an estimate of the numbers of servants and day-labourers drawn from four census totals:

O_1 = male occupiers with hired workers
O_2 = male occupiers without hired workers
W = male labourers in agriculture over twenty years of age
     (specifically including farm servants)
F = families in agriculture

In order to derive an estimate of the number of servants and of day-labourers, let:

o_j = male occupiers, aged twenty and under
o_f = female occupiers
l_a = male day-labourers, married, over twenty
l_b = male day-labourers, unmarried, over twenty
l_c = male day-labourers, married, twenty and under
l_d = male day-labourers, unmarried, twenty and under
s = male farm servants, over twenty

Families in agriculture are those headed by occupiers and married labourers;
thus $F \equiv O_1 + O_2 + o_j + o_f + l_a + l_c$ (1)
and $W \equiv l_a + l_b + s$ (2)

The crude estimate of the number of day-labourers, l_{a-d}, is given by equation (3):

$$F - (O_1 + O_2) = O_1 + O_2 + o_j + o_f + l_a + l_c - (O_1 + O_2) \qquad (3)$$
$$l \approx o_j + o_f + l_a + l_c$$

This is the sum of married agricultural day-labourers plus the small total of female occupiers (o_f) and male occupiers twenty and under (o_j). It does not include unmarried agricultural day-labourers. The crude estimate of s, the number of male farm servants over twenty, is the number of workers over twenty (W) less the number of labourers:

$$W - [F - (O_1 + O_2)] = l_a + l_b + s - [o_j + o_f + l_a + l_c] \qquad (4)$$
$$s \approx l_b - l_c + s - o_j - o_f$$

Table A8.1. *Servants as a proportion of the agricultural labour force, 1831*

Bucks.	0.147	Leics.	0.284
Wilts.	0.159	Herefords.	0.287
Hunts.	0.166	Lincs.	0.296
Beds.	0.175	Notts.	0.297
Dorset	0.190	Kent	0.304
Berks.	0.198	Sussex	0.313
Oxon	0.200	Devons.	0.354
Northants	0.201	Salop	0.357
Norfolk	0.208	Staffs.	0.362
Cambs.	0.210	Yorks., E.	0.369
Suffolk	0.218	Cornwall	0.376
Herts.	0.228	Northumb.	0.379
Essex	0.238	Durham	0.387
Warwicks.	0.239	Yorks., N.	0.407
Hants.	0.240	Yorks., W.	0.451
Rutland	0.243	Derbys.	0.458
Gloucs.	0.252	Chesh.	0.472
Worcs.	0.263	Cumberland	0.537
Somerset	0.264	Lancs.	0.603
Middlesex	0.267	Westmorland	0.616
Surrey	0.281		

Source: 1831 census

$$\frac{W - [F - (O_1 + O_2)]}{W}$$

The estimate of the number of farm servants is increased by the inclusion of unmarried day-labourers over twenty, and decreased by the numbers of married day-labourers, twenty and under, and female and minor male occupiers.

Notes

The following abbreviations are used in the notes.

Agri. HR	*Agricultural History Review.*
Am. Hist. Rev.	*American Historical Review.*
BRO	Bedfordshire Record Office, Bedford.
Camb. UL	University Library, Cambridge.
CG	Cambridge Group for the History of Population and Social Structure.
CJEPS	*Canadian Journal of Economics and Political Science.*
CRO	Cambridgeshire Record Office, Cambridge.
CSE	*Chettenham Settlement Examinations, 1815–1826,* ed. I. Gray, Record Society of the Bristol and Gloucester Archaeological Society, VII (1969)
EcHR	*Economic History Review.*
EEH	*Explorations in Economic History.*
ERO	Essex Record Office, Chelmsford.
ERRO	East Riding Record Office, Beverley.
GV	The Board of Agriculture Reports, 1793–1814, published individually under the general title *General View of the Agriculture of the County of* ....
H & L	P. L. Hughes and J. F. Larkin, eds. *Tudor Royal Proclamations,* 3 vols. (New Haven: Yale University Press, 1964–9).
HFR	Historical Farm Records, University of Reading.
HMC	Historical Manuscripts Commission.
HRO	Hertfordshire Record Office, Hertford.
JEH	*Journal of Economic History.*
JETR	J. E. T. Rogers, *A History of Agriculture and Prices in England,* 7 vols. (Oxford: Clarendon, 1866–1902).
J. Soc. Hist.	*Journal of Social History.*
LAO	Lincolnshire Archives Office, Lincoln.
LRO	Leicestershire Record Office, Leicester.
NRO	Norfolk Record Office, Norwich.
NRRO	North Riding Record Office, Northallerton.
Ox. Bod	Bodleian Library, Oxford.
PP	House of Commons, Sessional Papers.
PRO	Public Record Office, London.

SE Coll.   Settlement Examinations, from various counties (see
                  Bibliography).
SRO(B)   Suffolk Record Office, Bury.
SRO(I)   Suffolk Record Office, Ipswich.
VCH   Victoria County History.

1.   Servants: the problems

1 Gregory King, *Two Tracts*, ed. George E. Barnett (Baltimore: Johns
   Hopkins Press, 1936), p. 31.
2 Peter Laslett, 'Mean Household Size in England since the Sixteenth
   Century', in Peter Laslett and Richard Wall, eds., *Household and Family in
   Past Time* (Cambridge: University Press, 1972), p. 152.
3 Approximately 75 per cent of servants were aged fifteen to twenty-four;
   approximately 17.5 per cent of the population were aged fifteen to twenty-
   four.
4 Alan Macfarlane, *The Family Life of Ralph Josselin, A Seventeenth-Century
   Clergyman* (Cambridge: University Press, 1970), p. 146.
5 John Hajnal, 'European Marriage Patterns in Perspective', in D. V. Glass
   and D. E. C. Eversley, eds., *Population in History* (London: Arnold, 1965),
   p. 132.
6 E. A. Wrigley, 'Fertility Strategy for the Individual and the Group', in
   Charles Tilly, ed., *Historical Studies in Changing Fertility* (Princeton:
   University Press, 1978), p. 147.
7 In 1871, 89 per cent of all servants were domestics. 1871 census, PP 1873,
   LXXII.
8 PP 1852–3, LXXXVIII.
9 Laslett, 'Mean Household Size', p. 152; CG, Parish Listings Collection.
10 Ralph Josselin paid £100 to set up his elder son as an apprentice and £45
   to apprentice his younger son. Two of his five daughters were sent out to
   service. Macfarlane, *Family Life*, pp. 93, 120.
11 57 per cent of the farmers in CG, Parish Listings Collection, kept servants;
   36 per cent of the craftsmen and tradesmen did.
12 Wilhelm Hasbach, *History of the English Agricultural Labourer*, trans. Ruth
   Kenyon (1908; London: Cass, 1966). See also Ivy Pinchbeck, *Women
   Workers and the Industrial Revolution: 1750–1850* (London: Routledge, 1930)
   and E. J. Hobsbawm and George Rudé, *Captain Swing* (Harmondsworth,
   Middlesex: Penguin, 1973) for discussions of farm service in the later
   eighteenth and early nineteenth centuries.
13 Examples of drawing the distinctions and ignoring the consequences
   include Lord Ernle, *English Farming: Past and Present*, 3rd edn (London:
   Longmans Green, 1922); J. D. Chambers and G. E. Mingay, *The
   Agricultural Revolution, 1750–1880* (London: Batsford, 1966); Alan Everitt,
   'Farm Labourers', in J. Thirsk, ed., *The Agrarian History of England and
   Wales*, vol. IV, *1500–1640* (Cambridge: University Press, 1967). Eric
   Kerridge mentions servants only in a discussion of diet in *The Agricultural*

Revolution (London: Allen and Unwin, 1967). Notable exceptions to the rule are J. D. Chambers' posthumously published *Population, Economy, and Society in Pre-Industrial England* (London: Oxford University Press, 1972) and H. J. Habakkuk, *Population Growth and Economic Development since 1750* (Leicester: University Press, 1972).

14   Roger Schofield, basing his estimates on the signing and marking of marriage licences, found rates of illiteracy in 1754 to 1784 of 19 per cent for yeomen, 46 per cent for husbandmen, and 59 per cent for labourers and servants. See 'The Dimensions of Illiteracy, 1750–1850', *Explorations in Economic History*, X(1973), 437–54. The few autobiographies of servants that survive have acquired, through their rarity, a canonical status.

15   The only occasional appearance of servants in tax records is a pitfall into which Everitt and Hoskins have stepped, being less mindful than they might have been of which records would include servants (poll tax) and which would not (hearth tax, and subsidies, to the extent that the minimum wage liable to be taxed was higher than the money wages of most servants). Everitt, 'Farm Labourers'; George Hoskins, *Essays in Leicestershire History* (Liverpool: University Press, 1950).

16   *Rural Economy in Yorkshire in 1641, Being the Farming and Account Books of Henry Best of Elmswell in the East Riding of the County of York*, Surtees Society, XXXIII (1857), p. 176.

17   William Harrison, *The Description of England*, ed. Georges Edelen (1587; Ithaca: Cornell, 1968), pp. 117–18.

18   Anthony Fitzherbert, *The Boke of Husbandry* (London, 1534), pp. 57–9.

19   William Blackstone, *Commentaries on the Laws of England*, ed. Edward Christian, 4 vols. (London, 1803), vol. I, pp. 425–6. Italics in original.

20   1 William and Mary, c. 13.

21   PP 1833, V, 326; PP 1843, XII, 295.

22   Bertha Putnam, *The Enforcement of the Statute of Labourers during the First Decade after the Black Death, 1349–1359*, Columbia University Studies in History and Economics, no. 32 (New York: Columbia University Press, 1908), pp. 79–80.

23   11 Henry VII, c. 2.

24   Richard Burn, *The Justice of the Peace* (London, 1755), pp. 213, 350.

25   (London, 1779), n. pag.

26   PP 1852–53, LXXXVIII, pt 1, lxxviii.

27   See the Board of Agriculture reports for Northumberland and the North Riding: John Bailey and George Culley, *G. V. Northumberland* (London, 1794), p. 53, and John Tuke, *G. V. North Riding of Yorkshire* (London, 1794), p. 24.

28   For a discussion of *famuli*, see M. M. Postan, *The Famulus: The Estate Labourer in the XIIth and XIIIth Centuries*, Economic History Review Supplement, no. 2 (Cambridge: University Press, 1954); Edward Miller, *The Abbey and Bishopric of Ely* (Cambridge: University Press, 1951), p. 93; Hasbach, *History*, p. 7.

29   See, for example, Eleanor C. Lodge, *The Account Book of a Kentish Estate, 1616–1704* (London: Milford and Oxford University Press, 1927).

30 György Diósdi, *Ownership in Ancient and Pre-Classical Roman Law* (Budapest: Akadémiai Kiadó, 1970), pp. 19–30; A. Ernout and A. Meillet, *Dictionnaire Etymologique de la Langue Latine*, 3rd edn (Paris: Klincksieck, 1951), pp. 382–3; *Oxford English Dictionary*, 'family'.

31 Karen Kupperman kindly directed me to the possibility of a seventeenth-century use of 'family' in its older meaning. A letter of instruction from the New England Company in 1629 advised that 'for the better accomodation of business, we have divided servants into several families as we desire and intend they should live together'. Alexander Young, *Chronicles of the First Planters of Massachusetts Bay* (Boston, 1846), p. 167.

32 Richard Mayo, *A Present for Servants, ... Especially in Country Parishes* (London, 1693), p. 3.

33 Andrew Yarranton, *England's Improvement by Sea and Land, Shewing the Way to Out-Do the Dutch in Trade by Sea, to Set at Work all the Poor of England with the Growth of our own Lands*, 2 vols. (London, 1698), Vol. I, p. 171.

34 John Arbuthnot, *An Inquiry into the Connection between the Present Price of Provisions and the Size of Farms* (London, 1773), p. 26.

35 Gordon Schochet, *Patriarchalism in Political Thought: The Authoritarian Family and Political Speculations and Attitudes Especially in Seventeenth-Century England* (Oxford: Blackwell, 1975), p. 415 *et passim*.

36 See Appendix 1.

37 C. B. Macpherson, *Democratic Theory: Essays in Retrieval* (Oxford: Clarendon, 1973), p. 217.

38 Everitt, 'Farm Labourers', pp. 400, 433, 438.

39 Edward Chamberlayne, *Angliae Notitia, or the Present State of England*, 3rd edn (London, 1669), pp. 444–5.

40 For discussions of patriarchalism from a variety of points of view see Gordon Schochet, 'Patriarchalism, Politics, and Mass Attitudes in Stuart England', *Historical Journal*, XII (1969), 413–41; *idem, Patriarchalism in Political Thought*; Peter Laslett, *The World We Have Lost*, 2nd edn (London: Methuen, 1971); Christopher Hill, *Society and Puritanism in Pre-Revolutionary England* (1964; London: Panther, 1969); Mervyn James, *Family, Lineage, and Civil Society: A Study of Society, Politics, and Mentality in the Durham Region, 1500–1640* (Oxford: Clarendon, 1974).

41 1801 Census, PP 1801–2, VI, Preface.

42 Cf. C. B. Macpherson, *The Political Theory of Possessive Individualism* (Oxford: Clarendon, 1962); *idem, Democratic Theory*; Christopher Hill, 'Pottage for Freeborn Englishmen: Attitudes to Wage-Labour', in C. H. Feinstein, ed., *Socialism, Capitalism and Economic Growth* (Cambridge: University Press, 1967), rpt in Christopher Hill, *Change and Continuity in Seventeenth-Century England* (London: Weidenfeld and Nicolson, 1974).

43 Lawrence Stone, *The Family, Sex and Marriage in England, 1500–1800* (London: Weidenfeld and Nicolson, 1977), pp. 27–9.

44 J. L. and Barbara Hammond, *The Village Labourer* (London: Longmans Green, 1966); E. P. Thompson, *The Making of the English Working Class* (Harmondsworth, Middlesex: Penguin, 1968). Clapham and Saville were less careful. See J. H. Clapham, 'The Growth of an Agrarian Proletariat,

1688–1832: A Statistical Note', *Cambridge Historical Journal*, I (1932), 92–5, and John Saville, 'Primitive Accumulation and Early Industrialisation in Britain', *Socialist Register* (London, 1969), pp. 247–71.

45 Cf. D. C. Coleman, 'Labour in the English Economy of the Seventeenth Century', *Economic History Review*, 2nd ser., VIII (1956), 280–95.

2.   Incidence and understanding

1 The collection formed the statistical basis of much of Peter Laslett and Richard Wall, eds., *Household and Family in Past Time* (Cambridge: University Press, 1972).

2 Estimated from the population tables of E. A. Wrigley and R. S. Schofield, *The Population History of England, 1541–1871*, Studies in Social and Demographic History (London: Edward Arnold, 1980).

3 Conversely, some of those described as 'yeoman' may have been primarily engaged in manufacturing. See Mildred Campbell, *The English Yeoman under Elizabeth and the Early Stuarts* (New Haven: Yale University Press, 1942), pp. 163–5.

4 Contained in CG, Parish Listings Collection, Westmorland.

5 This and the following estimates are based on the sixteen listings dating before 1800, and exclude the large block of thirty-one Westmorland listings of 1787.

6 Mean = 0.58, s = 0.21.

7 John Smith, ed., *Men and Armour for Gloucestershire in 1608* (London: Southern, 1902); A. J. Tawney and R. H. Tawney, 'An Occupational Census of the Seventeenth Century', *EcHR*, V (1934), 25–64. Smith had doubts that the list would be of universal interest: 'a large proportion of the return being occupied with the trading, artizan and labouring class, few, perhaps, would really feel gratified by meeting an ancestor among them; but it also includes most of the leisured class of the country' (p. viii).

8 The lists were made under 30 Geo. II, c. 25 (1757), as amended by 31 Geo. II, c. 26 (1758); 32 Geo. II, c. 20 (1759); 33 Geo. II, c. 22 (1760); 2 Geo. III, c. 20 (1762); 4 Geo. III, c. 17 (1764); 19 Geo. III, c. 72 (1779); 26 Geo. III, c. 107 (1786); 37 Geo. III, c. 22 (1797); 42 Geo. III, c. 90 (1802). The principal amendments lowered the age of persons liable to serve from fifty to forty-five (1762); exempted poor men with three or more legitimate children (1762); established a minimum height of 5ft 4in. in 1764 (lowered to 5ft 2in. in 1797); and exempted any man with at least one legitimate child (1784).

9 Two copies exist, one in the Bucks. RO and the other in the British Library (Stowe MSS 805, 806).

10 If it can be assumed first that 55 per cent of late-eighteenth-century males were aged fifteen to fifty-nine, and second that the annual rate of population growth between 1798 and 1801 was 1.5 per cent, the 1798 figures can be compared with the 1801 census totals, with the result that

the 1798 Posse Comitatus apparently failed to include 12.01 per cent of Buckinghamshire males aged fifteen to fifty-nine.

11 Arthur Young, *A Farmer's Tour through the East of England*, 4 vols. (London, 1771); idem, *A Six Months' Tour through the North of England*, 4 vols. (London, 1770); idem, *A Six Weeks' Tour through the Southern Counties of England and Wales*, 3rd edn (London, 1772).

12 SE Coll. Some examinations recorded only the place of legal settlement; in others, where the settlement was established by the renting of a house or land, the examination did not record the history of service that preceded the renting.

13 The figure is higher than that given by James Stephan Taylor in his recent article; the discrepancy undoubtedly springs from our exclusive concern with rural parishes. See his 'The Impact of Pauper Settlement, 1691–1834', *Past and Present*, no. 73 (1976), 42–74.

14 PP 1852–3, LXXXVIII. In the median county in this distribution, 15 per cent of hired workers in agriculture were farm servants. The county mean is 0.21 ($s = 0.14$).

15 *Ibid.*, p. cxxxviii.

16 The county median of this distribution is 5.80, the mean 6.91 ($s = 3.45$).

17 Arthur Young, *A Farmer's Letters* (London, 1767), pp. 66–7. Emphasis in original.

18 John Clark, *G. V. Hereford*, 3 vols. (London, 1794), vol. III, p. 29.

19 William Marshall, *Minutes of Agriculture Made on a Farm of 300 Acres of Various Soils near Croydon, Surrey* (London, 1778), 15 June 1776; Arbuthnot, *Connection between the Present Price of Provisions and the Size of Farms*, p. 81. See also *Commercial and Agricultural Magazine*, III (1800), 165.

20 Adam Moore, *Bread for the Poor* (London, 1653), p. 6; see also Walter Blith, *The English Improver* (London, 1649), pp. 34–5.

21 Anon., *A Political Enquiry into the Consequences of Enclosing Waste Lands* (Holborn, 1785), pp. 43–5.

22 Marshall, *Minutes*, 20 Oct. 1775.

23 Joan Thirsk, 'Horn and Thorn in Staffordshire: The Economy of a Pastoral County', *North Staffordshire Journal of Field Studies*, IX (1969), 10.

24 See David G. Hey, 'A Dual Economy in South Yorkshire', *Agri. HR*, XVII (1969), 110–11, for examples of the extent of by-employment in this nail-making region. See also Joan Thirsk, 'Industries in the Countryside', in F. J. Fisher, ed., *Essays in the Economic and Social History of Tudor and Stuart England* (Cambridge: University Press, 1961), p. 73.

25 NRO, PD 78/72 (1827); SRO (B), N2/1/1 (1764); SRO (B), N2/1/6 (1781); SRO (B), N2/1/1 (1780); SRO (B), N2/1/2 (1765).

26 Thomas Hitt, *A Treatise of Husbandry on the Improvement of Dry and Barren Lands* (London, 1760), pp. 61–2.

27 June A. Sheppard, 'East Yorkshire's Agricultural Labour Force in the Mid-Nineteenth Century', *Agri. HR*, IX (1961), 50.

28 See Lutz Berkner, 'The Stem Family and the Developmental Cycle of the Peasant Household', *Am. Hist. Rev.*, LXXVII (1972), 398–418.

29 J. S. Nalson, *Mobility of Farm Families: A Study of Occupational and Residential Mobility in an Upland Area of England* (Manchester: University Press, 1968), p. 38.

30 See A. V. Chayanov, *On the Theory of Peasant Economy*, ed. D. Thorner, B. Kerblay, and R. E. Smith (1925; Homewood, Ill.: American Economic Association, 1966); Teodor Shanin, *The Awkward Class: Political Sociology of Peasantry in a Developing Country* (Oxford: Clarendon, 1972).

31 Berkner has provided an excellent description of this process at work in eighteenth-century Austria in his 'Stem Family', p. 418. He found servants to have been substitutes for adolescent offspring: the number of servants in peasant families declined as the number of children increased.

32 Richard Colebrook Harris, *The Seigneurial System in Early Canada: A Geographical Study* (Madison: University of Wisconsin Press, 1968), p. 159.

33 LAO, MM 8/51, 52, 55. Petty Sessions, 1588–96.

34 H. J. Habakkuk, 'Family Structure and Economic Change in Nineteenth-Century Europe', *JEH*, XV (1955), 8; Michael Anderson, *Family Structure in Nineteenth Century Lancashire* (Cambridge: University Press, 1971), p. 86.

35 David Sabean, 'Famille et tenure paysan: aux origines de la Guerre Paysans en Allemagne (1525)', *Annales: ESC*, XXVII (1972), 905–6.

36 [Charles Varley], *The Modern Farmer's Guide, by a Real Farmer* (Glasgow, 1768), p. xxxv.

37 See the essays by Margaret Spufford, Joan Thirsk, and E. P. Thompson in Jack Goody, Joan Thirsk, and E. P. Thompson, eds., *Family and Inheritance: Rural Society in Western Europe, 1200–1800* (Cambridge: University Press, 1976).

38 See Shanin, *Awkward Class*, pp. 81ff.

39 Wrigley, 'Fertility Strategy', pp. 135–54.

40 John Hajnal, 'European Marriage Patterns', pp. 101, 132.

41 Farm service is the specific case of the general argument of Eric R. Wolf, that nuclear families and wage-labour are closely associated (*Peasants* (Englewood Cliffs, N.J.: Prentice-Hall, 1966), p. 71). Wolf recognized the presence of servants and slaves in peasant households (p. 61). Daniel Thorner also included hired hands and slaves within his definition of the peasant household. See his 'Peasant Economy as a Category in Economic History', in T. Shanin, ed., *Peasants and Peasant Society* (Harmondsworth, Middlesex: Penguin, 1971), p. 205.

42 In several southeastern European communities cited by Laslett, servants were present, but they were typically married workers, living within the large households, and not the youthful unmarried servants of western Europe. See Peter Laslett, 'Characteristics of the Western Family Considered over Time', *Journal of Family History*, II (1977), 103–4.

43 *Ibid.*, p. 90. See, for discussions of service in western Europe: Berkner, 'Stem Family', for eighteenth-century Austria; Andrejs Plakans, 'Peasant Farmsteads and Households in the Baltic Littoral, 1797', *Comparative Studies in Society and History*, XVII (1975), 10; Hans Olaf Hansen, *Manntal 1729 I Þremur Syslum* (Reykjavik: Ríkisprentsmid jan Gutenberg,1975), pp.

34–7, an Icelandic census containing many male servants (*Karlhjú*); Martine Segalen, 'The Family Cycle and Household Structure: Five Generations in a French Village', *Journal of Family History*, II (1977), 223–36; Michael Drake, *Population and Society in Norway, 1735–1865* (Cambridge: University Press, 1969), p. 115. Emmanuel Todd, in his comparative study of Longuenesse, in Artois, in 1778 and Pratolino, Tuscany, in 1721 found many farm servants in the French parish and few in the Italian parish ('Seven Peasant Communities in Pre-Industrial Europe', unpublished Ph.D. thesis, Cambridge University, 1976, p. 77).

44   P. von Blackenburg, *The Position of the Agricultural Hired Worker* (Paris: OECD, 1962), pp. 26–7. He found that hired labourers living in the farm household were 85 to 95 per cent of the hired agricultural labour force in Luxembourg, 80 per cent in Denmark, 67 per cent in the German Federal Republic, 45 per cent in France, 38 per cent in Belgium, 11 per cent in the Netherlands, 7 to 8 per cent in Great Britain, and nonexistent in Italy. He called living-in a 'relic' of preindustrial society, and found it to predominate only on smaller farms.

45   See his comments on the religious training, diet, and future prospects of the poor tenant's servants in F. M. Powicke, ed., 'The Reverend Richard Baxter's Last Treatise' [*The Poor Husbandman's Advocate to Rich Racking Landlords*], *Bulletin of the John Rylands Library*, X (1926), 181, 183.

46   Young, *Farmer's Letters*, pp. 57, 66.

3.   Life and work

1   Suggestions were occasionally made that the contract should be explicit and written, rather than implicit and customary, to prevent abuses, but were never generally adopted. See [Giles Jacob], *The Compleat Parish Officer*, 5th edn (London, 1729), p. 114; Anon., *A Letter on the Subjects of Hiring, Service and Character, by a County Magistrate* (London, 1821; contained in HRO, 61720) includes in it a set of sample blank hiring certificates.

2   See below, Chapter 5.

3   Justices occasionally limited the size of the token payment to prevent total wages from exceeding the limits established by wage assessments. In Essex in 1612 the earnest was limited to one penny (ERO, Q/AA 1); in Lincolnshire in the mid eighteenth century earnests as high as 5s were given (LAO, Misc. Dep. 161).

4   Some contracts specified terms longer than a year. John Parker bound himself in 1604 for five years to serve George Hopwood for food, lodging, and 16s a year (*Lancashire Quarter Sessions Records 1590–1606*, J. Tait, ed., Chetham Society, n. s., LXXVII (1917), 216); the Hertfordshire settlement examinations contain an instance of a youth of fifteen being let for three years by his father to a farmer for food, lodging, and clothes (HRO, D/P 15/13/3, May 1782). The rigid annual form of the contract occasionally weakened in the nineteenth century. The Holland,

Lincolnshire Statute Sessions of that period show an increasing use of the provision of a month's wages or a month's warning'. William Rees was hired at Holbeach in May 1829, for one year 'subject to one month's warning each side' (LAO, Holland QS D3).

5 Putnam observed that the Statutes of Labourers represented a radical departure from previous customary practice. Until the mid thirteenth century, a master could force an unwilling servant to submit to his authority, but had no legal remedy if the servant escaped from his household; after that date, the servant could leave within the term on reasonable grounds of abuse and maltreatment, but the recapture of a runaway servant was made legal (*Enforcement of Statutes of Labourers*, p. 183). A provable cause was made the explicit grounds of voiding a contract in 1562–3 (5 Eliz. I, c. 4). See CRO, P/26/23/6 (1764) for an example of the return by warrant of a runaway servant. Quarter Sessions occasionally ordered servants to serve out the rest of their term. See *Quarter Sessions Order Book, 1642–1649*, B. C. Redwood, ed., Sussex Record Society, LIV (1954), 27, 38, 46. A Hertfordshire servant who left his master in mid May, without consent, and who tried to entice another servant away, was committed to Bridewell (HRO, D/P 29/13/3, July 1763). Quarter Sessions often ordered the payment of wages to servants. See, for examples, *Quarter Sessions Records 1605–1612*. J. C. Atkinson, ed., North Riding Record Society, I (1884), 142–4; County of Buckingham, *Calendar to the Sessions Records, 1678–1694*, W. Le Hardy, ed., I (1933), 52, 201, 464.

6 Burn, *Justice of the Peace*, p. 354. See also [Giles Jacob], *The Compleat Parish Officer*, 10th edn (London, 1744), pp. 164–7; Michael Dalton, *The Country Justice*, 5th edn (London, 1635), p. 85.

7 See, for example, *Norfolk Quarter Sessions Order Book, 1650 to 1657*, D. E. Howell James, ed., Norfolk Record Society, XXVI (1955), 70–1.

8 *Notes and Extracts from the Sessions Rolls, 1581 to 1698*, W. J. Hardy, ed., Hertfordshire County Record Society, I (1905), 146.

9 Hereford RO, Quarter Sessions Order Book, QSO/1 A, fol. 57B (1666).

10 Elizabeth King testified at her 1758 settlement examination that she had been discharged from service in Cambridgeshire on grounds of her pregnancy. HRO, D/P 29/13/3, Sept. 1758.

11 See, for example, *Calendar to the Sessions Books and Sessions Minute Books, 1658 to 1700*, W. Le Hardy, ed., Hertfordshire County Record Society, VI (1930), 197; *Quarter Sessions Order Book*, p. 44.

12 In Hertfordshire in 1653 a pregnant servant was sent back to her master and ordered to finish the term of service (*Calendar to the Sessions Books and Sessions Minute Books, 1619–1657*, W. J. Hardy, ed., Hertfordshire County Record Society, V (1928), 441).

13 William Perkins, [*Christian*] *Oeconomie, or Household Government, A Short Survey of the Right Manner of Erecting and Ordering a Family, According to the Scriptures*, in *Workes*, 3 vols. (London, 1631), vol. III, p. 697; Thomas Parkyns, *Subordination: An Essay on Servants, their Rates of Wages, and the*

Great Conveniency which will Accrue to every County, by Recording with all Chief Constables, etc., of the Same, 3rd edn (London, 1724), p. 26.

14 Dalton, *The Country Justice*, p. 79. The agreement of four Justices was necessary to terminate an apprentice's contract; see Gissing parish records, NRO, PD 50/83.

15 SRO (B), EL 119/7/280.

16 SRO (B), EL 158, 1797; NRO, PD 136/73, 1800. [Jacob], *The Compleat Parish Officer*, explicitly sanctioned parting by mutual consent (p. 166).

17 Several recent studies have made clear the dependent position of servants within the early modern patriarchal family. See Schochet, *Patriarchalism in Political Thought*, ch. 4; Schochet, 'Patriarchalism'; Hill, *Society and Puritanism*, ch. 13; Macfarlane, *Family Life*.

18 Stone, *Family, Sex and Marriage*, p. 22.

19 Subsidies of 1512–23 (4 Hen. VIII, c. 19; 5 Hen. VIII, c. 17; 6 Hen. VIII, c. 26; 14 and 15 Hen. VIII, c. 16); marriage, etc., taxes of 1696–7 (8 & 9 Wm III, c. 20); poll taxes of 1696–8 (8 & 9 Wm III, c. 6; 9 Wm III, c. 38); farm servants were specifically exempted from the weekly assessments of 1642–3 (C. H. Firth and R. S. Rait, eds., *Acts and Ordinances of the Interregnum 1642–1660*, 2 vols. (London: HMSO, 1911), 24 February 1642–3) and from the servant tax of 1776 (17 Geo. III, c. 39), which was to be paid by masters on those servants whom Adam Smith called, in the same year, 'unproductive'. For treatment of defaulters, see poll taxes of 1666–88 (18 & 19 Car. II, c. 1; 1 Wm and Mary, c. 13).

20 Firth and Rait, *Acts and Ordinances of Interregnum*, 13 Aug. 1651.

21 E. P. Thompson, *Whigs and Hunters: The Origin of the Black Act* (New York: Pantheon, 1975), pp. 84–5. No intensive attempt has been made to document the paucity of presentments. An example of the suggested practice is the Staffordshire Recusant Lists, and the lists of 'Trespasses, Contempts, and Offences', which contain within them the name of only one person identified as a servant, and he was servant to a gentleman (*Quarter Sessions, 1581–1589*, S. A. H. Bourne, ed., Historical Collections of Staffordshire, William Salt Archaeological Society, I (1929), 190ff).

22 It remained in force until the later eighteenth and early nineteenth centuries. Three aspects of the law will be discussed in detail in the pages that follow. Wage regulation will be considered in this chapter, in the section on wages; compulsory service will be treated in Chapter 5, and restrictions on mobility in Chapter 4.

23 The Webbs called Petty Sessions imitations of the older High Constable's Hundred Sessions. Sidney and Beatrice Webb, *The Parish and the County*, vol. I of *English Local Government*, 11 vols. (1906; rpt London: Cass, 1963), pp. 299n, 400, 489–91.

24 *Rural Economy*, p. 132.

25 David Jenkins, *The Agricultural Community of Southwest Wales at the Turn of the Twentieth Century* (Cardiff: University of Wales Press, 1971), pp. 77, 80; Marshall, *Minutes*, July 1774.

26 John Banister, 'Synopsis of Husbandry' [1799], *Commercial and Agricultural*

Magazine, III (1801), 189; Marshall, *Minutes*, 4 April 1776 and 19 May 1776.

27   Fred Kitchen, *Brother to the Ox: The Autobiography of a Farm-Labourer* (London: Dent, 1940) p. 139.

28   *Ibid.*, pp. 52, 55–9.

29   Thomas Tusser, *Five Hundred Pointes of Good Husbandrie* (London, 1580), fol. 69.

30   Gervase Markham, *Farewell to Husbandry*, 3rd edn (London, 1631), pp. 144–6.

31   Anon., *Boke of Thrift* (1509), in F. H. Cripps-Day, ed., *The Manor Farm* (London: Quaitch, 1931), pp. 2–3.

32   Rates were doubled in New Windsor (P. L. Hughes and J. F. Larkin, eds., *Tudor Royal Proclamations*, 3 vols. (New Haven: Yale University Press, 1964–9) (hereafter cited as H and I), vol. I, p. 219), in Lidd, Kent (H and L, I, 265), and in Rutland (H and L, I, 212–13); they were increased by smaller percentages in Lincolnshire (H and L, I, 221), in Northamptonshire (H and L, I, 286), and York (H and L, I, 223).

33   Minchinton reported that in 1972 there were 1,400 extant assessments. See W. E. Minchinton, ed., *Wage Regulation in Pre-Industrial England* (Newton Abbot: David and Charles, 1972), p. 19.

34   ERO, Calendar of Records, Quarter Sessions, II, 112; *Quarter Sessions Records*, North Riding Record Society, I (1884), 142–4, 207, 209; VII (1889), 34; E. M. Hampson, *The Treatment of Poverty in Cambridgeshire, 1597–1834* (Cambridge: University Press, 1934), pp. 55–6.

35   *Rural Economy*, pp. 163–4, compared with the 1658 assessment in *Quarter Sessions Records*, North Riding Record Society, VI (1888), 4; G. E. Fussell, ed., *Robert Loder's Farm Accounts, 1610–1620*, Camden Society, 3rd ser. LIII (1936), 90, compared with the Wiltshire assessment for 1703, in HMC, *Report on Manuscripts in Various Collections*, I (1901), 163; Lodge, *Account Book*, p. xxxii, compared with the Kent assessment of 1724, in Elizabeth L. Waterman, 'Some New Evidence on Wage Assessments in the Eighteenth Century', *English Historical Review*, XLIII (1928), 406.

36   ERO, Calendar of Records, Quarter Sessions, V (1573–4), 151, 175ff, compared with Colchester assessment of 1583 in H and L, I, 499; LAO, MM 8/51, 1588–91, compared with North Riding assessment of 1593 in J. E. T. Rogers, *A History of Agriculture and Prices in England*, 7 vols. (Oxford: Clarendon, 1866–1902); vol. VI, p. 687 (hereafter cited as JETR).

37   See Appendix 2.

38   LAO, Holland QS D2 (the mean proportion of female to male wages over the eighteen years was 0.44); LAO, Misc. Dep. 161 (the median proportion of female to male wages was 0.495, 1780–1803).

39   See Appendix 2.

40   In mid-twentieth-century Europe, the minimum age at which adult wages could be received by farm servants ranged from eighteen to twenty-three, as reported by von Blackenburg, *Position of Agricultural Hired Worker*, pp. 102–3.

41 *Annals of Agriculture*, XXX (1798), 10–12; XLV (1808), 317.
42 See Appendix 2.
43 SE Coll., SRO(B), HRO, CRO, ERO.
44 LAO, Holland QS D2.
45 LAO, Misc. Dep. 161.
46 Kitchen, *Brother to the Ox*, p. 187.
47 ERO, DP 80/13/4, 1803.
48 Tusser, *Five Hundred Pointes*, fol. 11.
49 Yarranton, *England's Improvement by Sea and Land*, vol. II, p. 127.
50 *Quarter Sessions Order Book*, p. 183.
51 *Brother to the Ox*, p. 98.
52 Nash Stevenson, 'On Statute Fairs: Their Evils and Their Remedy',
    Transactions of the National Association for the Promotion of Social Sciences
    (1858), p. 630.
53 *Rural Economy*, p. 134. Everitt reported an East Riding Village by-law of
    1632 that ordered that 'no man should allow his servant to keep above
    four shorn sheep and lambs' ('Farm Labourers', p. 459).
54 ERO, Calendar of Records, Quarter Sessions, VI, 176.
55 LAO, MM 8/51, 52, 55 (1588–96).
56 SRO (B), N2/1/6, Mar. 1784, and EL 97/7/6, Sept. 1794.
57 LAO, Holland QS D2.
58 LAO, 192/129 (1696) and 207/196 (1729).
59 Often clothing was also provided to servants. Sussex Quarter Sessions in
    1649 ordered a master to pay the back wages owed to a servant, taking
    into account the apparel she might have received. See *Quarter Sessions Order
    Book*, p. 183. Hertfordshire Quarter Sessions assessed wages for servants with
    and without 'leverye' (*Notes and Extracts*, pp. 11–12).
60 Von Blackenburg, *Position of Agricultural Hired Worker*, pp. 102–3. To
    think in terms of the real and money components of wages, however, is to
    be misleadingly anachronistic. Food and lodging were obligations mas-
    ters owed to servants. Masters were obliged to maintain their servants
    because they had hired them into their family for the year. Adopting this
    perspective has the advantage of making clearer the difficulties farmers
    faced when they tried to assess the relative costs of keeping farm servants
    and hiring day-labourers (see Chapter 6).
61 Gervase Markham, *The English Housewife* (London, 1683), p. 187.
    Markham's recipe, which includes peas and malt as well as grains, would
    please latter-day vegetarians. It is a well-balanced vegetable protein.
    William Vaughan reported in 1626 that servants in the North of
    England 'used to covenant heretofore with their masters to feed them
    with bread made of Beanes, and not of Barley, from Allhallowtide until
    May' (*The Golden Fleece* (London, 1626), p. 13). See also Richard
    Baxter's writings in praise of vegetarian diets in Powicke, 'The Reverend
    Richard Baxter's Last Treatise', 80 ('brown bread and milk and pease
    pies and apple pies and puddings and pancakes and gruel and flummery
    and furmety, yea dry bread').

62 Fussell, *Robert Loder's Farm Accounts*, pp. 86–7. The account book dates from the early seventeenth century.

63 See H. Leibenstein, 'The Theory of Underemployment in Backward Areas', *Journal of Political Economy*, LXV (1957), 91–103. Leibenstein discussed the relation of wages to strength and therefore productivity.

64 *Brother to the Ox*, p. 138.

65 Mayo, *Present for Servants*, p. 57.

66 *Five Hundred Pointes*, fol. 72.

67 *Synopsis of Husbandry*, p. 190.

68 Marshall, *Minutes*, 6 June 1776.

69 *Rural Economy*, pp. 175–6. He described the tasks of the eight (pp. 132–3), and Appendix A (p. 163) shows the hiring of nine servants at Martinmas 1641.

70 Jenkins, *Agricultural Community*, p. 123.

71 M. W. Barley, *The English Farmhouse and Cottage* (London: Routledge and Kegan Paul, 1961), p. 15. Barnaby Googe's ideal farmhouse had lodgings for servants arrayed around the threshing floor and stables; he also advocated the designation of a special 'sicke folkes' chamber. *The Whole Art of Husbandry* (London, 1614), p. 11.

72 Edmund S. Morgan, *The Puritan Family: Religion and Domestic Relations in Seventeenth-Century New England*, new edn (1944; New York: Harper and Row, 1966), p. 128.

73 Kitchen, *Brother to the Ox*, p. 109.

74 ERO, Calendar of Records, Quarter Sessions, v, 76.

75 *Brother to the Ox*, pp. 59, 67, 73. Richard Gough described a murder that could only have happened on a Sunday. Bandits came to a farmhouse on Sunday morning while all were at church and murdered the one maid servant who had been left behind making cheese. The murderers sneaked back to church after killing her, but were seen by another lone servant maid, from another farmhouse. Richard Gough, *Human Nature Displayed in the History of Myddle* (Fontwell, Sussex: Centaur Press, 1968), p. 71.

76 Kitchen, *Brother to the Ox*, p. 87; *Rural Economy*, p. 135; J. Skinner, *Facts and Opinions Concerning Statute Hirings* (London: Wertheim and Macintosh, 1861), p. 16.

77 Jenkins, *Agricultural Community*, p. 82.

78 Kitchen, *Brother to the Ox*, pp. 148–9, 160.

79 K. E. Wrightson, 'The Puritan Reformation of Manners, with Special Reference to the Counties of Lancashire and Essex, 1640–1660', Cambridge University PhD thesis, 1973, p. 95. By Wrightson's calculation, one in every eighteen Essex houses in 1647 was an alehouse; the figure for Lancashire was one in twelve (p. 91).

80 *Ibid.*, p. 96.

81 *Quarter Sessions Records for the County Palatine of Chester, 1559 to 1760*, J. H. E. Bennett and J. C. Dewhurst, eds., Record Society of Lancashire and

Cheshire, XCIV (1940), 177–8. She may have sold some of what she took; it was reported that she stole five or six eleven-pound cheeses.

82   Banister, *Synopsis of Husbandry*, p. 189.

83   Mayo, *Present for Servants*, pp. 39–40.

84   Historical Collections of Staffordshire, *Quarter Sessions, 1581 to 1589*, p. 338.

85   Wrightson, 'Puritan Reformation of Manners', p. 57.

86   *Ibid.*, pp. 57, 61.

87   *Brother to the Ox*, p. 100.

88   Timothy Nourse, *Campania Foelix, or a Discourse of the Benefits and Improvements of Husbandry* (London, 1700), p. 200. The example of perfidiousness Nourse gave was of a servant secretly bargaining with a new master, and then returning to the old, asking if he could beat the new wage (pp. 204–5).

89   *Ibid.*, p. 201.

90   Marshall, *Minutes*, 2 Sept. 1776.

91   *Rural Economy*, p. 136.

92   *Annals of Agriculture*, XI (1789), 77.

93   Arthur Young, *A Farmer's Calendar*, 2nd edn, rev. (London, 1778), p. 373.

94   Marshall, *Minutes*, 29 July 1775.

95   *Ibid.*, pp. 7–13.

96   *Ibid.*, p. 35.

97   *Ibid.*, 3 Mar. 1777.

98   *Ibid.*, 13 May 1775.

99   *Ibid.*, 4 Dec. 1775.

100 *Ibid.*, 29 July 1775.

101 *Ibid.*, 30 June 1775.

102 *Ibid.*, 10 April 1775.

103 *Ibid.*, 14 Mar. 1775.

104 *Ibid.*, 18 Mar. 1775.

105 *Ibid.*, 4 April 1775.

106 *Ibid.*, 3 Mar. 1777.

107 *Ibid.*, p. 35.

108 *Ibid.*, 13 April 1775.

109 *Ibid.*, pp. 36–7.

110 *Ibid.*, 2 Sept. 1776.

111 *Ibid.*, p. 37.

112 *Ibid.*, p. 38.

113 *Ibid.*, July 1777.

114 Nourse, *Campania Foelix*, p. 202.

115 Jenkins, *Agricultural Community*, p. 83.

116 Alan Macfarlane, ed., *The Diary of Ralph Josselin, 1616–1683* (London: Oxford University Press, 1976), p. 68.

117 SRO(B), EL 159/7/11.1, Jan. 1809.

118 ERO, D/P 8/13/4, Oct. 1764; LAO, Toynton St Peter, 13 Feb. 1786.

119 ERO, Calendar of Records, Quarter Sessions, VI (1574), 71–2.

4.   Hiring and mobility

1   See A. S. Kussmaul, 'The Ambiguous Mobility of Farm Servants', *EcHR* (forthcoming 1981).

2   The fifteen parishes are Ardeley, Aspenden, Bengeo, Braughing, Cottered, Great Hormead, Great Munden, Layston, Little Munden, Sacombe, Standon, Stapleton, Throcking, Walkern and Watton. Three men with names common to others in the lists were excluded from the search. HRO, Militia List Collection.

3   Northants RO, yz 4912.

4   Marshall, *Minutes*, 10 October 1775.

5   PP 1822, v, 40.

6   Marshall complained that Michaelmas was inconvenient, because it came in the midst of autumn seedtime (Marshall, *Minutes*, 10 Oct. 1775). It seems unlikely that all farmers would have placidly submitted to this inconvenience, had it been general. Two explanations suggest themselves. Marshall may have been planting earlier than his neighbours: Peter Timmer has suggested that one feature of the agricultural revolution was the shifting forward of seedtime (C. Peter Timmer, 'The Turnip, the New Husbandry, and the English Agricultural Revolution', *Quarterly Journal of Economics*, LXXXIII (1969), 393). The inconvenience may alternatively have been caused by the shift from the Julian to Gregorian calendar in 1752. Eleven days were dropped in the changeover, and Michaelmas, observed on the same date each year, occurred eleven days earlier in the agricultural year after the change. Many notations of hiring dates after 1752 specify that the date of hiring was Michaelmas Old Style (10 October, equivalent to pre-1752 29 September in the agricultural year) or New Style (29 September, equivalent to pre-1752 18 September).

7   William Marshall, *The Rural Economy of the West of England*, 2 vols. (London: Nicol, 1796), vol. I, p. 109. Charles Vancouver reported that the usual term in Devonshire was from Lady Day (25 March): *G. V. Devon* (1808; London: David and Charles, 1969), p. 361.

8   PRO, E 179 119/491.

9   LAO, Misc. Dep. 161.

10   HFR, BER/13.5.1. The account book covers three farms in Radley, Berkshire: Wick, Thrupp, and Gooseacre. The dates of hiring in the two books are consistent with the dates discovered in settlement examinations. The Tetney, Lincs. hirings ran from May Day to May Day; the Radley, Berks. hirings ran from Michaelmas to Michaelmas. No clear differences emerge between the patterns of mobility of male and female servants. More men than women remained at the Berkshire farms for only one year, but the order was reversed on the Lincolnshire farm.

11   The rates for Cogenhoe were calculated from data supplied to the author by Peter Laslett of the Cambridge Group. These, like the rates calculated for Orby and the Hertfordshire parishes, show movement away from parishes, not movement away from masters, and they thus underestimate real mobility.

12 LAO, LD 35/2.
13 HRO, Militia List Collection. A modified method of calculating r_m was used. Every servant appearing in the militia lists from 1758 to 1765 was classified by the number of years he appeared in the lists; the numbers were then combined to produce a table of the persistence that would have been observed had all these servants entered service in the same year. For example, if six servants remained only one year, three remained two years, and one remained a third year, we can imagine that $6 + 3 + 1 = 10$ servants were present at time 0, that $3 + 1 = 4$ remained to appear at time 1, and that 1 remained to time 2. Rates of persistence and mobility can be estimated to approximate the declining sequence.
14 The ages are drawn from the parish listings of Corfe Castle (Dorset), Ardleigh (Essex), and Ealing (Middlesex), all Cambridge Group's parish listings, and from the 1851 Census (PP 1852–3, LXXXVIII).
15 Using the distribution of total years served gleaned from the roughly 5 per cent of settlement examinations detailed enough to reveal them, we can estimate that 16 per cent of farm servants would leave service altogether at the end of the year. The proportion was calculated by making the best estimate of annual rates of departure as if all eighty-one servants in the sample had entered service in the same year.
16 *Annals of Agriculture*, III (1785), 51.
17 Four places were filled each year; in addition, the farmer hired a shepherd who was kept in a separate cottage. Only four men held this post in the forty-nine years.
18 See Appendix 6.
19 James Woodforde, *The Diary of a Country Parson, 1758–1802*, ed. John Beresford (Oxford: University Press, 1978). At the time of Woodforde's death, his household consisted of six ageing celibates and a servant boy. Woodforde was sixty-three, his unmarried niece lived with him, and his four adult servants had been with him for twenty-six, eighteen, seventeen and eight years.
20 'On Statute Fairs' p. 624.
21 Kitchen, *Brother to the Ox*, p. 138.
22 Jenkins, *Agricultural Community*, p. 84.
23 II (1800), 97.
24 I am indebted to David Levine for this observation.
25 Tusser, *Five Hundred Pointes*, fol. 70.
26 William Marshall, *The Rural Economy of the Midland Counties*, 2 vols. (London, 1796), vol. II, p. 18n.
27 *Brother to the Ox*, p. 138.
28 Young, *Farmer's Letters*, p. 66.
29 LAO, Misc. Dep. 161; lads are taken to be those males paid low wages and given an 'earnest' half that received by other servants.
30 For a recent discussion of settlement law and practices, see Taylor, 'Impact of Pauper Settlement'.
31 SRO (B), EL 66/7/4.
32 LAO, Holland QS D2 and D3. See Appendix 5.

33   Spalding mean male distance is 12.32 km; Suffolk mean male distance is 8.24 km. These differ significantly at the 0.003 level of error $(t = 3.119)$.

34   The proportions differ significantly at the 3.61×10^{-9} level of error $(Z = 5.79)$.

35   The proportions differ significantly at the 0.03 level of error $(Z = 1.816)$.

36   PP 1833, V, 246; Marshall, *Rural Economy of the West of England*, vol. I, p. 109.

37   Kitchen, *Brother to the Ox*, pp. 138, 174.

38   ERO, Calendar of Records, Quarter Sessions, V, 24.

39   HRO, D/P 3/16/1.

40   Gough, *Human Nature Displayed in the History of Myddle*, pp. 60–1.

41   See my 'Statute Sessions and Hiring Fairs', forthcoming.

42   The maximum distance a master travelled to the Spalding Spring Sessions in 1773 and 1784 was 22.5 km, giving a maximum diameter of the area of 45 km, or nearly 30 miles. The maximum distance travelled by sixty-three farmers to a variety of Sessions in Gloucestershire, Oxfordshire, Worcestershire, and Warwickshire around 1800 was 25 km (*Cheltenham Settlement Examinations, 1815–1826*, I. Gray, ed., Record Society of the Bristol and Gloucester Archaeological Society, VII (1969)). The median distance of the Spalding set is 9 km, and of the Cheltenham set, 6 km. It should be noted that while the mean distance for Spalding (8.47 km) is higher than the mean distance for Cheltenham (7.25 km), the difference between the means is not significant $(t = 1.573,$ 162 d.f., 0.1097 level of error).

43   Besides the Spalding Sessions, spring and autumn sessions were held in Holbeach, Fleet, or Long Sutton each year; north of Spalding, sessions were held in Leake, Freistone, Kirton, Swineshead, and Sutterton (LAO, Holland QS D2 and D3).

44   *Suffolk Mercury*, XVI, no. 18 (30 Aug. 1725), p. 8.

45   See the notices for Mickfield, Suffolk in 1642 (SRO (I), FB 19/I1/2) and Horham in 1600 (SRO (I), FC 85/I1/7).

46   Marshall, *Rural Economy of the Midland Counties*, vol. II, p. 18.

47   LAO, Holland QS D2.

48   *Cheltenham Settlement Examinations, 1815–1826*.

49   *Rural Economy*, p. 135.

50   Kitchen, *Brother to the Ox*, p. 97.

51   John Cowell, *The Interpreter, or Booke Containing the Signification of Words* (Cambridge, 1607), n. p.

52   Contracts made outside the session were declared void and masters were presented for failing to record new contracts with Constables (*Calendar to the Sessions Books* (1930), pp. 246, 410); for examples of orders to attend sessions and presentments for failing to attend, see, *Quarter Sessions Records*, North Riding Record Society, I (1884), 11 and 68 (1605–8); *Quarter Sessions Records*, Northants Record Society, p. 62 (1630); *Calendar to the Sessions Books* (1930), pp. 346, 410 (1681–2, 1698); H. H. Copnall, ed.,

Nottinghamshire County Records: Notes and Extracts from the Nottinghamshire County Records of the Seventeenth Century (Nottingham, 1915), p. 66.

53 *Rural Economy*, pp. 134–5. See also A. F. J. Brown, *Essex at Work: 1700–1815*, ERO Publication, no. 49 (Chelmsford, 1969), p. 129; Margaret Gay Davies, *The Enforcement of England's Apprenticeship: A Study in Applied Mercantilism* (Cambridge, Mass.: Harvard University Press, 1956), p. 192; Parkyns, *Subordination*, p. 32; S. A. Peyton, ed., *Minutes of the Proceedings in Quarter Sessions held for Parts of Kesteven in the County of Lincoln, 1674–95*, I (1931), cxiii.

54 Within the limits set by the assessments, however, some bargaining was possible.

55 John Monk, *G. V. Leics.* (London, 1794), p. 49; John Farey, *G. V. Derbyshire*, 3 vols. (London, 1815), vol. III, p. 184.

56 Kenneth Tweedale Meaby, ed., *Nottinghamshire: Extracts from the County Records of the Eighteenth Century* (Nottingham: Forman and Sons, 1947), p. 233.

57 H. E. Strickland, *G. V. East Riding of Yorkshire* (York, 1812), p. 261.

58 E. P. Thompson, writing of grain riots in the eighteenth century, argued that it was in the regulated open market places that the people felt strong. 'The Moral Economy of the English Crowd in the Eighteenth Century', *Past and Present*, no. 50 (1971), 76-136.

59 T. E. Kebble, *The Agricultural Labourer* (London: Chapman and Hall, 1870), p. 123.

60 Kitchen, *Brother to the Ox*, p. 100.

61 Kebble, *Agri. Labourer*, pp. 123–4.

62 R. W. Malcolmson, *Popular Recreation in English Society, 1700–1815* (Cambridge: University Press, 1973), p. 23.

63 Kebble, *Agri. Labourer*, p. 127.

64 LAO, Banks Collection, Lincs. Coll. 3, folder M 1796, item 14.

65 William Howitt, *The Rural Life of England*, 2 vols. (London: Longman, Orme, Brown, Green and Longmans, 1838), vol. II, p. 250.

66 Skinner, *Facts and Opinions Concerning Statute Hirings*, pp. 5–7.

67 *Ibid.*, p. 16.

68 Topography might account for the difference; so might a tendency for poorer children to remain near their home to remit their wages to their parents.

69 $t = 0.3118$, level of error $= 0.756$. Two extreme values (27 and 29 km) were excluded from the calculation. Had they been included, they would have raised the mean distance from place of birth to place of last service of the other thirty servants from 6.31 to 7.30.

70 However, 9.34 per cent of the hirings record that the servant came to the Sessions 'from home', or from a household headed by someone with the servant's surname.

71 $t = 0.689$, level of error of 0.492.

72 These findings contradict the conclusion of R. S. Schofield that, for servants, distance from home increased with age. He based his argument on a valuable and unusual listing for Cardington, Beds., that listed the

ages and residences of the children who had left the parish for service. See R. S. Schofield, 'Age-Specific Mobility in an Eighteenth-Century Rural English Parish', *Annales de démographie historique*, 1970, pp. 268, 273.

73 Figure 4.1 shows the approximate late-eighteenth-century extent of the Wash; it is drawn from Arthur Young, *GV Lincoln* (London, 1799).

74 Table 4.10 provides the empirical base of the chi-square test. The values shown are both the observed frequencies (e.g. eight servants moved from Spalding to the north and northwest) and the values expected had all moves been distributed randomly. The chi-square test is based on the squared differences between the observed and expected values. The probability that the moves were in fact randomly distributed is shown by the large value of chi-square with 9 degrees of freedom [(rows − 1) (columns − 1)] to be 0.58 per cent.

75 John Monk found the only advantage of public hiring to be 'the facility with which persons get into service without any reference to character' (*G. V. Leics.*, p. 49); Arthur Young hoped that a quick study of a servant's physiognomy might be helpful (*A Farmer's Calendar*, p. 374).

76 G. William Skinner, 'Marketing and Social Structure in Rural China', *Journal of Asian Studies*, XXIV (1964), 32–5.

77 Everitt's work on marketing would support the existence of the supra-village marketing community. He wrote of the small village market that played 'a vital role in the lives of several thousand husbandmen and labourers'. See 'The Marketing of Agricultural Produce', in J. Thirsk, ed., *The Agrarian History of England and Wales*, vol. IV, *1500–1640* (Cambridge: University Press, 1967), p. 478.

78 E. J. Buckatzsch, 'Places of Origin of a Group of Immigrants into Sheffield, 1624–1799', *EcHR*, II (1949–50), 303–6.

79 T. C. Smith suggested that wage-labour in Japanese agriculture prepared Japan for wage-directed mobility. See *The Agrarian Origins of Modern Japan* (Palo Alto: Stanford University Press, 1959), p. 212; see also his 'Farm Family By-Employment in Pre-Industrial Japan', *JEH*, XXIX (1969), 712.

80 Adam Smith, *An Inquiry into the Nature and Causes of the Wealth of Nations*, 2 vols. (London: Strahon and Cadell, 1776), vol. I, p. 91.

81 E. E. Rich, 'The Population of Elizabethan England', *EcHR*, 2nd ser., II (1950), 247–65. The annual rate of mobility that can be calculated from Rich's data is 0.20, for all males aged sixteen to sixty (including servants). Mortality alone would have contributed a rate of 0.03; how much more would the special mobility of servants have contributed to this rate?

82 Jethro Tull, *The Horse-Hoeing Husbandry* (London, 1733), p. vi.

83 Kitchen, *Brother to the Ox*, p. 71.

84 Carlo Cipolla, 'Diffusion of Innovations in Early Modern Europe', *Comparative Studies in Society and History*, XIV (1972), 48.

85 Basil Quayle, *G. V. Isle of Man* (London, 1794), p. 15.

86 Matthew Peters, *The Rational Farmer*, 2nd edn (London, 1771), p. 94.

87 *Annals of Agriculture*, II (1784), 379–81.

88 William Marshall, *The Rural Economy of Norfolk*, 2 vols., 2nd edn (London, 1795), vol. I, p. 55.

89 William Stevenson, *G. V. Surrey* (London, 1813), pp. 541–2.

5.   **Entry into and exit from service**

1   These three populations are taken from the only three listings of rural populations in the Cambridge Group's collection that permit the simultaneous identification of age, household status, and occupation.

2   The inferences are based upon two assumptions. First, it is assumed that the cross-sectional listings are representative of changes in status over time. Second, it is assumed that the parishes gained servants from other parishes in the same numbers, and at the same ages, that their own children left the parish for service, apprenticeship, or other positions.

3   PP 1843, XII, 297.

4   [Christopher Tancred], *A Scheme for an Act of Parliament for the Better Regulating Servants* ... (London, 1724); p. viii.

5   [Varley], *Modern Farmer's Guide*, p. 393.

6   CRO, P/25/13/4, July 1789.

7   *Farmer's Magazine* (Edinburgh), VIII (1807), 334.

8   NRO, PD 17/37, Mar. 1826.

9   See C. Stella Davies, *The Agricultural History of Cheshire, 1750–1850*, Chetham Society, 3rd series, X (1960), p. 91.

10 Settlement examination from CRO, P 25/13/4, October 1784; parish registers (Bishop's transcripts) for Hardwick from Camb. UL. Spalding hiring records provide an occasional glimpse of the phenomenon. The matching of successive hirings into fragmentary biographies of individuals very occasionally produced sequences in which a servant came to the fair 'from home' after having, in a previous session, been hired as a servant. LAO, Holland QS D2.

11 Macfarlane, *Family Life*, p. 205. See also E. P. Thompson's review of the book, which casts doubt upon the psychological interpretation (*Midland History*, no. 13 (1972), 43–4).

12 Hervé Le Bras, 'Parents, grands-parents, bisaieux', *Population*, XXVII (1973), 34.

13 See Peter Laslett, 'Parental Deprivation in the Past: A Note on the History of Orphans in England', *Local Population Studies*, no. 13 (1974), 11–18.

14 See SRO (B), N2/1/1 and N2/1/6.

15 [Varley], *Modern Farmer's Guide*, p. v; George Bourne, *Memoirs of a Surrey Labourer* (London: Duckworth, 1907), p. x; *idem*, *The Bettesworth Book: Talks with a Surrey Peasant* (London: Lamley, 1901), p. 19; Kitchen, *Brother to the Ox*, p. 18.

16 [Varley], *Modern Farmer's Guide*, p. 393.

17 Kitchen, *Brother to the Ox*, p. 91.

18 HRO, D/P 15/13/3, May 1782; HRO, D/P 7/13/1, Dec. 1795.

19 Macfarlane, *Family Life*, p. 209.
20 John Moore, *A Scripture-Word against Inclosure viz such as Doe Un-People Townes, and Un-Corne Fields* (London, 1656), p. 8.
21 Kitchen, *Brother to the Ox*, p. 74; LAO, Misc. Dep. 161. The lower the wage, the more likely it was to have been collected during the course of the year rather than at the end of the year.
22 [Varley], *Modern Farmer's Guide*, p. xvii.
23 Leics. RO, DE 432/3.
24 J. P. D. Dunbabin, 'The Incidence and Organization of Agricultural Trades Unionism in the 1870s', *Agri. HR*, XVI (1968), 122; Davies, *Agricultural History of Cheshire*, p. 91; Hoskins, *Essays in Leics. History*, p. 129; William M. Williams, *The Sociology of an English Village: Gosforth* (London: Routledge and Kegan Paul, 1956), p. 40.
25 See LAO, Belchford Settlement Examinations, November 1825, for an example of a carpenter's son who entered farm service at ten and returned home to learn the trade of carpentry at sixteen.
26 I am grateful to Tony Wrigley for the germ of this last speculation.
27 Ivy Pinchbeck and Margaret Hewitt, *Children in English Society*, 2 vols. (London: Routledge and Kegan Paul, 1969), vol. I, p. 26.
28 *Rural Economy of Midland Counties*, vol. I, p. 84.
29 William Fleetwood, *The Relative Duties of Parents and Children, Husbands and Wives, Masters and Servants* (London, 1705), p. 359.
30 Alan Macfarlane, *The Origins of English Individualism* (Oxford: Basil Blackwell, 1978), p. 76.
31 Assumption one is reasonable, for the survival of listings is unlikely to have been related to a tendency of a parish to import more servants and send away fewer of its own children. Assumption two is a rough compromise derived from the age-distribution of servants in the three listings noted at the beginning of the chapter. Assumption three is less arbitrary; it is derived from the monumental back-projection of the English population of the Cambridge Group. The range in the proportion that 15–24-year-olds represented between 1601 and 1811 was 16.3 per cent (1681) to 19.4 per cent (1601). Assumption four can only be posited, in the absence of firm estimates of differential rates of fertility between occupational groups.
32 Jenkins, *Agricultural Community*, pp. 77–8.
33 *Annals of Agriculture*, XXXVII (1801), 556; see also XXXII (1799), 85–98; XXXVI (1801), 202; XLI (1804), 434.
34 J. C. Loudon, *Encyclopaedia of Agriculture* (London: Longman, 1825), p. 728.
35 Googe, *Whole Art of Husbandry*, p. 10.
36 Northants RO, YZ 4912 (June 1797). Perhaps the married couple would be more footloose because their place of settlement was fixed forever; the settlement of a single servant was contingent upon the successful completion of a full year's service.
37 Very occasionally, people covertly returned to service after their marriage to establish settlements. Varley told the story of the couple who had

been reduced to this (*Modern Farmer's Guide*, p. xxvi). Essex Quarter Sessions debated the case of a married woman who had openly contracted to serve a master: they wondered whether a married woman could make a contract since 'her husband hath power to command her away as his wife'. See ERO, Q/S Ba 2/34; I am indebted to Keith Wrightson for having called my attention to this debate.

38 Source SE Coll., SRO (B). $Z = 2.77$, significant at 0.01 level.

39 For example, a pauper testified in 1826 that he had been born in Norfolk, served several farmers in the neighbourhood, and then had entered the militia. He was examined in Derbyshire. NRO, PD 17/37.

40 SE Coll., HRO, SRO (B), CRO, LAO, Leics. RO, Northants RO, NRO, ERO.

41 SE Coll., HRO, SRO (B), CRO, LAO, Leics. RO, Northants RO, NRO.

42 Tusser, *Five Hundred Pointes*, fol. 66. Cf. Leonore Davidoff, 'Mastered for Life: Servant and Wife in Victorian England', *J. Soc. Hist.*, VII (1974), 406–28.

43 Howitt, *Rural Life of England*, vol. I, p. 163.

44 See Kebble, *Agricultural Labourer*, p. 110; E. L. Jones, *Seasons and Prices: The Role of Weather in English Agricultural History* (London: Allen and Unwin, 1964); Yong Sam Cho, *'Disguised Unemployment' in Underdeveloped Areas with Special Reference to South Korean Agriculture* (Berkeley: University of California Press, 1963), pp. 84 and 147; Davies, *Agricultural History of Cheshire*, p. 81.

45 Minchinton, *Wage Regulation*, pp. 24–5. Even when the day rates covered labourers whose food and drink was provided, they work out at two to three times the annual wages.

46 William Pomeroy, *G. V. Worcs.* (London, 1794), p. 18.

47 Jenkins, *Agricultural Community*, pp. 77, 80.

48 Hasbach, *History*, p. 177.

49 Kebble, *Agri. Labourer*, p. 110.

50 Arthur Young, *The Farmer's Guide in Hiring and Stocking Farms*, 2 vols. (London, 1770), vol. I, p. 110; Young, *Farmer's Letters*, p. 60.

51 Young, *The Farmer's Guide*, pp. 110–25.

52 Davies, *Agricultural History of Cheshire*, p. 91.

53 Anon., *A Political Enquiry*, pp. 43–4; J. Howlett, *Enclosures: A Cause of Improved Agriculture* (London, 1789), p. 76.

54 William Pitt, *G. V. Stafford* (London, 1813), p. 219.

55 Young, *Farmer's Letters*, pp. 60, 72.

56 III (1800), 49.

57 LAO, Addlethorpe 13, 1811; Belchford 13, 1812.

58 pp. 43–4.

59 See HRO, D/P 13/13/3, Oct. 1749, and HRO, D/P 29/13/1, April 1779 for examples of servants becoming cottagers.

60 Hitt, *Treatise of Husbandry*, p. 61.

61 SRO (B), N2/1/1, Sept. 1759.

62 VI (1766), 145.

63 *Museum Rusticum et Commerciale*, VI (1766), 138. To have been 'celibate', in
    this usage, was to have been unmarried, not necessarily to have been
    chaste. See J. L. Flandrin's thorough discussion of the options open to
    celibates such as these in 'Mariage tardif et vie sexuelle', *Annales: ESC*,
    XXVII (1972), 1351–78.

64 Hitt, *Treatise of Husbandry*, p. 39; Arbuthnot, *Connection between the Present
    Price of Provisions and the Size of Farms*, pp. 26–8.

65 Howitt, *Rural Life of England*, vol. I, p. 163.

66 P. E. H. Hair has estimated that one-fifth of English brides who married
    between 1540 and 1700 were pregnant when they married, and two-fifths
    of those marrying from 1700 to the early-nineteenth century were. See P.
    E. H. Hair, 'Bridal Pregnancy in Rural England in Earlier Centuries',
    Population Studies, XX (1966), 240; *idem*, 'Bridal Pregnancy in Earlier Rural
    England Further Examined', *Population Studies*, XXIV (1970), 59–70.
    Neither Hair nor Laslett and Oosterveen considers the possibility that
    youths delayed marriage until the woman became pregnant, nor the effect
    that annual contracts might have on the relative timing of pregnancy and
    marriage. See Peter Laslett and Karla Oosterveen, 'Long-Term Trends in
    Bastardy in England', *Population Studies*, XXVII (1973), 269–70.

67 CG, Parish Listings Collection, Essex.

68 The number of lodgers in preindustrial households is difficult to know.
    Many listings contain no lodgers, but this may well have been because list-
    makers excluded lodgers from their consideration. See Peter Laslett,
    'Mean Household Size', p. 134.

69 John R. Gillis, *Youth and History: Tradition and Change in European Age-
    Relations, 1770–present* (New York: Academic Press, 1974), pp. 47–8.

70 Macfarlane, *Family Life*, p. 94.

71 Arthur Young, *Northern Tour*, vol. IV, p. 396; *Southern Tour*, pp. 316–
    17.

72 Joseph Mayett's memoirs are in pencil manuscript in the Bucks. RO (D/x
    371).

6.   Cycles: 1540–1790

1 See Appendix 7 for a necessarily speculative consideration of farm service
   in medieval England.

2 The calculation of marriage seasonality on such a large scale and in such
   detail is possible only because of the massive file of counts of baptisms,
   marriages, and burials, by parish, and by months within each year,
   compiled by the Cambridge Group, and because of the Group's generosity
   in welcoming me back to their archives, and their assistance in providing
   access to the machine-readable records. All the counts are derived from
   parish registers. The computer file from which the sample parishes were
   selected consists of 404 exceptionally continuous registers; the file forms a
   large part of the basis of Wrigley and Schofield's *Population History of
   England*. The sample chosen for the October index consists of a subset of

fifty-six parishes meeting two criteria: all are in the ten counties of Hampshire, Oxfordshire, Buckinghamshire, Berkshire, Hertfordshire, Bedfordshire, Cambridgeshire, Norfolk, Suffolk, and Essex, and each parish was predominantly agricultural in 1831, in that in the census of that year, at least twice as many families in each parish were employed in agriculture as in trades and crafts.

3 Dorothy McLaren, 'The Marriage Act of 1653: Its Influence on Parish Registers', *Population Studies*, XXVIII (1974), 319–27.

4 See Wrigley and Schofield, *Population History of England*, Tables 7.8 and A.3.1.

5 I am grateful to David Souden for having suggested to me the potential importance of changes in age composition and the number of youths.

6 See Macfarlane, *Origins of English Individualism*, pp. 87–8.

7 E. A. Wrigley, 'A Simple Model of London's Importance in Changing English Society and Economy, 1650–1750', *Past and Present*, no. 37 (1967), 44–70.

8 Nourse, *Campania Foelix*, p. 213.

9 *Ibid.*, p. 211; N. L. Tranter, ed. *Population and Industrialization* (London: Black, 1973), p. 56.

10 The cost of living series is taken from E. H. Phelps Brown and Sheila V. Hopkins, 'Seven Centuries of the Prices of Consumables, Compared with Builders' Wage Rates', in E. M. Carus-Wilson, ed., *Essays in Economic History*, vol. II (London: Edward Arnold, 1962), pp. 179–96.

11 Marshall, *Minutes*, 6 June 1776.

12 Fussell, *Robert Loder's Farm Accounts*, pp. 68 and 72.

13 Jan De Vries, *The Economy of Europe in an Age of Crisis* (Cambridge: University Press, 1976), pp. 176–80.

14 The index patches Bowden's estimates of the relative prices of animal products and grain, 1450–1649 (Peter Bowden, 'Agricultural Prices, Farm Profits, and Rents', in Thirsk, *The Agrarian History of England and Wales*, vol. IV, pp. 815–21, 839–45), onto an index of the relative prices of wheat (Exeter College, from B. R. Mitchell and Phyllis Deane, *Abstract of British Historical Statistics* (Cambridge: University Press, 1971), pp. 486–7 and average prices of British corn, *ibid.*, p. 488) and beef (mean prices at King's College, from Rogers, *History of Agriculture*, vol. V, and at Winchester, Westminster, and Charterhouse, from William Beveridge, *Prices and Wages in England from the Twelfth to the Nineteenth Century* (London: Longmans Green, 1939)), corrected for varying measures of the weight of beef. The moving average was centred on the last year (the twentieth) to convey the impression of trends that a farmer of that year, who could only look to the past, might have had.

15 Joan Thirsk, 'The Farming Regions of England', in Thirsk, *The Agrarian History of England and Wales*, vol. IV, p. 4.

16 Joan Thirsk, 'Seventeenth-Century Agriculture and Social Change', *Agri. HR*, XVIII (1970), 155; *idem*, 'Enclosing and Engrossing', in Thirsk, *The Agrarian History of England and Wales*, vol. IV, pp. 248–9.

17 Joan Thirsk, 'Farming Techniques', in Thirsk, *The Agrarian History of England and Wales*, vol. IV, p. 196.

18 The evidence of new techniques presented by Eric Kerridge in *The Agricultural Revolution* and by Joan Thirsk in *Economic Policy and Projects* (London: Oxford University Press, 1978) documents the existence of novelty, but not its incidence relative to the persistence of old practices.

19 E. L. Jones, 'Agriculture and Economic Growth in England, 1660–1750: Agricultural Change', *JEH*, XXV (1965), 1–18.

20 Chambers and Mingay, *The Agricultural Revolution*, pp. 59–61; Kerridge, *The Agricultural Revolution*, pp. 219–20.

21 See Jones, 'Agriculture and Economic Growth'.

22 E. L. Jones, 'Agricultural Origins of Industry', *Past and Present*, no. 40 (1968), 58–71.

23 For an analysis of Willingham in the sixteenth and seventeenth centuries see Margaret Spufford, *Contrasting Communities: English Villagers in the Sixteenth and Seventeenth Centuries* (Cambridge: University Press, 1974), pp. 121–64.

24 David Levine, *Family Formation in an Age of Nascent Capitalism* (New York: Academic Press, 1977), p. 47.

25 *Ibid.*, pp. 116–26.

26 Habakkuk, *Population Growth*, pp. 37–8.

27 The new real wage series, a revision of the Phelps Brown and Hopkins series, appears in Wrigley and Schofield, *Population History of England*, Table A. 9.2.

28 In *Population History of England*, Wrigley and Schofield argue that movements in real wages were the major determinants of family formation and population growth in the English past.

29 A. W. Coats, 'Changing Attitudes to Labour in the Mid-Eighteenth Century', *EcHR*, 2nd ser., XI (1958), 35–51.

30 See Arthur Redford, *Labour Migration in England, 1800–1850*, 2nd edn, rev. by W. H. Chaloner (1926; Manchester: University Press, 1964), p. 77; J. T. Krause, 'Some Neglected Factors in the English Industrial Revolution', *JEH*, XIX (1959), 537; Habakkuk, *Population Growth*, pp. 38–9; Chambers, *Population, Economy, and Society*, p. 3.

31 'An Essay on the Proper Size of Farms', *Farmer's Magazine* (Edinburgh), I (1800), 380–1.

32 *Northern Tour*, vol. IV, pp. 402–3.

33 Arbitrarily defined as districts in which 50 per cent or more of the male labourers were identified as agricultural labourers.

34 The proportion never married is the only proxy available from the 1851 census for age at marriage. It is a weak measure in that it encompasses the effect both of age at marriage and the numbers who never marry, but it is a good proxy in relation to farm service because service was a niche both for those who married late and those who never married.

35 Males: $p_m = 0.257 + 0.204x$; $r = 0.5060$; $F_{1,37} = 12.93$. Females: $p_m = 0.238 +$

$0.139x$; $r = 0.5645$; $F_{1,37} = 16.84$ (where p_m = proportion of married males, females twenty and older in the populations of predominantly agricultural registration districts). Both F-values are significant at the 0.01 level.

36 Krause, 'Neglected Factors', p. 113; *idem*, 'English Population Movements between 1700 and 1850', in M. Drake, ed., *Population in Industrialization* (London: Methuen, 1969), pp. 118–27. Habakkuk calculated that a decline of less than two years in the mean age at first marriage of women could have produced an increase in the annual rate of population increase of 0.5 per cent (*Population Growth*, pp. 38–9).

37 K. F. Helleiner, 'The Vital Revolution Reconsidered', in D. V. Glass and D. E. C. Eversley, eds., *Population and History* (London: Arnold, 1965), pp. 79–86, first published in *CJEPS*, XXIII (1957); *idem*, 'The Population of Europe from the Black Death to the Eve of the Vital Revolution', in E. E. Rich and C. H. Wilson, eds., *The Cambridge Economic History of Europe*, vol. IV, (Cambridge: University Press, 1967), pp. 92–3; P. E. Razzell, 'Population Change in Eighteenth-Century England', in Drake, *Population in Industrialization*, pp. 128–56, first published in *EcHR*, XVIII (1965); D. E. C. Eversley, 'General Discussion', in F. C. Bechhofer, ed., *Population Growth and the Brain Drain* (Edinburgh: University Press, 1969), p. 230; Andrew B. Appleby, 'Disease or Famine? Mortality in Cumberland and Westmorland, 1580–1640', *EcHR*, XXVI (1973), 403–31; Gordon Philpot, 'Enclosure and Population Growth in Eighteenth-Century England', *EEH*, XII (1975), 29–46.

38 E. A. Wrigley 'Family Limitation in Pre-Industrial England', in Drake, *Population in Industrialization*, pp. 156–94, reprinted from *EcHR*, XIX (1966); G. S. L. Tucker, 'English Pre-Industrial Population Trends', *EcHR*, XVI (1963), 205–18; Wrigley and Schofield, *Population History of England*.

39 A marked decline in the hiring of either male or female servants could have caused the fall in the age at marriage of women, the proposed cause of population increase. The effect of a decreased hiring of female servants would have been direct. If males were suddenly to begin marrying earlier, they would have had to marry either members of the same cohort they would eventually have married, or women who would have married still later, or married not at all. From whichever group marriage partners were chosen, the age at marriage of women or the proportion unmarried would have declined, contributing to the population increase.

40 Phyllis Deane and W. A. Cole, *British Economic Growth 1688–1959: Trends and Structure*, 2nd edn (Cambridge: University Press, 1967), p. 119; Levine, *Family Formation*, chs. 5 and 6. See also Habakkuk, *Population Growth*, p. 44; Krause, 'English Population Movements', pp. 123–6; R. Braun, 'The Impact of Cottage Industry on an Agricultural Population', in D. S. Landes, ed., *The Rise of Capitalism* (New York: Macmillan, 1966), pp. 53–64; W. Fischer, 'Rural Industrialization and Population Change', *Comparative Studies in Society and History*, XV (1973), 158–70.

41 Hajnal, 'European Marriage Patterns', p. 132; Habakkuk, *Population Growth*, pp. 11–12.

42 J. D. Chambers, 'Enclosure and the Labour Supply in .the Industrial Revolution', *EcHR*, 2nd ser. V (1953), 319–43; Chambers and Mingay, *The Agricultural Revolution*, pp. 98–100; Thirsk, *Economic Policy and Projects*, pp. 158–9. A correspondent to *Annals of Agriculture* noted in 1792 that labour requirements at the taking up of a lease by an improving farmer were 50 per cent higher than they were after the improvements had been undertaken (XVII, 567). See also Blith, *The English Improver*.

43 J. A. Yelling, *Common Field and Enclosure in England, 1450–1850* (London: Macmillan, 1977). Champions of enclosure often wrote of the beneficial effect that hedging would have on the employment of the poor. See Board of Agriculture, *Report of the Committee Appointed by the Board of Agriculture to Take into Consideration the State of Waste Lands and Common Fields of this Kingdom* (London, 1795), p. 5; Joseph Lee, *A Vindication of Regulated Enclosure* (London, 1656), p. 4; Moore, *Bread for the Poor*, p. 30.

44 Timmer, 'The Turnip, the New Husbandry, and the English Agricultural Revolution', p. 394; Jones, *Seasons and Prices*, p. 60; Pinchbeck, *Women Workers*, p. 39.

45 G. E. Mingay, 'The Size of Farms in the Eighteenth Century', *EcHR*, XIV (1962), 469; Arthur H. Johnson, *The Disappearance of the Small Landowner* (Oxford: Clarendon, 1909), p. 147. In the parish listings discussed in Chapter 2, the mean ratio of workers to farmers increases from 2.8 in 1694–1705 to 4.4 in 1776–1801 in southern and eastern counties.

46 Barley, *English Farmhouse and Cottage*, pp. 159, 220, 248; *idem*, 'Rural Housing in England', in Thirsk, *The Agrarian History of England and Wales*, vol. IV, p. 741.

47 *Commercial and Agricultural Magazine*, III (1800), 182; Marshall, *Minutes*, 6 June 1776.

48 Fussell, *Robert Loder's Farm Accounts*, pp. 72, 87.

49 *Annals of Agriculture*, IV (1785), 174.

50 HFR, Reading: KEN 19/1/1, Account Book of Forestall Farm, Burmarsh, Kent (October 1769).

51 *Collection of Letters for the Improvement of Husbandry and Trade*, 2 vols. (London, 1681–3).

52 *Farmer's Magazine* (London), I (1776), 268.

53 Marshall, *Minutes*, 6 June 1776; Young, *Northern Tour*, vol. III, pp. 6, 369, 377, 393; *idem*, *The Farmer's Guide*, p. 70; *Commercial and Agricultural Magazine*, III (1800), 182; John Trusler, *The Way to be Rich and Respectable, Addressed to Men of Small Fortune* (London, [1775]), p. 44n.

54 Markham, *Farewell to Husbandry*, pp. 144–6. See also Anon., *Boke of Thrift* in Cripps-Day, *The Manor Farm*, pp. 2–3.

55 Pehr Kalm, *An Account of His Visit to England* (1753), trans. Joseph Lucas (London: Macmillan, 1892), p. 173.

7. Extinction

1 John Wilkinson, 'The Farming of Hampshire', *Journal of the Royal Agricultural Society*, XXII (1861), 368.

2 'Country Life', *Punch*, 18 Nov. 1973.

3 The likelihood of a lagged response to what we can now recognize as cyclical turning points is great. In the 1770s, Arthur Young was urging the consolidation of farms to promote population growth, as if population growth were not already, as we know, well under way. *Northern Tour*, vol. IV, pp. 402–3.

4 Thomas Stone, *Suggestions for Rendering the Inclosure of Common Fields and Waste Lands a Source of Population and Riches* (London, 1787), pp. 29–30.

5 The tendency towards larger farms had become strong enough by 1800 to evoke the law-like judgement of the *Commercial and Agricultural Magazine* that 'farms are constantly consolidating, never dividing, in an improving country'. III, 48.

6 Young, *Farmer's Letters*, pp. 75–6. John Arbuthnot assumed a large farmer would hire both labourers and servants, while small farmers would hire only servants. *Connection between the Present Price of Provisions and the Size of Farms*, pp. 26–7.

7 Thomas Robertson simply found servants to be an 'alien element in the economy of the large farm'. *Outline of the General Report upon the Size of Farms* (Edinburgh, 1796), p. 43. See also Young, *Farmer's Letters*, pp. 68–9; *idem, Northern Tour*, vol. IV, p. 403; Marshall, *Minutes*, 6 June 1776.

8 Chambers, 'Enclosure and the Labour Supply', 336. My 'incumbrance' is Chambers' memorable 'thin and squalid curtain'.

9 William Mavor, *G. V. Berks.* (London, 1808), pp. 416–17.

10 David Grigg, 'Small and Large Farms in England and Wales: Their Size and Distribution', *Geography*, XLVIII (1963), 277–8; Robertson, *Outline of the General Report upon the Size of Farms*, pp. 26–7.

11 The difference in the ratios of wages for servants and labourers between the industrializing north and agricultural south reflects the greater need for servants in the agrarian economy of the north. The 1793–5 series of Board of Agriculture county reports yields a ratio of mean annual wages for male servants to mean winter weekly wages for day-labourers (both expressed in shillings) of 14.4 in the north and west (Cheshire, Cumberland, Derbyshire, Devon, Durham, Gloucestershire, Herefordshire, Lincolnshire, Northumberland, Nottinghamshire, Shropshire, Staffordshire, Warwickshire, Westmorland, Worcestershire, Yorkshire, East and North Ridings) and only 10.4 in the south and east (Berkshire, Buckinghamshire, Cambridgeshire, Essex, Hampshire, Hertfordshire, Huntingdonshire, Kent, Leicestershire, Middlesex, Norfolk, Northamptonshire, Rutland, Somerset, Suffolk, Surrey, Sussex, Wiltshire). The ratios of mean annual wages of male servants to mean weekly wages in the hay harvest are 10.8 in the north and west and 8.4 in the south and east.

12   R. I. Hodgson, 'The Progress of Enclosure in County Durham, 1550–1870', in H. S. A. Fox and R. A. Butlin, eds., *Change in the Countryside: Essays on Rural England, 1500–1900* (London: Institute of British Geographers, 1979), pp. 95–6; E. L. Jones, 'The Arable Depression after the Napoleonic Wars and the Agricultural Development of the Hampshire Chalklands', BA Diss., University of Nottingham, 1958, p. v.

13   Stuart Macdonald, 'The Role of the Individual in Agricultural Change: the Example of George Culley of Fenton, Northumberland', in Fox and Butlin, *Change in the Countryside*, p. 12.

14   William Marshall, *Review and Abstract of the County Reports to the Board of Agriculture*, 4 vols. (York, 1818), vol. IV, p. 589; Pitt, *GV Stafford*, pp. 217–18; John Middleton, *GV Middlesex* (London, 1813), p. 509; Stevenson, *GV Surrey*, p. 545; R. W. Dickson, *GV Lancs.* (London, 1815), p. 598.

15   See note 11 for the sample from which the wages were drawn. The method of computation of the wage increases was to work out the compound annual rates of increase for each county between the dates of its first and second reports, and then calculate the mean of all county annual rates. The wages used were weekly wages, out of harvest, and annual wages for the best male servant. The cost of living series was drawn from Phelps Brown and Hopkins, 'Seven Centuries'.

16   See Chapter 5, p. 90.

17   Mark Neuman, 'Speenhamland in Berkshire', in E. W. Martin, ed., *Comparative Development in Social Welfare* (London: Allen and Unwin, 1972), pp. 85–127; Mark Blaug, 'The Myth of the Old Poor Law and the Making of the New', *JEH*, XXIII (1963), 151–84.

18   'From a Country Clergyman', *Annals of Agriculture*, XXXVII (1801), 103.

19   These actions had their parallel in the system of 'open' and 'closed' parishes, attempts to prevent actual, as opposed to legal, settlement.

20   See, for example, an agreement of sixteen farmers in Bampton, Oxfordshire, to hire none but 'certificate' labour in 1741. Bodleian, Bampton MSS DD Par. 16.

21   BRO, T46/6, pp. 53ff. I am indebted to David Souden for having provided me with this information.

22   Bucks. RO, D/x 371.

23   Stuart Macdonald, 'The Progress of the Early Threshing Machine', *Agri. HR*, XXIII (1975), 53ff; N. E. Fox, 'The Spread of the Threshing Machine in Central Southern England', *Agri. HR*, XXXVI (1978), 26–8; Macdonald, 'Rejoinder', *Agri. HR*, XXXVI (1978), 29–32.

24   Board of Agriculture, *Communications to the Board of Agriculture* (London, 1797), vol. I, plate xxiii.

25   James Donaldson, *GV Northants* (Edinburgh, 1794), p. 11; Arthur Young, *GV Norfolk* (London, 1804), p. 484; *idem, GV Essex*, 2 vols. (London, 1807), vol. II, p. 373; Banister, *Synopsis of Husbandry*, reprinted in *Commercial and Agricultural Magazine*, III (1801), 190.

26   Thomas Rudge's absolute minima were a man and a boy for every five horses, and two women for every twenty-five cows. *GV Gloucs.* (London,

1813), p. 329. See also Donaldson, *GV Northants*, p. 11; John Boys, *GV Kent* (Brentford, 1794), p. 25; George Rennie *et al.*, *GV West Riding* (London, 1794), p. 25.

27 The increase can be observed in both the Tetney, Lincolnshire, account books (LAO, Misc. Dep. 161) and in those from Radley, Berkshire (HFR, Reading: BER/13.5.1). In addition, the Tetney books show a marked break in the pattern of hirings after 1802. Before that date, the household had always contained at least one adult male and a lad; from 1803 to 1816, however, only one male servant, either a man or lad, was hired, and after 1816, only lads.

28 James Malcolm, *GV Surrey*, 3 vols. (London, 1805), vol. I, p. 181; Middleton, *GV Middlesex*, p. 509. Pinchbeck noted that the wives of farmers were often blamed for the detachment. *Women Workers*, p. 33.

29 Middleton, *GV Middlesex*, p. 510.

30 See Hobsbawm and Rudé, *Captain Swing*, ch. 4, for an excellent discussion of the period and its effects upon relations between workers and masters.

31 Blaug, 'The Myth of the Old Poor Law'.

32 Keith Snell, 'The Standard of Living, Social Relations, the Family, and Labour Mobility in South-Eastern and Western Counties, 1700–1860', unpublished PhD thesis, Cambridge University, 1980, pp. 55–8.

33 Marshall, *Review and Abstract*, p. 588; Mavor, *GV Berks.*, p. 416; Arthur Young, *GV Sussex* (1813; Newton Abbot: David and Charles, 1970), p. 404; Middleton, *GV Middlesex*, p. 496; Strickland, *GV East Riding*, p. 260.

34 Select Committee on the Depressed State of Agriculture, PP 1822, V, 401, 49, 122; Select Committee on Agriculture, PP 1833, V, 48, 117, 195, 246, 308, 326, 440, 456, 483, 573.

35 PP 1833, V, 440.

36 Blaug, 'The Myth of the Old Poor Law'. The measure of correlation used was the Spearman rank correlation; $r_s = 0.762$, which, with $(41-2)$ degrees of freedom, shows significant correlation between the two ranks with the infinitesimal error of 7.26×10^{-9}.

37 PP 1834, XXXIII, Appendix B, Part IV.

38 A Rutland correspondent noted that servants were hired for fifty-one weeks, but 'continue in the same service under different hirings'.

39 Some respondents gave a variety of explanations for the decline; in Table 7.1 each explanation was counted separately.

40 LAO, Holland QS D3.

41 See Snell, 'The Standard of Living', pp. 67–9.

42 Howitt, *The Rural Life of England*, vol. I, pp. 149–51.

43 Because the figures given for each district included only males twenty and over, they underestimate the true relative weight of servants by excluding both women and male servants under twenty.

44 That threshing machines were more common in the high-wage north than in the south has been observed by Macdonald ('The Progress of the Early Threshing Machine'); he noted a remark by Culley in 1801 that one

advantage of them was that grain could be 'thrashed by the ordinary servants on the farm' (p. 71).

45 E. H. Hunt, *Regional Wage Variations in Britain, 1850–1914* (Oxford: Clarendon, 1973).

46 PP 1834, XXXIII, Appendix B, Part IV, Byfield, Northants.

47 Kent, in every record from Board of Agriculture reports, Parliamentary reports, the Poor Law Report, to the 1851 census, is clearly divided between regions where few servants were hired and those where few labourers were.

48 Dunbabin, 'Agricultural Trades Unionism', pp. 123–4.

49 Kebble, *Agri. Labourer*, pp. 106–7.

50 Williams, *Gosforth*, pp. 37–40.

Appendix 1   'Servants' and 'labourers' in early modern English

1 Nourse, *Campania Foelix*, p. 203.

2 Macpherson, *Possessive Individualism*, pp. 279–92; Peter Laslett, 'Market Society and Political Theory', *Historical Journal*, VII (1964) 150–4; Macpherson, *Democratic Theory*, pp. 207–23.

Appendix 2   Age and sex

1 Cho, '*Disguised Unemployment*'; S. S. Gill, 'Unemployment and Underemployment of Permanent Farm Workers', *Artha Vijñāna*, II (1960), 249–61.

2 Derbyshire, 1634, in J. Charles Cox, *Three Centuries of Derbyshire Annals*, 3 vols. (London: Bemrose, 1890), vol. II, pp. 239–40; Devonshire, 1566, in Hughes and Larkin, *Tudor Royal Proclamations*, vol. II, pp. 283–5 (hereafter cited as H & L); Devonshire, 1588, in H & L, III, 18–19; Devonshire, 1595, in H & L, III, 150–1; Essex, 1583, in H & L, II, 499–500; Kent, 1563, in H & L, II, 215–18; Kent, 1565, in H & L, II, 265–70; Kent, 1576, in H & L, II, 405–7; Kent, 1589, in H & L, III, 36–8; Kent, 1724, in Waterman, 'Some New Evidence on Wage Assessments', 405–8; Lancashire, 1595, in H & L, III, 149–50; Lincolnshire, 1563, in H & L, II, 221–3; Lincolnshire, 1563, in H & L, II, 225–7; New Sarum, 1595, in H & L, III, 147–8; New Windsor, 1563, in H & L, II, 219–20; Nottinghamshire, 1723, in Meaby, *Nottinghamshire*, p. 232; Rutland, 1563, in H & L, II, 212–14; Shropshire, 1732, in *Orders of the Shropshire Quarter Sessions*, R. L. Kenyon, ed., Shropshire County Records, 4 vols. (1901–13), II, 79; Staffordshire, 1606, in *Quarter Sessions*, Historical Collections of Staffordshire, pp. 324–6; Suffolk, 1630, in Cambridge UL, Add. Ms. 22, no. 76, fol. 72–4; Suffolk, 1682, in Rogers, *History of Agriculture*, vol. VI, pp. 698–9; Wiltshire, 1603, in HMC, *Various*, I, 162–6; Wiltshire, 1655 and 1685, in B. H. Cunningham, ed., *Records of the County of Wiltshire* (Devizes: Simpson, 1932), pp. 290–6; Yorkshire, 1563, in H & L, II, 223–24; Yorkshire, 1570, in H & L, II, 337–9; Yorkshire, 1593, in Rogers,

History of Agriculture, vol. VI, 686–9; Yorkshire, 1658, in *Quarter Sessions Records*, North Riding Record Society, VI (1888), 3–5; Yorkshire, 1703, in Rogers, *History of Agriculture*, vol. VII, pp. 610–14.

3 Cho, *'Disguised Unemployment'*, pp. 70–1; Gill, 'Unemployment and Under-employment', p. 251.

Appendix 3 Legal control of mobility

1 23 Hen. VI, c. 12.
2 *Notes and Extracts*, 4 (1590–1); County of Buckingham, *Calendar to the Sessions Records*, I (1933), 151 and 159 (1684); *Quarter Sessions Records*, North Riding Record Society, I (1884), 2, 33, 37–8, 41, 59 (1605–1606/7); *West Riding Sessions Records, 1611 to 1642*, J. Lister, ed., Yorkshire Archaeological Society. Record Series, LIV (1915), 218 (1640); ERO; Calendar of Records, Quarter Sessions, II, 100 (1566).
3 ERO, D/P 135/1/1.
4 *Calendar of State Papers, Domestic*, Charles I, 27 January 1637–8, p. 193.
5 [Tancred], *A Scheme for an Act of Parliament*, p. 15.
6 Roger Thompson, *Women in Stuart England and America* (London: Routledge and Kegan Paul, 1974), p. 64.
7 14 Car. II, c. 12.

Appendix 5 The Holland, Lincolnshire, Statute Sessions

1 LAO, Holland Quarter Sessions Minutes, January 1777.
2 David Grigg, *The Agricultural Revolution in South Lincolnshire* (Cambridge: University Press, 1966), pp. 30–1.
3 *Ibid*. p. 32.

Appendix 6 Compulsory service

1 Hampson, *Treatment of Poverty*, p. 55.
2 ERO, Calendar to Records, Quarter Sessions, I, 51; II, 101, 103, 222; III, 44, 46, 55; IV, 105, 151, 179, 186.
3 Bucks., 1685, 1687, 1689–90: County of Buckingham, *Calendar to the Sessions Records, 1678–1694*, pp. 176–7, 234, 322, 336; Herts., 1675: *Notes and Extracts*, p. 254; N. Riding, 1605–6, 1611, 1670: *Quarter Sessions Records*, North Riding Record Society, I (1884), 27, 220 and VI (1880); West Riding, 1641: *West Riding Sessions Records*, pp. 11, 333.
4 HMC, *Various*, I (1901), 132.
5 14 Eliz. I, c. 5.

Appendix 7 Speculations on the origin of the institution

1 M. M. Postan mentioned the likelihood that some wage-workers on demesne lands boarded and lodged with lords, but thought them to have

been far less common than smallholding *famuli* (Postan, *The Famulus*, p. 14). Raftis found many references to servants (*serviens, ancilla, manupastus, homo, garcon, famulus*) of tenants in the Court Rolls of Ramsey Abbey in the late thirteenth and early fourteenth centuries (J. A. Raftis, 'Social Structures in Five East Midland Villages', *EcHR*, XVIII (1965), 97–8). Servants of tenants also are recorded in the charters of Peterborough Abbey (C. N. L. Brooke and M. M. Postan, eds., *Carte Nativorum: A Peterborough Abbey Cartulary of the Fourteenth Century*, Northamptonshire Record Society, XX (1960), xl). The cartulary is thought to date from c. 1340.

2   Harry A. Miskimin, *The Economy of Early Renaissance Europe, 1300–1460* (Englewood Cliffs, NJ: Prentice-Hall, 1969), pp. 32–3.

Bibliography

Manuscripts

Bedfordshire Record Office
  Settlement examinations
    Ampthill parish records, 1741–99
    DDP 1/13/4 Bedford St Paul's, 1743–92
    P 35/13/4 Caddington, 1829–32
    P 5/13/4 Eaton Socon, 1764–1819
    Henlow parish records, 1816
    T46/6 pp. 53ff. Lease requiring the hiring of no servants
    QSR 5 1738/36. Quarter Sessions
Berkshire Record Office
  Settlement examinations
    D/P 35/13/1 Brightwell, 1741–85
    D/P 34/13/3 Chieveley, 1816–28
    D/P 48/13/1 Drayton, 1732–1800
    D/P 110/13/1 Shinfield, 1703–1819
    D/P 115/13/3 Sparsholt, 1787
    D/P 128/13/4 Sutton Courtenay, 1768–1813
    D/P 130/13/1 Thatcham, 1764–1836
    D/P 132/13/4 Tilehurst, 1744–99
    D/P 143/13/5 Wantage, 1723–69
Bodleian Library, Oxford
  Settlement examinations, MSS DD
    Adderbury, 1743
    Brampton, 1739–69
    Claydon, 1752
    Garsington, 1705–67
    Lewknor, 1705–98
    Oxford St Clements, 1766–86
    Oxford St Giles, 1774–94
    Oxford St Peters in the East, 1715–70
    Rotherfield Greys, 1750–99
    Stanton Harcourt, 1740–90
  Bampton MSS par. 16. Farmers' agreement to hire no servants
British Library
  Stowe MSS 805, 806. Bucks. Posse Comitatus
Buckinghamshire Record Office
  Settlement examinations

PR 36/13/6 Chalfont St Peter, 1800–23
PR 44/13/200–37 Chesham, 1702–39
PR 51/16/1 East Claydon, 1740–1809
PR 71/13/106/111 Emberton, 1735–88
PR 115/13/4 Iver, 1800–9
PR 159/13/121 Olney, 1713–86
PR 169/13/2 Quainton, 1711–1815
PR 174/13/37–41 Ravenstoke, 1761–90
PR 223/13/31–7 Westbury, 1700–80
D/x 371. Manuscript memoir of Joseph Mayett
Cambridge Group for the History of Population and Social Structure
Parish Listings Collection
  Melbourn, Cambs., 1831
  Barlborough, Cambs., 1792
  Littleover, Derbys., 1811
  Mickleover, Derbys., 1811
  Smalley, Derbys., 1801
  Corfe Castle, Dorset, 1790
  Melbury Osmond, Dorset, 1800
  Sturminster Newton, Dorset, 1801
  Ardleigh, Essex, 1796
  fforthampton and Swinley, Gloucs., 1752
  Barkway and Reed, Herts., 1801
  Adisham, Kent, 1705
  Ash (Chilton), Kent, 1705
  Ash (Overland), Kent, 1705
  Stadmarsh, Kent, 1705
  Carlton Rode, Norfolk, 1777
  Ealing, Middlesex, 1599
  Clayworth, Notts., 1674
  Clayworth, Notts., 1688
  Askham, Westmorland, 1787
  Hutton Roof, Westmorland, 1695
  Killington, Westmorland, 1695
  Kirkby Lonsdale, Westmorland, 1695
  Bampton, Westmorland, 1787
  Barton, Westmorland, 1787
  Bragill, Westmorland, 1787
  Birkbeckfells, Westmorland, 1787
  Crosby Ravensworth, Westmorland, 1787
  Colby, Westmorland, 1787
  Clifton, Westmorland, 1787
  Cliburn, Westmorland, 1787
  Burton, Westmorland, 1787
  Brougham, Westmorland, 1787
  Morland, Westmorland, 1787
  Milburn Grange, Westmorland, 1787

Milburn, Westmorland, 1787
Lowther, Westmorland, 1787
Lowther (Huckthorpe and Whale), Westmorland, 1787
Longmarton, Westmorland, 1787
King's Meaburn, Westmorland, 1787
Kaber, Westmorland, 1787
Dutton, Westmorland, 1787
Knock, Westmorland, 1787
Murton, Westmorland, 1787
Newbiggen, Westmorland, 1787
Newby, Westmorland, 1787
Rosgill and Iledale, Westmorland, 1787
Stainmore, Westmorland, 1787
Great Strickland, Westmorland, 1787
Temple Sowerby, Westmorland, 1787
Thrimby, Westmorland, 1787
Cambridgeshire Record Office
Settlement examinations
P/7/13/2 Burrough Green, 1764–1822
P/24/13/3 Cambridge St Andrew, 1725–91
P/25/13/4 Cambridge St Benet, 1753–1835
P/27/13/31/6 Chippenham, 1797–9
P/135/13/4 Royston, 1750–87
Cambridge University Library
Add. Ms. 22, no. 76, fol. 72–4, Suffolk Quarter Sessions Assessment, 1630
Bishop's Transcript of Hardwick Parish Registers
Cheshire Record Office
Settlement examinations
Audlem, Chester St Mary, Church Hulme, Handforth, Little Budworth,
Lymm, Macclesfield Forest, Middlewich, Partington, Preston on the
Hill, Tattenhall, Warburton
Dorset Record Office
Settlement examinations
Beaminster, Bere Regis, Blandford Forum, Bradford Abbas, Broadwey,
Buckland Newton, Canford Magna, Castleton, Cerne Abbas, Charlton
Marshall, Corfe Castle, Corscombe, Folke, Fontmell Magna,
Fordington, Hammoon, Hilton, Holwell, Kington Magna, Leigh,
Lillington, West Lulworth, Lydlinch, Milton Abbas, Mosterton,
Motcombe, West Orchard, Pimperne, Powerstock, Puddletown,
Sherbourne, Shipton Gorge, Stoke Abbott, Sydling St Nicholas,
Thornford, Wimborne Minster, Winterbourne Kingston, Wootton
Glanville, Wyke Regis
East Riding Record Office
Settlement examinations
DDBD/5/133 Beverley, 1799–1836
PR 662 Beverley, 1824–35
PR 500 Beverley, 1790–2

PR 708 Seaton Ross, 1786–1834
Essex Record Office
Settlement examinations
　　D/P 18/13/4 Ashdon, 1726–1807
　　D/P 80/13/4 Little Clacton, 1723–1803
　　D/P 134/13/4 Kelvedon, 1740–1801
　　D/P 21/13/4 Steeple Bumpstead, 1745–1809
　　D/P 8/13/4 Thorpe le Soken, 1764–82
Calendar of Records, Quarter Sessions, vols. IV–VIII (typescript), 1572–8
D/P 135/1/1. Register for servants departing from Heydon Parish,
　　1563–85
Q/AA 1. Assessment of wages, 1612
Q/S Ba 2/34. Question of power of married woman to make a contract
Gloucestershire Record Office
Settlement examinations
　　Avening, Badgeworth, Bibury, Bishop's Cleeve, Bisley, Blockley, South
　　Cerney, Charfield, Charlton Kings, Chedworth, Chipping Camden,
　　Coln Rogers, Coln St Denis, Deerhurst, Duntisborne Abbots, Dymock,
　　Hawkesbury, Kempsford, Kingswood, Mickleton, Mitcheldean, Moreton
　　Valence, Newnham, North Nibley, Painswick, Rodborough, Saintbury,
　　Upper Slaughter, Slimbridge, Stinchcombe, Stonehouse, Tetbury,
　　Welford, Wickwar, Woolaston
Hampshire Record Office
Settlement examinations
　　3M70/53 Basingstoke, 1709–1818
　　4M70/12 Eling, 1733–66
　　19M76 Kingsclere, 1718–1821
Herefordshire Record Office
Settlement examinations
　　Aymestrey, Bodenham, Eye, Kingsland, Lyonshall, Mathon, Ocle
　　Pitchard, Orcop, Peterstow, Stoke Edith, Titley, Yarpole
QSO/1 A, fols. 27B, 28A. Assessment, 1665
Hertfordshire Record Office
Settlement examinations
　　D/P 3/16/1 Aldenham, 1754–93
　　D/P 4/13/2 Great Amwell, 1779–1823
　　D/P 7/13/1 Ashwell, 1835
　　D/P 8/13/1 Aspenden, 1789–1827
　　D/P 13/13/3 Barkway, 1737–99
　　D/P 29/13/1–5 Cheshunt, 1750–96
　　D/P 15/13/3 Chipping Barnet, 1767–85
　　D/P 15/18/1 Chipping Barnet, 1717–1805
　　D/P 55/13/1 Great Hormead, 1800–18
　　D/P 107/13/2 Therfield, 1784–94
D/P 87/8/1. Announcement of available parish apprentices, Royston, 1786
Militia List Collection, 1758–96

Aldenham, Great Amwell, Anstey, Ardeley, Aston, Barkway, Barley, Bayford, Bengeo, Bennington, Little Berkhamstead, Braughing, Buckland, Cottered, Datchworth, Eastwick, Essendon, Gilston, Much Hadham, Hertingfordbury, Hexton, Great Hormead, Hunsdon, Kimpton, Layston, Lilley, Great Munden, Little Munden, Pirton, Reed, Sacombe, Shephall, Standon, Stanstead St Abbot's, Stanstead St Margaret's, Stapleton, Tewin, Therfield, Thorley, Throcking, Stagenhoe, St Paul's Warden, Walkern, Watton, Westmill, Widford, Wyddial

18278. 'Labourers' Book' of Beechwood Farm, 1774

Historical Farm Records, University of Reading

BER/13.5.1. Farm account book, three farms in Berkshire, 1797–1822

KEN/6/1/1. Diary of Richard Hayes, yeoman, 1760–78, typescript

KEN/19/1/1. Farm account book of Forestall Farm, Burmarsh, Kent, 1764–75

Leicestershire Record Office

Settlement examinations

DE 432/3 Ashby de la Zouch, 1692–1785

DE 390/25 Ibstock, 1765–86

Lincolnshire Archives Office

Settlement examinations

Addlethorpe parish records, 1796–1817

Algarkirk parish records, 1774–1843

Belchford parish records, 1794–1827

Coningsby parish records, 1792–1800

Quadring parish records, 1817

Saleby parish records, 1750–1815

Toynton St Peter's parish records, 1766–1823

Dixon 21/5/6/3. Advice from minister to parishioners (mid nineteenth century)

Banks Collection, Lincs. Coll. 3, folder M 1796, item 14. Letter to Sir Joseph Banks

Holland Quarter Sessions Minutes, 1766–9. Proclamation of wage rates

Holland Quarter Sessions Minutes, 1777–80. Orders to hold Statute Sessions

Holland QS D2, D3. Statute Sessions records, eighteenth and nineteenth centuries

LD 35/2. Poll-tax assessments, Orby, Lincs., 1692, 1694

MM 8/51,52,55. Petty Sessions Records in court rolls of Ingoldmells and Addlethorpe, 1588–96

Misc. Dep. 161. Farm account book, probably from Tetney, 1780–1837

192/129 (1696). Post mortem inventory; 207/196 (1729). Post mortem inventory

Norfolk Record Office

Settlement examinations

PD 111/103 Bressingham, 1752–1811

PD 124/41 Carbrooke, 1771–1813
PD 136/73 Denton, 1755/1819
PD 108/95 Kenninghall, 1740–1817
PD 80/57 Shelfanger, 1732–1816
PD 17/37 Sparham, 1754–1833
PD 119/114 Starston, 1748–1805
PD 122/44 Stratton, 1785–1810
PD 78/72 Winfarthing, 1766–1830
1014362/4, 1014364/4, 164353, 164354, 164355. North Walsham Court
    Rolls, petty sessions, 1570–80
PD 50/83. Orders terminating contracts, 1726–43

Northamptonshire Record Office
Settlement examinations
    PSJ 224 Peterborough, 1762–93
Militia lists, 1762 and 1777. All parishes in Huxloe, Nassaborough,
    Orlingbury, Rothwell and Willybrook Hundreds
YZ 4912. Letter to Duke of Buccleuch, June 1797

North Riding Record Office
Settlement examinations
    PR/NO 4/1 North Allerton, 1765–1808
    PR/TAW 13/2 Tawfield, 1763–1826
    PR/TH 6/5 Thirsk, 1760–1837

Nottinghamshire Record Office
PR 1745. Order to make list of masters and servants, 1726
PR 2661. Register of hirings, East Leake, 1818–33
PR 2728–2731. Forms for assessment of taxes on unproductive servants,
    1778–89
PR 5773/8,11. Notices of holding of hiring sessions, 1814 and 1822
PR 6380. East Drayton militia list, 1825

Oxfordshire Record Office
Settlement examinations
    Mil. VI/iii/a Milton, 1720–85
    Woot. Pc/lx/iii Wooton, 1729–83

Shropshire Record Office
Settlement examinations
    Acton Burnell, Cardington, Chetwynd, Claverly, Cleobury Mortimer,
    Condover, Great Ness, Great Wollaston, Hodnet, Kinnerly, Loppington,
    Pontesbury, Prees, Ryton, Shawbury, Smethcott, Stanton, Stapleton

Somerset Record Office
Settlement examinations
    Ashcott, Babcary, Baltonsborough (Glastonbury), Batcombe, Bishop's
    Hull, Broomfield, West Buckland, Carhampton, Charlton Mackrell,
    Chew Magna, Churchill, Congresbury, Croscombe, Ditcheat, Fitzhead,
    Hemington, Huish Episcopi, Hutton, Kewstoke, Mark, Mells, Othery,
    Penselwood, Pitney, Queen Camel, Somerton, Staple Fitzpaine, Weare,
    Winsford, Worle

Staffordshire Record Office
Settlement examinations
Abbot's Bromley, Aldridge, Alrewas, Armitage, Ashley, Baswich, Betley,
Bushbury, Cheekley, Church Eaton, Clifton Campville, Colton,
Colwich, Darlaston, Dilhorn, Drayton Bassett, Enville, Fradswell,
Gnossal, Hatherton, Haughton, Kingsley, Kinver, Madeley, Patshull,
Rocester, Sandon, Tettenhall
Suffolk Record Office, Bury
Settlement examinations
TEM 529/4 Badwell Ash, 1775–1834
EL 25 7/18 Brandon, 1761–1809
N 2/1/1–6 Bury, 1757–1818
EL 47/7/12 Debden, 1771–1806
TEM 535 52/2 Clare, 1777
EL 66/7 Groton, 1758–1818
EL 97/7 Lakenheath, 1760–94
EL 110/7 Mildenhall, 1763–1820
EL 119/7 Norton, 1791–1835
EL 158 Little Waldingfield, 1766–1815
EL 159/7 Walsham le Willows, 1791–1814
EL 169/7 Wickhambrook, 1795–9
2341/4/3 Worlington, 1765–1808
EL 119/7/280. Order terminating servant's contract, 1733
Suffolk Record Office, Ipswich
Settlement examinations
FB 191/63 East Bergholt, 1708–46
FC 101/G9 Framlingham, 1783–1832
FC 121/G14 Great Glenham, 1745–1817
FC 85/G2 Horham, 1778–1814
FB 95/G3 Ipswich St Matthew, 1710–1811
FB 101/G3 Ipswich St Peter's, 1778–85
Kettleburgh parish records, 1768–1819
FB 78/G5 Polstead, 1745–1820
FC 123/G2 Snape, 1797–1822
FC 84/G3 Wingfield, 1779–1823
FC 94/G4 Worlingworth, 1796–1810
FB 19/I1/2. Notice to attend statute sessions, 1642
FC 85/I1/7–96. Orders to prepare lists of masters and servants, 1600–39
FC 105/64/1. Acknowledgement of hiring of parish apprentice, 1809
FC/127/G2/11. Order dissolving contract, 1792
FC 195/64/1. Indenture of parish apprentice, 1809
FB 161/I1/8. Order to make list of masters and servants, 1745
Warwickshire Record Office
Settlement examinations
Alcester, Astley, Aston Cantelow, Austrey, Barston, Bedworth,
Berkswell, Bulkington, Claverdon, Fenny Compton, Corley,

Cubbington, Exhall (Coventry), Temple Grafton, Hampton in Arden, Hartshill, Hatton Haseley, Hillmorton, Kenilworth, Kineton, Monk's Kirby, Leamington Hastings, Butler's Marston, Newbold on Avon, Newbold Pacey, Newton Regis, Nuneaton, Great Packington, Little Packington, Quinton, Radford Semele, Rowington, Southam, Tanworth, Wellesbourne, Weston under Wetherley, Nether Whitacre

Wiltshire Record Office
Settlement examinations
Bradford upon Avon, Bromham, Great Cheverell, Chippenham with Tytherton Lucas, Cricklade St Sampson, Cricklade St Mary's, Devizes, Ebbesbourne Wake with Fifield Bavant and Alvediston, Enford Pewsey, Hilmarton, Hilperton, Horningsham, Lacock, Longbridge Deverill, Lydiard Millicent, Nunton, Ogbourne St George, Potterne, Seend, Sherston Magna, Little Somerford, Stratford sub Castle, Trowbridge, Wroughton

Worcestershire Record Office
Settlement examinations
Astley, Bengeworth, Bredon, Claines, Hanley Castle, Ombersley, Powick

Printed material

Anderson, Michael. *Family Structure in Nineteenth Century Lancashire.* Cambridge: University Press, 1971.

Annals of Agriculture. London, 1784–1808.

Anon. *The Advantages and Disadvantages of Inclosing Waste Lands.* n.p., [1772].

Anon. *Boke of Thrift* (1509), in F. H. Cripps-Day, ed., *The Manor Farm.* London: Quaitch, 1931.

Anon. *Compleat Parish Officer.* 10th edn. London, 1744.

Anon. *Jus Imperij et Servitutis or the Law Concerning Masters, Apprentices, Bayliffs, Receivers, Stewards, Attornies, Factors, Deputies, Carriers, Covenant-Servants,* etc. London, 1707.

Anon. *A Letter on the Subjects of Hiring, Service and Character, by a County Magistrate.* London, 1821.

Anon. *A Political Enquiry into the Consequences of Enclosing Waste Lands.* Holborn, 1785.

Appleby, Andrew B. 'Disease or Famine? Mortality in Cumberland and Westmorland, 1580–1640', *Economic History Review,* XXVI (1973), 403–31.

Arbuthnot, John. *An Inquiry into the Connection between the Present Price of Provisions and the Size of Farms.* London, 1773.

Arch, Joseph. *The Story of His Life.* London: Hutchinson, 1898.

Bailey, John. *A General View of the Agriculture of the County of Durham.* London, 1810.

and George Culley. *A General View of the Agriculture of Cumberland.* London, 1794.

A General View of the Agriculture of the County of Northumberland. London, 1794.

Banister, John. *A Synopsis of Husbandry, being Cursory Observations in the Several Branches of Rural Oeconomy.* London, 1799, pp. 458–61, rpt in *Commercial and Agricultural Magazine*, III (1801), 189–91.

Barley, M. W. *The English Farmhouse and Cottage.* London: Routledge and Kegan Paul, 1961.

'Rural Housing in England', in Joan Thirsk, ed., *The Agrarian History of England and Wales*, vol. IV, *1500–1640*. Cambridge: University Press, 1967, pp. 696–766.

Berkner, Lutz. 'The Stem Family and the Developmental Cycle of the Peasant Household', *American Historical Review*, LXXVII (1972), 398–418.

Beveridge, William. *Prices and Wages in England from the Twelfth to the Nineteenth Century.* London: Longmans Green, 1939.

von Blackenburg, P. *The Position of the Agricultural Hired Worker.* Paris: OECD, 1962.

Blackstone, William. *Commentaries on the Laws of England.* Edited by Edward Christian. 4 vols. London, 1803.

Blagrave, Joseph. *The Epitome of the Art of Husbandry.* London, 1675.

Blalock, Hubert M. *Social Statistics.* New York: McGraw Hill, 1960.

Blanchard, Ian. 'Population Change, Enclosure, and the Early Tudor Economy', *Economic History Review*, 2nd ser., XXIII (1970), 427–45.

Blaug, Mark. 'The Myth of the Old Poor Law and the Making of the New', *Journal of Economic History*, XXIII (1963), 151–84.

Blith Walter. *The English Improver.* London, 1649.

Board of Agriculture. *Communications to the Board of Agriculture*, London, 1797.

Report of the Committee Appointed by the Board of Agriculture to Take into Consideration the State of Waste Lands and Common Fields of this Kingdom. London, 1795.

Bourne, George. *The Bettesworth Book: Talks with a Surrey Peasant.* London: Lamley, 1901.

Memoirs of a Surrey Labourer. London: Duckworth, 1907.

Bowden, Peter. 'Agricultural Prices, Farm Profits, and Rents', in Joan Thirsk, ed., *The Agrarian History of England and Wales*, vol. IV, *1500–1640*. Cambridge: University Press, 1967.

Boys, John. *General View of the Agriculture of the County of Kent.* Brentford, 1794.

Bradley, Richard. *Complete Body of Husbandry.* Dublin, 1727.

Braun, R. 'The Impact of Cottage Industry on an Agricultural Population', in D. S. Landes, ed., *The Rise of Capitalism.* New York: Macmillan, 1966, pp. 53–64.

Brears, Charles. *Lincolnshire in the Seventeenth and Eighteenth Centuries.* London: A. Brown, 1940.

[Bridges, J.] *A Book of Fairs, or a Guide to the West Country Travellers.* [n.p.], [n.d.].

Brome, Richard. *Britannia*. London, 1673.

Brooke, C. N. L. and M. M. Postan, eds. *Carte Nativorum: A Peterborough Abbey Cartulary of the Fourteenth Century*. Northamptonshire Record Society, XX (1960).

Brown, A. F. J. *Essex at Work: 1700–1815*. Essex Record Office Publication, no. 49. Chelmsford, 1969.

Brown, Robert. *A General View of the Agriculture of the West Riding of Yorkshire*. Edinburgh, 1799.

Buckatzsch, E. J. 'The Constancy of Local Populations and Migration in England Before 1800', *Population Studies*, V (1951), 62–9.

'Places of Origin of a Group of Immigrants into Sheffield, 1624–1799', *Economic History Review*, II (1949–50), 303–6.

Burn, Richard. *The Justice of the Peace*. London, 1755.

Calendar of State Papers, Domestic. Charles I. (1637–8).

Calendar to the Sessions Books and Sessions Minute Books, 1619 to 1657. W. J. Hardy, ed. Hertfordshire County Record Society, V (1928).

Calendar to the Sessions Books and Sessions Minute Books, 1658 to 1700. W. Le Hardy, ed. Hertfordshire County Record Society, VI (1930).

Campbell, Mildred. *The English Yeoman under Elizabeth and the Early Stuarts*. New Haven: Yale University Press, 1942.

Chamberlayne, Edward. *Angliae Notitia, or the Present State of England*. 3rd edn. London, 1669.

Chambers, J. D. 'Enclosure and the Labour Supply in the Industrial Revolution', *Economic History Review*, 2nd ser., V (1953), 319–43.

Population, Economy, and Society in Pre-Industrial England. London: Oxford University Press, 1972.

and G. E. Mingay. *The Agricultural Revolution, 1750–1880*. London: Batsford, 1966.

Chayanov, A. V. *On the Theory of Peasant Economy*. Edited by D. Thorner, B. Kerblay, and R. E. Smith. Homewood, Illinois: American Economic Association, 1966.

Cheltenham Settlement Examinations, 1815–1826, I Gray, ed. Record Society of the Bristol and Gloucester Archaeological Society, VII (1969).

Chester, Greville J. *Statute Fairs (A Sermon)*. London, 1858.

Cho, Yong Sam. *'Disguised Unemployment' in Underdeveloped Areas with Special Reference to South Korean Agriculture*. Berkeley: University of California Press, 1963.

Cipolla, Carlo. 'Diffusion of Innovations in Early Modern Europe', *Comparative Studies in Society and History*, XIV (1972), 46–52.

Clapham, J. H. 'The Growth of an Agrarian Proletariat, 1688–1832: A Statistical Note', *Cambridge Historical Journal*, I (1932), 92–5.

Clark, John. *A General View of the Agriculture of the County of Hereford*. 3 vols. London, 1794.

Clarke, Desmond, ed. *The Unfortunate Husbandman: An Account of the Life and Travels of a Real Farmer in Ireland, Scotland, England, and America*. London: Oldbourne, 1964.

Coats, A. W. 'Changing Attitudes to Labour in the Mid-Eighteenth Century', *Economic History Review*, 2nd ser., XI (1958), 35–51.

Coleman, D.C. 'Labour in the English Economy of the Seventeenth Century', *Economic History Review*, 2nd ser., VIII (1956), 280–95.

Commercial and Agricultural Magazine (London), 1800.

Communications to the Board of Agriculture, 1797–1811. London, 1797.

Copnall, H. H., ed. *Nottinghamshire County Records: Notes and Extracts from the Nottinghamshire County Records of the Seventeenth Century*. Nottingham, 1915.

County of Buckingham. *Calendar to the Sessions Records, 1678–1694*. W. Le Hardy, ed. I (1933).

Calendar to the Sessions Records, 1699–1704, W. Le Hardy and G. Reckitt, eds. II (1936).

Calendar to the Sessions Records, 1705–1712. W. Le Hardy and G. Reckitt, eds. III (1939).

Cowell, John. *The Interpreter, or Booke Containing the Signification of Words*. Cambridge, 1607.

Cox, J. Charles. *Three Centuries of Derbyshire Annals*. 3 vols. London: Bemrose, 1890.

Craigie, P. G. 'The Size and Distribution of Agricultural Holdings in England and Abroad', *Journal of the Royal Statistical Society*, L (1887), 86–142.

Cunningham, B. H., ed. *Records of the County of Wiltshire*. Devizes: Simpson, 1932.

Dalton, Michael. *The Country Justice*. 5th edn. London, 1635.

Darby, H. C., ed. *A New Historical Geography of England*. Cambridge: University Press, 1973.

Davidoff, Leonore. 'Mastered for Life: Servant and Wife in Victorian England', *Journal of Social History*, VII (1974), 406–28.

Davies, C. Stella. *The Agricultural History of Cheshire, 1750–1850*. Chetham Society, 3rd series, X (1960).

Davies, David. *The Case of Labourers in Husbandry Stated and Considered, in Three Parts*. Bath, 1795.

Davies, Margaret Gay. *The Enforcement of England's Apprenticeship: A Study in Applied Mercantilism*. Cambridge, Mass.: Harvard University Press, 1956.

Davies, Thomas. *A General View of the Agriculture of the County of Wiltshire*. London, 1794.

Deane, Phyllis and W. A. Cole. *British Economic Growth, 1688–1959: Trends and Structure*. 2nd edn. Cambridge: University Press, 1967.

Deloney, Thomas. *Thomas of Reading*. London, 1612.

De Vries, Jan. *The Economy of Europe in an Age of Crisis*. Cambridge: University Press, 1976.

Dickson, R. W. *General View of the Agriculture of Lancashire*. London, 1815.

Diósdi, György. *Ownership in Ancient and Pre-Classical Roman Law*. Budapest: Akadémiai Kiadó, 1970.

Donaldson, James. *General View of the Agriculture of the County of Northampton*. Edinburgh, 1794.

Douglas, Robert. *A General View of the Agriculture in the Counties of Roxburgh and Selkirk*. Edinburgh, 1798.

Drake, Michael. 'Age at Marriage in the Pre-Industrial West', in F. Bechhofer, ed., *Population Growth and the Brain Drain*. Edinburgh: University Press, 1969.

'The Census, 1801–1891', in E. A. Wrigley, ed., *Nineteenth-Century Society: Essays in the Use of Quantitative Methods for the Study of Social Science*. Cambridge: University Press, 1962.

Population and Society in Norway, 1735–1865. Cambridge: University Press, 1969.

ed. *Population in Industrialization*. London: Methuen, 1969.

Dunbabin, J. P. D. 'The Incidence and Organization of Agricultural Trades Unionism in the 1870s', *Agricultural History Review*, XVI (1968), 114–41.

Ernle, Lord. *English Farming: Past and Present*. 3rd edn. London: Longmans Green, 1922.

Ernout, A. and A. Meillet. *Dictionnaire Etymologique de la Langue Latine*. 3rd edn. Paris: Klincksieck, 1951.

Everitt, Alan. 'Farm Labourers', in Joan Thirsk, ed., *The Agrarian History of England and Wales*, vol. IV, *1500–1640*. Cambridge: University Press, 1967, pp. 396–465.

'The Marketing of Agricultural Produce', in Joan Thirsk, ed., *The Agrarian History of England and Wales*, vol. IV, *1500–1640*. Cambridge: University Press, 1967, pp. 466–592.

Eversley, D. E. C. 'General Discussion', in F. C. Bechhofer, ed., *Population Growth and the Brain Drain*. Edinburgh: University Press, 1969.

Farey, John. *General View of the Agriculture and Minerals of Derbyshire*. 3 vols. London, 1815.

Farmer's Magazine. Edinburgh, 1800–7.

Farmer's Magazine. London, 1776–9.

Farmer's Magazine. *A General Dictionary of Husbandry*. 2 vols. Bath, 1779.

Firth, C. H. and R. S. Rait, eds. *Acts and Ordinances of the Interregnum, 1642–1660*. 2 vols. London: HMSO, 1911.

Fischer, W. 'Rural Industrialization and Population Change', *Comparative Studies in Society and History*, XV (1973), 158–70.

Fitzherbert, Anthony. *The Boke of Husbandry*. London, 1534.

Flandrin, J. L. 'Mariage tardif et vie sexuelle', *Annales: ESC*, XXVII (1972), 1351–78.

Fleetwood, William. *The Relative Duties of Parents and Children, Husbands and Wives, Masters and Servants*. London, 1705.

Fox, N. E. 'The Spread of the Threshing Machine in Central Southern England', *Agricultural History Review*, XXXVI (1978), 26–8.

Fussell, G. E., ed. *Robert Loder's Farm Accounts, 1610–1620*. Camden Society, 3rd ser., LIII (1936).

and K. R. Fussell. *The English Countryman: His Life and Work*. London: Melrose, 1955.

Gill, S. S. 'Unemployment and Underemployment of Permanent Farm Workers', *Artha Vijñāna*, II (1960), 249–61.

Gillis, John R. *Youth and History: Tradition and Change in European Age-Relations, 1770–present*. New York: Academic Press, 1974.

'Youth in History: Progress and Prospects', *Journal of Social History*, VII (1974), 201–7.

Glass, D. V. 'Gregory King's Estimate of the Population of England and Wales, 1695', *Population Studies*, III (1950), 338–74.

Goody, Jack, Joan Thirsk and E. P. Thompson, eds. *Family and Inheritance: Rural Society in Western Europe, 1200–1800*. Cambridge: University Press, 1976.

Googe, Barnaby. *The Whole Art of Husbandry*. London, 1614.

Gough, Richard. *Human Nature Displayed in the History of Myddle*. Fontwell, Sussex: Centaur, 1968.

Grant, I. F. *Everyday Life on an Old Highland Farm, 1769–82*. London: Longmans Green, 1924.

Great Britain. *Census of Population, 1801*. PP 1801–2, VI–VII.

Census of Population, 1851. PP 1851, XLIII, PP 1852–3, LXXXVIII.

Census of Population, 1871. PP 1873, LXXII.

Papers on the State of Agriculture and the Condition of the Population in Europe. PP 1836, XLVII.

Report from the Select Committee on the Several Petitions Complaining of the Depressed State of Agriculture of the UK. PP 1821, IX.

Reports from the Committees on Emigration from the United Kingdom. PP 1827, V.

Report from the Select Committee Appointed to Inquire into the Present State of Agriculture, and Persons Appointed in Agriculture, in the United Kingdom. PP 1833, V.

Report from the Select Committee on Labourers' Wages. PP 1824, VI.

Report of the Select Committee on the Poor Law. PP 1834, XXIII, Appendix B, Part iv.

Reports of the Special Assistant Poor Law Commissioners on the Employment of Women and Children in Agriculture. PP 1843, XII.

Royal Commission on Market Rights and Tolls. PP 1888, LIII.

Grigg, David. *The Agricultural Revolution in South Lincolnshire*. Cambridge: University Press, 1966.

'Small and Large Farms in England and Wales: Their Size and Distribution', *Geography*, XLVIII (1963), 268–79.

H. 'An Essay on the Proper Size of Farms', *Farmer's Magazine* (Edinburgh), I (1801), 376–86.

Habakkuk, H. J. 'La Disparition du paysan anglais', *Annales: ESC*, XX (1965), 649–63.

'English Landownership, 1680–1740', *Economic History Review*, X (1940), 2–17.

'Family Structure and Economic Change in Nineteenth-Century Europe', *Journal of Economic History*, XV (1955), 1–12.

Population Growth and Economic Development since 1750. Leicester: University Press, 1972.

Hair, P. E. H. 'Bridal Pregnancy in Earlier Rural England Further
  Examined', *Population Studies*, XXIV (1970), 59–70.
  'Bridal Pregnancy in Rural England in Earlier Centuries', *Population
  Studies*, XX (1966), 233–43.
Hajnal, John. 'European Marriage Patterns in Perspective', in D. V. Glass
  and D. E. C. Eversley, eds., *Population in History*. London: Arnold, 1965.
Hammond, J. L. and Barbara Hammond. *The Village Labourer*. London:
  Longmans Green, 1966.
Hampson, E. M. *The Treatment of Poverty in Cambridgeshire, 1597–1834*.
  Cambridge: University Press, 1934.
Hansen, Hans Olaf. *Manntal 1729 I Þremur Syslum*. Reykjavik: Ríkisprentsmid
  jan Gutenberg, 1975.
Hardwick, Charles. *History of the Borough of Preston and Its Environs*. Preston:
  Worthington, 1857.
Harris, Richard Colebrook. *The Seigneurial System in Early Canada: A
  Geographical Study*. Madison: University of Wisconsin Press, 1968.
Harrison, William. *The Description of England*. Edited by Georges Edelen.
  Ithaca: Cornell, 1968.
Hasbach, Wilhelm. *History of the English Agricultural Labourer*. Translated by
  Ruth Kenyon. London: Cass, 1966.
Helleiner, K. F. 'The Population of Europe from the Black Death to the
  Eve of the Vital Revolution', in E. E. Rich and C. H. Wilson, eds., *The
  Cambridge Economic History of Europe*, vol. IV. Cambridge: University
  Press, 1967, pp. 1–96.
  'The Vital Revolution Reconsidered', in D. V. Glass and D. E. C.
  Eversley, eds., *Population in History*. London: Arnold, 1965, pp. 79–86.
Henderson, John. *A General View of the Agriculture of the County of Caithness*.
  London, 1812.
Hey, David G. 'A Dual Economy in South Yorkshire', *Agricultural History
  Review*, XVII (1969), 108–19.
Hill, Christopher. *Change and Continuity in Seventeenth-Century England*. London:
  Weidenfeld and Nicolson, 1974.
  'Pottage for Freeborn Englishmen: Attitudes to Wage-Labour', in C. H.
  Feinstein, ed., *Socialism, Capitalism and Economic Growth*. Cambridge:
  University Press, 1967.
  Society and Puritanism in Pre-Revolutionary England. London: Panther, 1969.
Historical Manuscripts Commission. *Report on Manuscripts in Various
  Collections*, vol. I.
  Rutland, Vol. I.
  Seventh Report, Appendix.
Hitt, Thomas. *A Treatise of Husbandry on the Improvement of Dry and Barren
  Lands*. London, 1760.
Hobsbawm, E. J. and George Rudé. *Captain Swing*. Harmondsworth,
  Middlesex: Penguin, 1973.
Hodgson, R. I. 'The Progress of Enclosure in County Durham, 1550–1870',
  in H. S. A. Fox and R. A. Butlin, eds., *Change in the Countryside: Essays*

on Rural England, 1500–1900. London: Institute of British Geographers, 1979.

Holdsworth, W. S. *A History of English Law.* 3rd edn, vol. II. London: Methuen, 1923.

Holland, Henry. *General View of the Agriculture of Cheshire.* London, 1808.

Hollingsworth, T. H. *Historical Demography.* London: Hodder and Stoughton, 1969.

Hone, William. *The Table Book.* 2 vols. London: Hunt and Clark, 1827.

Hoskins, George. *Essays in Leicestershire History.* Liverpool: University Press, 1950.

'The Farm Labourer through Four Centuries', in W. G. Hoskins and H. P. R. Finberg, eds., *Devonshire Studies.* London: Cape, 1952.

'The Leicestershire Farmer in the Seventeenth Century', in G. Hoskins, *Provincial England: Essays in Social and Economic History.* London: Macmillan, 1963, pp. 149–69.

The Midland Peasant: The Economic and Social History of a Leicestershire Village. London: Macmillan, 1957.

Houghten, John. *Collection of Letters for the Improvement of Husbandry and Trade.* 2 vols. London, 1681–3.

Howitt, William. *The Rural Life of England.* 2 vols. London: Longman, 1838.

Howlett, J. *Enclosures: A Cause of Improved Agriculture.* London, 1789.

Enquiry into the Influence Which Enclosures Have Had Upon the Population of the Kingdom. London, 1786.

The Insufficiency of the Causes to Which the Increase of our Poor and of the Poor Rates have been Commonly Ascribed. London, 1788.

Hughes, P. L. and J. F. Larkin, eds. *Tudor Royal Proclamations.* 3 vols. New Haven: Yale University Press, 1964–9.

Hunt, E. H. *Regional Wage Variations in Britain, 1850–1914.* Oxford: Clarendon, 1973.

[Jacob, Giles]. *The Compleat Parish Officer.* 10th edn. London, 1744.

James, Mervyn. *Family, Lineage, and Civil Society: A Study of Society, Politics, and Mentality in the Durham Region, 1500–1640.* Oxford: Clarendon, 1974.

James, William and Jacob Malcolm. *General View of the Agriculture of the County of Buckingham.* London, 1794.

Jenkins, David. *The Agricultural Community of Southwest Wales at the Turn of the Twentieth Century.* Cardiff: University of Wales Press, 1971.

John, A. H. 'Introduction' to J. Howlett, *Enclosure and Population.* London: Gregg International Publishers, 1973.

Johnson, Arthur H. *The Disappearance of the Small Landowner.* Oxford: Clarendon, 1909.

Johnson, W. B., ed. *'Memorandums for . . .', Diary of 1798–1810 of John Carrington, Farmer, Chief Constable.* London: Phillimore, 1973.

Jones, E. L. 'The Agricultural Labour Market in England, 1793–1872', *Economic History Review*, 2nd ser., XVII (1964), 322–38.

'Agricultural Origins of Industry', *Past and Present*, no. 40 (1968), 58–71.

'Agriculture and Economic Growth in England, 1660–1750: Agricultural Change', *Journal of Economic History*, XXV (1965), 1–18.

'The Arable Depression after the Napoleonic Wars and the Agricultural Development of the Hampshire Chalklands', BA Diss., University of Nottingham, 1958.

Seasons and Prices: The Role of Weather in English Agricultural History. London: Allen and Unwin, 1964.

and S. J. Woolf, eds. *Agrarian Change and Economic Development: The Historical Problems.* London: Methuen, 1969.

Kalm, Pehr. *Account of His Visit to England* (1753). Translated by Joseph Lucas. London: Macmillan, 1892.

Kebble, T. E. *The Agricultural Labourer.* London: Chapman and Hall, 1870.

Kelsall, Keith. 'Wages of Northern Farm Labourers in the Mid-Eighteenth Century', *Economic History Review*, VIII (1937), 80–1.

Kent, Nathaniel. *A General View of the Agriculture of the County of Norfolk.* London, 1794.

Kerr, Robert. *A General View of the Agriculture of the County of Berwick.* London, 1809.

Kerridge, Eric. *The Agricultural Revolution.* London: Allen and Unwin, 1967.

King, Gregory. *Two Tracts.* Edited by George E. Barnett. Baltimore: Johns Hopkins Press, 1936.

Kitchen, Fred. *Brother to the Ox: The Autobiography of a Farm-Labourer.* London: Dent, 1940.

Krause, J. T. 'English Population Movements between 1700 and 1850', in M. Drake, ed., *Population in Industrialization.* London: Methuen, 1969, pp. 118–27.

'Some Aspects of Population Change, 1690–1790', in E. L. Jones and G. E. Mingay, eds., *Land, Labour, and Population in the Industrial Revolution.* London: Arnold, 1967.

'Some Implications of Recent Work in Historical Demography', *Comparative Studies in Society and History*, I (1958), 164–88.

'Some Neglected Factors in the English Industrial Revolution', *Journal of Economic History*, XIX (1959), 528–40.

Kussmaul, Ann. 'The Ambiguous Mobility of Farm Servants', *Economic History Review* (forthcoming 1981).

Lambard, William. *The Duties of Constables, Borsholders, Tythingmen, and Such other Lowe and Lay Ministers of the Peace.* London, 1610.

Lancashire Quarter Sessions Records, 1590–1606, J. Tait, ed. Chetham Society, n.s., LXXVII (1917).

Laslett, Peter. 'Characteristics of the Western Family Considered Over Time', *Journal of Family History*, II (1977), 89–116.

'Market Society and Political Theory', *Historical Journal*, VII (1964), 150–4.

'Mean Household Size in England since the Sixteenth Century', in Peter Laslett and Richard Wall, eds., *Household and Family in Past Time.* Cambridge: University Press, 1972.

'Parental Deprivation in the Past: A Note on the History of Orphans in England', *Local Population Studies*, no. 13 (1974), 11–18.

'Size and Structure of the Household of England over Three Centuries', *Population Studies*, XXIII (1969), pp. 199–223.

The World We Have Lost. 2nd edn. London: Methuen, 1971.

and John Harrison, 'Clayworth and Cogenhoe', in H. E. Bell and R. L. Ollard, eds., *Historical Essays Presented to David Ogg*. London: Adam and Charles Black, 1963.

and Karla Oosterveen. 'Long-Term Trends in Bastardy in England', *Population Studies*, XXVII (1973), 255–86.

Laurence, Edward. *The Duty of a Steward to His Lord.* London, 1727.

Laurence, John. *A New System of Agriculture.* London, 1726.

Leatham, Isaac. *A General View of the Agriculture of the East Riding of Yorkshire.* London, 1794.

Le Bras, Hervé. 'Parents, grands-parents, bisaieux', *Population*, XXVII (1973), pp. 9–37.

[Lee, Joseph]. *Considerations Concerning Common Fields and Inclosures.* London, 1653.

A Vindication of Regulated Enclosure. London, 1656.

Leibenstein, H. 'The Theory of Underemployment in Backward Areas', *Journal of Political Economy*, LXV (1957), 91–103.

Levine, David. *Family Formation in an Age of Nascent Capitalism.* New York: Academic Press, 1977.

Levy, Hermann. *Large and Small Holdings: A Study of English Agricultural Economics.* Cambridge: University Press, 1911.

Lisle, Edward. *Observations in Husbandry.* 2 vols. London, 1757.

Lodge, Eleanor C. *The Account Book of a Kentish Estate, 1616–1704.* London: Milford and Oxford University Press, 1927.

Loudon, J. C. *Encyclopaedia of Agriculture.* London: Longman, 1825.

Macdonald, Stuart. 'The Progress of the Early Threshing Machine', *Agricultural History Review*, XXIII (1975), 63–77.

'Rejoinder', *Agricultural History Review*, XXXVI (1978), 29–32.

'The Role of the Individual in Agricultural Change: The Example of George Culley of Fenton, Northumberland', in H. S. A. Fox and R. A. Butlin, eds., *Change in the Countryside: Essays on Rural England, 1500–1900*. London: Institute of British Geographers, 1979.

Macfarlane, Alan. *The Family Life of Ralph Josselin, A Seventeenth-Century Clergyman.* Cambridge: University Press, 1970.

The Origins of English Individualism: The Family, Property and Social Transition. Oxford: Blackwell, 1978.

ed. *The Diary of Ralph Josselin, 1616–1683.* Records of Social and Economic History, n.s., III, British Academy, London: Oxford University Press, 1976.

McLaren, Dorothy. 'The Marriage Act of 1653: Its Influence on Parish Registers', *Population Studies*, XXVIII (1974), 319–27.

Macpherson, C. B. *The Political Theory of Possessive Individualism*. Oxford:
Clarendon, 1962.
  Democratic Theory: Essays in Retrieval. Oxford: Clarendon, 1973.
Malcolm, James. *General View of the Agriculture of the County of Surrey*. 3 vols.
London, 1805.
Malcolmson, R. W. *Popular Recreation in English Society, 1700–1815*.
Cambridge: University Press, 1973.
Markham, Gervase. *The English Housewife*. London, 1683.
  Farewell to Husbandry. 3rd edn. London, 1631.
Marshall, William. *Minutes of Agriculture Made on a Farm of 300 Acres of
Various Soils near Croydon, Surrey*. London, 1778.
  Review and Abstract of the County Reports to the Board of Agriculture. 4 vols.
York, 1818.
  The Rural Economy of Gloucestershire. 2 vols. Gloucester, 1789.
  The Rural Economy of the Midland Counties. 2 vols. London, 1796.
  The Rural Economy of Norfolk. 2 vols. 2nd edn. London, 1795.
  The Rural Economy of the West of England. 2 vols. London: Nicol, 1796.
Mavor, William. *General View of the Agriculture of Berkshire*. London, 1808.
Maxwell, George. *A General View of the Agriculture of the County of Huntingdon*.
London, 1793.
Mayo, Richard. *A Present for Servants, . . . Especially in Country Parishes*.
London, 1693.
Meaby, Kenneth Tweedale, ed. *Nottinghamshire: Extracts from the County
Records of the Eighteenth Century*. Nottingham: Forman and Sons, 1947.
Middleton, John. *General View of the Agriculture of Middlesex*. London, 1813.
Miller, Edward. *The Abbey and Bishopric of Ely*. Cambridge: University Press,
1951.
  'Pre-Industrial Society', *Historical Journal*, IX (1966), 374–88.
Minchinton, W. E., ed. *Wage Regulation in Pre-Industrial England*. Newton
Abbot: David and Charles, 1972.
Mingay, G. E. 'The Size of Farms in the Eighteenth Century', *Economic
History Review*, XIV (1962), 469–88.
Miskimin, Harry A. *The Economy of Early Renaissance Europe, 1300–1460*.
Englewood Cliffs, NJ: Prentice-Hall, 1969.
Mitchell, B. R. and Phyllis Deane. *Abstract of British Historical Statistics*.
Cambridge: University Press, 1971.
Monk, John. *General View of the Agriculture of the County of Leicester*. London,
1794.
Moore, Adam. *Bread for the Poor*. London, 1653.
Moore, John. *The Crying Sin of England of not Caring for the Poor*. London,
1653.
  *A Scripture-Word against Inclosure viz. such as Doe Un-People Townes, and Un-
Corne Fields*. London, 1656.
Morgan, Edmund S. *The Puritan Family: Religion and Domestic Relations in
Seventeenth-Century New England*. New edn. New York: Harper and Row,
1966.

Mortimer, John. *The Whole Art of Husbandry*. London, 1707.

Museum Rusticum et Commerciale. London, VI (1766).

Nalson, J. S. *Mobility of Farm Families: A Study of Occupational and Residential Mobility in an Upland Area of England*. Manchester: University Press, 1968.

Neuman, Mark. 'Speenhamland in Berkshire', in E. W. Martin, ed., *Comparative Development in Social Welfare*. London: Allen and Unwin, 1972, pp. 85–127.

Norfolk Quarter Sessions Order Book, 1650 to 1657, D. E. Howell James, ed. Norfolk Record Society, XXVI (1955).

Northamptonshire Militia Lists, 1777, V. A. Hatley, ed. Northamptonshire Record Society, XXV (1973).

Norwich Mercury, 1743–69.

Notes and Extracts from the Sessions Rolls, 1581 to 1698, W. J. Hardy, ed., Hertfordshire County Record Society, I (1905).

Nourse, Timothy. *Campania Foelix, or a Discourse of the Benefits and Improvements of Husbandry*. London, 1700.

Orders of the Shropshire Quarter Sessions R. L. Kenyon, ed., Shropshire County Records, 4 vols. (1901–13).

Owen, W. *New Book of Fairs*. New edn. London, 1805.

Parkyns, Thomas. *Subordination: An Essay on Servants, their Rates of Wages, and the Great Conveniency which will Accrue to every County, by Recording with all Chief Constables, etc., of the Same*. 3rd edn. London, 1724.

Perkins, William. *[Christian] Oeconomie, or Household Government, A Short·Survey of the Right Manner of Erecting and Ordering a Family, According to the Scriptures*, in his *Workes*. 3 vols. London, 1631.

Peters, Matthew. *The Rational Farmer*. 2nd edn. London, 1771.

Peyton, S. A., ed. *Minutes of the Proceedings in Quarter Sessions Held for the Parts of Kesteven in the County of Lincoln, 1674–95*. vol. I. Lincoln, 1931.

Phelps Brown, E. H. and Sheila V. Hopkins. 'Seven Centuries of the Prices of Consumables, Compared with Builders' Wage Rates', in E. M. Carus-Wilson, ed., *Essays in Economic History*, vol. II. London: Edward Arnold, 1962.

Philpot, Gordon. 'Enclosure and Population Growth in Eighteenth-Century England', *Explorations in Economic History*, XII (1975), 29–46.

Pinchbeck, Ivy. *Women Workers and the Industrial Revolution: 1750–1850*. London: Routledge, 1930.

Pinchbeck, Ivy, and Margaret Hewitt. *Children in English Society*. 2 vols. London: Routledge and Kegan Paul, 1969.

Pitt, William. *General View of the Agriculture of the County of Leicester*. London, 1809.

General View of the Agriculture of the County of Northampton. London, 1813.

General View of the Agriculture of the County of Stafford. London, 1813.

A General View of the Agriculture of the County of Worcester. London, 1810.

Plakans, Andrejs. 'Peasant Farmsteads and Households in the Baltic Littoral, 1797', *Comparative Studies in Society and History*, XVII (1975), 2–35.

Plymley, Joseph. *A General View of the Agriculture of Shropshire*. London, 1803.

Pollock, Frederick and Frederick William Maitland. *The History of English Law*. 2 vols. 2nd edn. Cambridge: University Press, 1968.

Pomeroy, William. *General View of the Agriculture of the County of Worcester*. London, 1794.

Postan, M. M. *The Famulus: The Estate Labourer in the XIIth and XIIIth Centuries*. Economic History Review Supplement, no. 2. Cambridge: University Press, 1954.

[Powell, Robert]. *Depopulation Arraigned, Convicted, and Condemned, by the Laws of God and Man*. London, 1636.

Powicke, F. M., ed. 'The Reverend Richard Baxter's Last Treatise', *Bulletin of the John Rylands Library*, X (1926), 163–218.

Priest, St John. *General View of the Agriculture of the County of Buckingham*. London, 1813.

Pringle, Andrew. *A General View of the Agriculture of the County of Westmorland*. Edinburgh, 1805.

Putnam, Bertha. 'The Earliest Form of Lambard's "Eirenarcha" and a Kent Wage Assessment of 1563', *English Historical Review*, XLI (1926), 260–73.

The Enforcement of the Statutes of Labourers during the First Decade After the Black Death, 1349–1359. Columbia University Studies in History and Economics, no. 32. New York: Columbia University Press, 1908.

Quarter Sessions, 1581–1589, S. A. H. Bourne, ed. Historical Collections of Staffordshire, William Salt Archaeological Society, 1929.

Quarter Sessions Order Book, 1642–1649, B. C. Redwood, ed. Sussex Record Society, LIV (1954).

Quarter Sessions Records. Northamptonshire Record Society, I (1924).

Quarter Sessions Records 1605–1612, J. C. Atkinson, ed. North Riding Record Society, I–VII (1884–9).

Quarter Sessions Records for the County Palatine of Chester, 1559–1760, J. H. E. Bennett and J. C. Dewhurst, eds. Record Society of Lancashire and Cheshire, XCIV (1940).

Quarter Sessions Records for the County of Somerset, 1607 to 1625, E. H. Bates, ed. Somerset Record Society, XXIII (1907).

Quarter Sessions Records for the County of Somerset, 1625 to 1639, E. H. Bates Harbin, ed. Somerset Record Society, XXIV (1908).

Quarter Sessions Records for the County of Somerset, 1646 to 1660, E. H. Bates Harbin, ed. Somerset Record Society, XXVIII (1912).

Quarter Sessions Rolls. Historical Collections of Staffordshire, William Salt Archaeological Society, V (1940).

Quayle, Basil. *General View of the Agriculture of the Isle of Man*. London, 1794.

Quayle, Thomas. *A General View of the Agriculture of the Isle of Man*. London, 1812.

Raftis, J. A. 'Social Structures in Five East Midland Villages', *Economic History Review*, XVIII (1965), 83–99.

Razzell, P. E. 'Population Change in Eighteenth-Century England', in M.

Drake, ed., *Population in Industrialization*. London: Methuen, 1969, pp. 128–56.

Redford, Arthur. *Labour Migration in England, 1800–1850*. 2nd edn. Revised by W. H. Chaloner. Manchester: University Press, 1964.

Rennie, George, *et al. General View of the Agriculture of the West Riding of Yorkshire*. London, 1794.

Rich, E. E. 'The Population of Elizabethan England', *Economic History Review*, 2nd ser., II (1950), 247–65.

Roberts, George. *The Social History of the People of the Southern Counties of England in Past Centuries*. London: Longman Green, 1856.

Robertson, James. *A General View of the Agriculture of the County of Inverness*. London, 1808.

Robertson, Thomas. *Outline of the General Report Upon the Size of Farms*. Edinburgh, 1796.

Rogers, J. E. T. *A History of Agriculture and Prices in England*. 7 vols. Oxford: Clarendon, 1866–1902.

Rudge, Thomas. *General View of the Agriculture of the County of Gloucester*. London, 1813.

Rural Economy in Yorkshire in 1641, Being the Farming and Account Books of Henry Best of Elmswell in the East Riding of the County of York. Surtees Society, XXXIII (1857).

Sabean, David. 'Famille et tenure paysan: aux origines de la Guerre Paysans en Allemagne (1525)', *Annales: ESC*, XXVII (1972), 903–22.

Saville, John. 'Primitive Accumulation and Early Industrialisation in Britain', *Socialist Register* (London, 1969), 247–71.

Schochet, Gordon. *Patriarchalism in Political Thought: The Authoritarian Family and Political Speculations and Attitudes Especially in Seventeenth-Century England*. Oxford: Blackwell, 1975.

 'Patriarchalism, Politics, and Mass Attitudes in Stuart England', *Historical Journal*, XII (1969), 413–41.

Schofield, R. S. 'Age-Specific Mobility in an Eighteenth-Century Rural English Parish', *Annales de démographie historique* (1970), 261–74.

 'The Dimensions of Illiteracy, 1750–1850', *Explorations in Economic History*, X (1973), 437–54.

Segalen, Martine. 'The Family Cycle and Household Structure: Five Generations in a French Village', *Journal of Family History*, II (1977), 223–36.

Shanin, Teodor. *The Awkward Class: Political Sociology of Peasantry in a Developing Country*. Oxford: Clarendon, 1972.

 ed. *Peasants and Peasant Society*. Harmondsworth: Penguin, 1971.

Sheppard, June A. 'East Yorkshire's Agricultural Labour Force in the Mid-Nineteenth Century', *Agricultural History Review*, IX (1961), 43–54.

Simon, Daphne. 'Master and Servant', in John Saville, ed., *Democracy and the Labour Movement*. London: Lawrence and Wishart, 1954, pp. 160–200.

Skinner, G. William. 'Marketing and Social Structure in Rural China', *Journal of Asian Studies*, XXIV (1964), 1–43.

Skinner, J. *Facts and Opinions Concerning Statute Hirings*. London: Wertheim and Macintosh, 1861.

Smith, Adam. *An Inquiry into the Nature and Causes of the Wealth of Nations*. 2 vols. London: Strahan and Cadell, 1776.

Smith, John, ed. *Men and Armour for Gloucestershire in 1608*. London: Southern, 1902.

Smith, T. C. *The Agrarian Origins of Modern Japan*. Palo Alto: Stanford University Press, 1959.

'Farm Family By-Employments in Pre-Industrial Japan', *Journal of Economic History*, XXIX (1969), 687–715.

Snell, Keith. 'The Standard of Living, Social Relations, the Family, and Labour Mobility in South-Eastern and Western Counties', unpublished PhD thesis, Cambridge University, 1980.

Spufford, Margaret. *Contrasting Communities: English Villagers in the Sixteenth and Seventeenth Centuries*. Cambridge: University Press, 1974.

Steele, Richard. *The Husbandman's Calling*. 2nd edn. London, 1672.

Stevenson, Nash. 'On Statute Fairs: Their Evils and Their Remedy', *Transactions of the National Association for the Promotion of Social Sciences* (1858), 624–63.

Stevenson, William. *A General View of the Agriculture of the County of Dorset*. London, 1812.

A General View of the Agriculture of the County of Surrey. London, 1813.

Stone, Lawrence. *The Family, Sex and Marriage in England, 1500–1800*. London: Weidenfeld and Nicolson, 1977.

Stone, Thomas. *Suggestions for Rendering the Inclosure of Common Fields and Waste Lands a Source of Population and Riches*. London, 1787.

Strickland, H. E. *General View of the Agriculture of the East Riding of Yorkshire*. York, 1812.

Suffolk Mercury, 1725–6.

Surrey Quarter Sessions Records, Order Book and Sessions Rolls, 1659 to 1661, D. L. Powell and H. Jenkinson, eds. Surrey Record Society, XIII (1934).

Surrey Quarter Sessions Records, Order Book and Sessions Rolls, D. L. Powell and H. Jenkinson, eds. Surrey Record Society, XIV (1935).

Surrey Quarter Sessions Records, Order Book and Sessions Rolls, D. L. Powell and H. Jenkinson, eds. Surrey Record Society, XVI (1938).

[Tancred, Christopher]. *A Scheme for an Act of Parliament for the Better Regulating Servants, and Ascertaining their Wages, and Lessening the Future Growth of the Poor and Vagrants of the Kingdom*. London, 1724.

Tawney, A. J. and R. H. Tawney. 'An Occupational Census of the Seventeenth Century', *Economic History Review*, V (1934), 25–64.

Tawney, R. H. 'The Assessment of Wages in England by the Justices of the Peace', in W. E. Minchinton, ed., *Wage Regulation in Pre-Industrial England*. Newton Abbot: David and Charles, 1972.

Taylor, James Stephan. 'The Impact of Pauper Settlement, 1691–1834', *Past and Present*, no. 73 (1976), 42–74.

Thirsk, Joan, ed. *The Agrarian History of England and Wales*, vol. IV, *1500–1640*. Cambridge: University Press, 1967.

Economic Policy and Projects. London: Oxford University Press, 1978.

'Enclosing and Engrossing', in Joan Thirsk, ed., *The Agrarian History of England and Wales*, vol. IV, *1500–1640*. Cambridge: University Press, 1967, pp. 200–55.

English Peasant Farming: The Agrarian History of Lincolnshire from Tudor to Recent Times. London: Routledge and Kegan Paul, 1957.

'The Farming Regions of England', in Joan Thirsk, ed., *The Agrarian History of England and Wales*, vol. IV, *1500–1640*. Cambridge: University Press, 1967, pp. 1–112.

'Farming Techniques', in Joan Thirsk, ed., *The Agrarian History of England and Wales*, vol. IV, *1500–1640*. Cambridge: University Press, 1967, pp. 161–99.

Fenland Farming in the Sixteenth Century. Department of English Local History, Occasional Papers, no. 3, University of Leicester. Leicester, 1953.

'Horn and Thorn in Staffordshire: The Economy of a Pastoral County', *North Staffordshire Journal of Field Studies*, IX (1969), 1–16.

'Industries in the Countryside', in F. J. Fisher, ed., *Essays in the Economic and Social History of Tudor and Stuart England*. Cambridge: University Press, 1961, pp. 70–85.

'Seventeenth-Century Agriculture and Social Change', *Agricultural History Review*, XVIII (1970), 148–77.

Thompson, E. P. *The Making of the English Working Class*. Harmondsworth: Penguin, 1968.

'The Moral Economy of the English Crowd in the Eighteenth Century', *Past and Present*, no. 50 (1971), 76–136.

'Review', *Midland History*, no. 13 (1972), 43–53.

Whigs and Hunters: The Origin of the Black Act. New York: Pantheon, 1975.

Thompson, Roger. *Women in Stuart England and America*. London: Routledge and Kegan Paul, 1974.

Thorner, Daniel. 'Peasant Economy as a Category in Economic History', in T. Shanin, ed., *Peasants and Peasant Society*. Harmondsworth: Penguin, 1971, pp. 202–18.

Timmer, C. Peter. 'The Turnip, the New Husbandry, and the English Agricultural Revolution', *Quarterly Journal of Economics*, LXXXIII (1969), 375–95.

Todd, Emmanuel. 'Seven Peasant Communities in Pre-Industrial Europe', Unpublished Ph.D. thesis, Cambridge, 1976.

Tranter, N. L., ed. *Population and Industrialization*. London: Black, 1973.

Trusler, John. *Practical Husbandry, or the Art of Farming*. 3rd edn. London, 1790.

The Way to be Rich and Respectable, Addressed to Men of Small Fortune. London, [1775].

Tucker, G. S. L. 'English Pre-Industrial Population Trends', *Economic History Review*, XVI (1963), 205–18.

Tuke, John. *A General View of the Agriculture of the North Riding of Yorkshire*. London, 1794.

Tull, Jethro. *The Horse-Hoeing Husbandry*. London, 1733.

Tusser, Thomas. *Five Hundred Pointes of Good Husbandrie*. London, 1580.

Vancouver, Charles. *General View of the Agriculture of the County of Cambridge*. London, 1794.

    General View of the Agriculture of the County of Devon. London: David and Charles, 1969.

    A General View of the Agriculture of the County of Essex. London, 1795.

    General View of the Agriculture of Hampshire, including the Isle of Wight. London, 1810.

[Varley, Charles]. *The Modern Farmer's Guide, by a Real Farmer*. Glasgow, 1768.

    A New System of Husbandry. York, 1770.

Vaughan, William. *The Golden Fleece*. London, 1626.

Walker, D. *General View of the Agriculture of the County of Hertford*. London, 1795.

Waterman, Elizabeth L. 'Some New Evidence on Wage Assessments in the Eighteenth Century', *English Historical Review*, XLIII (1928), 398–408.

Webb, Sidney and Beatrice Webb. *English Local Government*. 11 vols. Vol. I, *The Parish and the County*. London: Cass, 1963.

West Riding Sessions Records, 1611 to 1642. J. Lister, ed. Yorkshire Archaeological Society, Record Series, LIV (1915).

Whitford, Richard. *Worke for Householders, or for them that have the Gydynge or Governaunce of any Company*. [n.p.], [1553].

Wilkinson, John. 'The Farming of Hampshire', *Journal of the Royal Agricultural Society*, XXII (1861), 239–371.

Williams, William M. *The Sociology of an English Village: Gosforth*. London: Routledge and Kegan Paul, 1956.

Willis, Arthur J., ed. *Winchester Settlement Papers, 1667–1842*. Hambledon, Kent: 1967.

Wiltshire Quarter Sessions and Assizes, 1736. J. P. M. Fowle, ed. Wiltshire Archaeological and Natural History Society, Record Branch, XI (1955).

Wolf, Eric R. *Peasants*. Englewood Cliffs, NJ: Prentice-Hall, 1966.

Woodforde, James. *The Diary of a Country Parson, 1758–1802*. Edited by John Beresford. Oxford: University Press, 1978.

Wright, A. R. *British Calendar Customs, England*. 3 vols. London: Glaisher, 1936–40.

Wrightson, K. E. 'The Puritan Reformation of Manners, with Special Reference to the Counties of Lancashire and Essex, 1640–1660', PhD thesis, Cambridge University, 1973.

Wrigley, E. A. 'Family Limitation in Pre-Industrial England', in M. Drake, ed., *Population in Industrialization*. London: Methuen, 1969, pp. 156–94.

    'Fertility Strategy for the Individual and the Group', in Charles Tilly, ed., *Historical Studies in Changing Fertility*. Princeton: University Press, 1978.

    'A Simple Model of London's Importance in Changing English Society and Economy', *Past and Present*, no. 37 (1967), 44–70.

and R. S. Schofield. *The Population History of England 1541–1871*. Studies in Social and Demographic History. London: Edward Arnold, 1980.

Wunderlich, Frieda. *Farm Labour in Germany, 1810–1945*. Princeton: University Press, 1961.

Wyczański, Andrzej and Jerzy Topolski. 'Peasant Economy Before and During the First Stage of Industrialisation', General Report, *6th International Congress on Economic History*, Copenhagen, 1974, pp. 11–31.

Yarranton, Andrew. *England's Improvement by Sea and Land, Shewing the Way to Out-Do the Dutch in Trade by Sea, to Set at Work all the Poor of England with the Growth of our own Lands*. 2 vols. London, 1698.

Yelling, J. A. *Common Field and Enclosure in England, 1450–1850*. London: Macmillan, 1977.

Young, Alexander. *Chronicles of the First Planters of Massachusetts Bay*. Boston, 1846.

Young, Arthur, the elder. *A Farmer's Calendar*. 2nd edn. London, 1778.
The Farmer's Guide in Hiring and Stocking Farms. 2 vols. London, 1770.
A Farmer's Letters. London, 1767.
A Farmer's Tour through the East of England. 4 vols. London, 1771.
General View of the Agriculture of the County of Essex. 2 vols. London, 1807.
General View of the Agriculture of the County of Lincoln. London, 1799.
General View of the Agriculture of the County of Norfolk. London, 1804.
A Six Months' Tour through the North of England. 4 vols. London, 1770.
A Six Weeks' Tour through the Southern Counties of England and Wales. 3rd edn. London, 1772.

Young, Arthur, the younger. *General View of the Agriculture of the County of Sussex*. Newton Abbot: David and Charles, 1970.

Index

Numbers in italics refer to tables and figures.

account books, accounting, 118–19
Adisham (Kent), *12*
age at marriage, *see* marriage
age of servants, 11, 37–8, 133, *134*; and wages, 143–7; at entry into service, 70–2; at departure from service, 79–80
Aldenham (Herts.), 110, *111*
Alphamstone (Essex), 41–2
apprentices and apprenticeship, 4, 66, 73–4; parish apprentices, 166–7
Arbuthnot, John, 7, 83
Ardleigh (Essex), *13*, 70, *71, 77*, 84
Ash Chilton (Kent), *12*
Ash Overland (Kent), *12*
autobiographies and diaries, 5, 74, 85–93

Banister, John, 40, 43, 45
Banks, Sir Joseph, 62
Barkway and Reed (Herts.), *13*
Barlborough (Derbys.), *13*
Battlesden (Beds.), 123–4
Baxter, Richard, 27
Berkshire, 121
Best, Henry, 5, 34, 36, 39, 41, 43, 45, 61
Bettesworth, 75
Blackstone, William, 6
Board of Agriculture reports, 125–6
board wages, 7, 118, 124
Boke of Thrift, 35
Bottesford (Leics.), 110, *111*
Buccleuch, Duke of, 79
Buckinghamshire, 18
Burn, Richard, 6, 32
by-employment, 13–14, 23

Cambridge Group for the History of Population and Social Structure, 11, 110
Cambridgeshire, *51*
Carlton Rode (Norfolk), *13*
census of 1831, 126, 170–1; of 1851, 4, 6–7, 19–22, 115, 130–1, 133, 134
Chamberlayne, Edward, 8

children, 9, 14; of farmers, 76–7; of labourers and poor, 76
China, 65
Clayworth (Notts.), *12*
Cogenhoe (Northants), *53*
Coke of Norfolk, 68
commons and wastes, 22
Commonwealth, 97, 98
compulsory service, 33–4, 166–7
constables, 34, 61
contract between servant and master, 31–4
Corfe Castle (Dorset), *13*, 70, *71, 77*
Cornwall, *15*, 60
cost of living, 101–3, 121, 122
courts, 31
Cowell, John, 51
crafts and trades, 11, 14, 23, 100–1; *see also* by-employment
Cumberland, *15*

dairy farming, 22
Dalton, Michael, 33
day-labourers, *see* labourers
death of farmer, wife, 26
Defoe, Daniel, 101
demand for servants and labourers, 22–6, 107, 116–17, 120–1, 122
depression, agricultural, 124–5, 129
Devonshire, *15*
diaries, *see* autobiographies
diet, *see* food
Digswell (Herts.), *13*
discipline, 44–8
disorder, 33
domestic servants, 4, 5, 6, 9–10
Doncaster (Yorks.), 60, 62
Donhead (Wilts.), *12*
Dydsey (Herefords.), 51

Ealing (Middlesex), *12*, 70, *71, 77*
earnest, 32
education and training, 75, 77
Elloe (Lincs.), 164–5
Elmswell (Yorks.), 5, 41
enclosure, 116, 121

230